LIGHT
OF THE
FEATHER

LIGHT
OF THE
FEATHER

*A Teacher's Journey
into Native American
Classrooms and Culture*

Mick Fedullo

ANCHOR BOOKS
DOUBLEDAY
New York   London   Toronto   Sydney   Auckland

AN ANCHOR BOOK
PUBLISHED BY DOUBLEDAY
a division of Bantam Doubleday Dell Publishing Group, Inc.
1540 Broadway, New York, New York 10036

ANCHOR BOOKS, DOUBLEDAY, and the portrayal of an anchor
are trademarks of Doubleday, a division of Bantam Doubleday
Dell Publishing Group, Inc.

Light of the Feather was originally published in hardcover by
William Morrow and Company, Inc. in 1992. The Anchor Books edition is
published by arrangement with William Morrow and Company, Inc.

Library of Congress Cataloging-in-Publication Data
Fedullo, Mick, 1949–
Light of the feather : a teacher's journey into Native American
classrooms and culture / Mick Fedullo. — 1st Anchor Books ed.
p. cm.
Originally published: New York : Morrow, © 1992.
1. Fedullo, Mick, 1949– . 2. Teachers—United States—
Biography. 3. Indians of North America—Education. 4. Children of
minorities—Education—United States. 5. Indians of North America—
Social life and customs. I. Title.
[E97.F44A3   1993]
371.1′092—dc20
[B]   93-16837
CIP

ISBN 0-385-47136-X
Copyright © 1992 by Mick Fedullo

During the course of this book, a young Indian friend hands me a feather from his powwow costume, saying, "Have it." I whisper, "Thank you." More words than that, which would have been nothing more than words heaped on words, would have diminished the giving, the receiving. The gift was such.

Friend, the feather is still safe. Because of it, I have not lost my way. Giving and receiving, these are the powers that bind us. The tip of the feather pointed out a direction, and I followed. Friend, I thank you again, and offer you this book. I say only "Have it," for it was written by the light of that feather.

Acknowledgments

My sincerest thanks go to Dorothy Small, whose constant support, encouragement, and criticism, as well as whose stories, helped shape this book; and to Lynn Vanderburg, for her heartfelt and intelligent guidance. Thanks also to Kim Meilicke Douglas, Angela Branz-Spall, and Katherine Douglass.

Contents

10 CONTENTS

Author's Note

FIVE HUNDRED YEARS ago this year, Christopher Columbus came to America and mistakenly called the indigenous people "Indians." The name stuck. The voyager's error is recognized in the term "American Indians." More recently, a move to replace both designations with "Native Americans" has been endorsed by many. A Cheyenne friend of mine prefers "Native American Indians"; and I have heard offered several others—among them "Indigenous Americans" and "Indigenous People."

There is no absolute consensus in the matter, even among the first Americans. Nowadays, "Native American" is widely used in the media and academia, as well as among some young Indians. It seems, also, to be favored by certain tribes, such as the Navajo. Yet one simple fact remains; when Native Americans who live on reservations refer to themselves collectively, most still use, by a large majority, the single word "Indians." It is for this simple reason that I, more often than not, use that term.

Indians of any given group, it should be noted, have always and still prefer to be called by their particular tribal name.

Introduction

THE HITCHHIKING OLD man climbed into the front seat of my car; his wife got in the back. Each carried a grocery bag full of provisions. We were somewhere south of Blanding, Utah, in the middle of the biggest nowhere I had ever seen. I'd been driving from the East on my way to visit friends in Phoenix, and this openness of land, this eternity of sky, this determination of primeval rock, had been slamming at my senses the way light slams at a newborn. The West, as it does to so many first-time visitors, reduced me. I felt a need for company, for someone with whom I could share a little small talk. The sound of voices would insulate me from a vastness I could see but not comprehend. The old man and his wife, I thought, would be my company.

The man wore faded jeans, scuffed cowboy boots, a sky-blue western-style shirt, and a black felt hat. His skin was dark and covered with a thin film of dust. The woman was dressed in a long red velveteen skirt, a pink cotton blouse, bracelets and necklaces of silver and turquoise, and canvas tennis shoes. Her narrow eyes sparkled behind the wrinkles of a rich bronze face. The hair of both had been pulled back and tied into tight bundles with white yarn.

"You got a cigarette?" the old man asked with a heavy guttural accent. I pulled out a pack of plastic-filtered cigarettes.

The man took one, broke off the filter along with half the tobacco, passed this half to his wife in the backseat, and lit up what was left.

His wife said, "Thanks."

"Where you people going?" I asked.

"Back to the reservation," the woman answered.

"Where's that?"

"Up ahead."

All I saw up ahead was more of the same stark nothingness I had been leaving in my wake all day. I squinted hard to look for some sign of humanity.

"Where you coming from?" I asked, but the question sounded ridiculous even as I formed it. There was no other place to be coming from but Blanding.

The woman politely answered, "Town. Had to do a little shopping." The man grumbled something in a language like none I had ever heard.

The miles rolled by endlessly. After a while, we passed the tiny settlement of Bluff. Eventually, we dipped down into Mexican Hat, crossed the San Juan River, and began climbing a sage-speckled plateau of red earth. Very little small talk passed between my company and me. The questions I wanted to ask would have sounded foolish: What kind of people are you? What, exactly, is a reservation?

Several miles beyond Mexican Hat, the old woman said, "Stop here. We get off here." I pulled to the side of the road and looked around. There was nothing there but the powdery red desert and distant towering vermilion cliffs. I looked hard, hoping to spot something I might identify as a reservation: a cluster of buildings, a faraway water tank.

Nothing. Why on earth did these people want to get out here?

"Take care," I said, still baffled.

"Thanks for the ride," the woman said.

"Got another cigarette?" the old man mumbled.

The two left the car with their bags and began walking straight into the heart of the desert, along two dirt tracks faintly carved by an occasional vehicle. Soon the old man and woman disappeared over a ridge and into the vast emptiness. I felt as though two ghosts had appeared in my car and now had floated off.

They were not ghosts, of course, unless they were ghosts of my future. Little did I know that we had already entered the enormous Navajo Nation. And I hardly could have imagined that within several years I would be living among American Indians of many tribes, including the Navajo, working with their children, and learning about a world that now escaped me.

This happened in 1975. In 1978, having been thunderstruck by the desert, I moved to Arizona. I began to write this book in 1987; the stories took place between 1979 and 1990. I had originally told many of the stories to friends, both Indian and non-Indian, who encouraged me to write them down.

The stories represent a bridging of cultures made possible by the good graces of the many Indians I have befriended—friendships for which I will forever be grateful. I believe these stories were gifts, like the feather my young Indian friend gave me from his powwow outfit, and I believe, as my Navajo friend and colleague Chester Henry told me, that they should be shared.

The stories are told more or less chronologically. They sometimes zigzag around the country, especially between Arizona and Montana, because since 1984 that is exactly what I have been doing—zigzagging around the country to work on many reservations. Having breakfast in Oakland, California, lunch in Tuscon, Arizona, and dinner in Choctaw, Mississippi, *all in the same day*, is the kind of thing I have become accustomed to. In the last few chapters, I have switched the tense from past to present, mainly because I wrote the end of this book virtually while the stories happened.

All of the stories are true. In some cases, though, I have changed the names of certain individuals, especially of some of the children and of some adults with whom I no longer have contact.

The Navajo tribe is one of many tribes whose people I wound up spending much time with, and in that time one of the things I learned about Navajos was that for them the word "beauty" has special significance. More than just indicating physical attractiveness and aesthetically pleasing qualities, beauty, to the Navajo, means harmony. "To go in beauty" means to proceed, to live, in harmony with oneself and with all of nature—to be relaxed into that which we are. May the reader who proceeds through this book go in beauty.

1
Sacaton School

I HAD NO PLAN. I had just earned a graduate degree from the University of Iowa; I was single and didn't want to live in the East where I was raised; and I was pushing thirty. So, free of responsibility and with all the time in the world, I packed my bags and headed for the Wild West, specifically the town of Tucson.

I unloaded my pride and took a part-time job at a convenience market, and it paid enough, almost, to fill my stomach. For a year and a half, I basked in the wonderful, dry climate of my own dream. Up at seven, I'd hike out onto the desert, soaking in a heat that goes to the bone and transforms ordinary comfort into ecstatic rhythms of slow, deep breathing. When money was less than scarce, I'd bring home a dinner of prickly pear cactus—sauté the pads and eat the fruit for dessert.

Then, a year and a half later, the Arizona Commission on the Arts hired me to teach poetry writing at a school seventy-five miles north of Tucson, in the middle of the Sonoran Desert. I was to work there two days a week for one school year.

Two weeks before I started as writer-in-residence, a representative from the arts commission and I visited the campus of Sacaton Middle School to meet with administrators and schedule the days I would be there. As we walked toward the office, two things startled me: All the children passing through the open-air hallway to their next classes were dark-skinned with blue-black hair; and when they talked to each other, much of what they said, spoken with a thick accent of glottal stops and phonetic oddities, I found incomprehensible.

Stopping short of the office, I asked the arts-commission liaison, "Are these Mexican children?"

She laughed. "Nobody told you? They're Indian. Pima Indians. We're on a reservation."

"Oh . . ."

"I'm sorry you didn't know. But I really think you'll enjoy it here. The last writer we sent here had a terrific time." Then she offered the fine print. "Listen, if you have any difficulty with the situation here, don't feel bad. Several other artists we've sent couldn't adjust to Indian kids and had to give it up after several weeks. If you have trouble and want to call it quits, let me know. No problem."

Part of me wanted to flash white tail. The other part was curious, intrigued.

As it turned out, understanding the Pima children was indeed difficult, but luckily the human ear adapts rather quickly. Soon I made sense of the English under the thickest accents, and I came to enjoy the way these children sounded.

As we slowly grew to know each other better, I wanted to find out more about their community, their families, their way of life, which were different from any I had ever encountered. By October, I was volunteering a third day's work and visiting four additional classes on Wednesdays.

The students often wrote stirring poems. I began to get positive reactions from their parents, who told me they were surprised that their children could be brought to enjoy writing so much.

I edited a photocopied student poetry magazine and started talking about having the students give recitations later in the spring. My year at Sacaton could end with a bang. I envisioned introducing students to the school board and to parent advisory committees, before whom they would read their writings. In fact, I was beginning to think it would be nice to hang around another year or two and build a solid creative-writing program.

One teacher encouraged me to write a proposal setting up such a program. Other teachers were less enthusiastic. Said one, "These kids don't need creative writing. They need basics. Hell, they can't even spell correctly."

Then something happened that helped set my course. I had already been aware that some of the non-Indian teachers at Sacaton did not think highly of Indian students in general, or of Pima students in particular. One day in the teachers' lounge, I mentioned my plan to have several students recite their poems before audiences. I explained that such an experience could only bolster their self-confidence. The three teachers, a man and two women, sat silently on couches, exchanging glances. Then one of the women spoke up. "Look, you've been here a month and a half, and you think you've got it all figured out. I've been here eight years, and I still don't know what these people are about. But one thing I do know is that you'll never get Pima kids to stand up in front of an audience, much less open their mouths. They're just too damned withdrawn. Maybe they speak up in a classroom, but in front of outside people they're too shy to do anything."

The second female teacher said, "Don't get us wrong. We like you. But it would be a waste of your time and energy to try to get these Pima kids to perform before a crowd. You'll only wind up frustrated."

The man stood up and walked out of the lounge, chuckling to himself.

I thought, Why are these teachers here if they don't believe the students can achieve? What right do they have going into a classroom of children for whom they have set the lowest expectations? Granted, most of the non-Indian staff didn't harbor these not-so-hidden prejudices, but what of the children who spent seven hours a day with an adult who believed they were incapable? The effects on those young lives must be devastating.

Within a week, a second incident sealed my fate. After lunch, I walked outside to the playground at the elementary school. The children were at recess, and two teachers, on playground duty, sat on a concrete bench in the shade of a wispy palo verde tree. No sooner had I joined them when the male teacher called out a student's name: "Leonard! Come here!"

A fourth-grade boy ambled over. "What?"

The teacher said, "You know you failed this morning's math test. You missed almost every problem."

The boy was defiant. "So?"

The teacher looked at me and at his colleague. "You know, Leonard here comes to school every day. Never absent. And you know the reason he shows up all the time?" The question hung only a second. "It's not to learn. No, the only reason Leonard here comes to school is to get a free lunch. Maybe if their parents had to pay for their lunches, well, maybe the only ones who'd come to class would be the ones who wanted to learn."

Leonard squinted his eyes, let out a snakelike hiss, then ran off to join his classmates. Seething inside, I said nothing, convinced that no argument would change the teacher's mind. I did, however, decide I could *do* something.

By mid-November, I had drafted a proposal outlining a creative-writing program that emphasized classroom instruction, publication of student writing, *and* recitations by the best student authors. The plan was circulated through the administration, the Indian school board, and a parent advisory committee.

The administrators and board members were mildly receptive, while the Indian parents were especially interested. One morning at the school, one of the officers of the parent group visited me. Betty Perez was a large-boned, well-proportioned woman, whose black hair had been permed into tight curls. She walked with me down the corridor as I hurried to my first class. "You have my son, Joey," she said. "He really likes you, and he likes writing now. Oh, we've read your proposal. Don't worry." Then she said good-bye and vanished.

I didn't know it, but I was receiving my first lesson in Indian-style communication. When Indians address someone they don't know, they often keep what they say short and to the point. Translated into Anglo verbosity, Mrs. Perez had told me that since I was achieving unexpected, positive results, the parent committee looked favorably upon my proposal and would make every effort to see that funding for the program would come from a Title IV grant over which the parents themselves had considerable control. In effect, Mrs. Perez had told me I was about to become Arizona's first and only writer-in-residence paid by and working for Indians on a reservation.

As it turned out, I spent the next five years at Sacaton, five years that changed everything. Everything, that is, but a few teachers' minds. They remained unimpressed that by my last year at the school I was flying my best students to Indian education conferences as far away as Spokane, Washington, where they'd confidently recite their poetry to as many as five hundred people.

2
The Perezes

SACATON: A SMALL, inconspicuous mark on the Sonoran Desert. Interstate 10 runs northwest to Phoenix and southeast to Tucson about six miles west of the tiny village. For thousands of travelers passing between the Casa Grande and Casa Blanca Road exits, two distant water towers shimmering in desert heat are the only evidence that anyone lives "out there." The casual tourist, on a hunt for Indian curios, might venture toward these towers knowing he is approaching the tribal capital of the Gila River Indian Community. But Sacaton, for anyone driving over ten miles an hour, is truly a now-you-see-it-now-you-don't town. Many Pimas live in scattered smaller villages across the fifty-by-twenty-five-mile reservation: Bapchule, Blackwater, San Tan, Stotonic, Casa Blanca, Olberg, Komatke. And many live between these villages, surrounding themselves with nothing more than plain old desert. Eight or nine thousand in all.

The Pimas were the probable descendants, I would learn, of the Hohokam, that ancient civilization that irrigated the desert and constructed the astonishing three-story adobe complex known as Casa Grande in the middle of the hottest, driest area in North America.

Around 1400, the Hohokam culture disappeared, and some time later Spanish explorers came across a sturdy people eking out an existence from sand and wind. They called themselves *O'odham*. But when the Spanish asked these people, in Spanish, who they were, the confused Pimas responded in their own language by saying, "I don't understand what you're saying." The words, shortened, sounded like "*Pee-mah*." Thus the O'odham were "blessed" with a new name.

The I-don't-understand-what-you're-saying tribe was, like the Hohokam, mainly agricultural, harvesting beans and squash. To supplement their diet, the Pima hunted rabbit and quail, sometimes deer, and gathered cactus fruit and mesquite beans.

Unfortunately, they were destined to suffer the cultural decline that goes with being a "conquered" people, though they had never really raised objections to the encroaching settlements of the *Mil-gahn*—that is, the whites, or as they are commonly known among many southern Indians, Anglos.

The settlement, then town, then city, of Phoenix had determined to minimize contact with these "savages." Into the twentieth century, it was unlawful to enter city limits dressed in anything but full, Anglo-style attire. An invisible sign hung at every point of entry: NO BARE-ASSED BROWN SONS OF BITCHES PERMITTED BEYOND THIS POINT.

The Pimas, money-poor as they were, suffered no lack of ingenuity. Near town, in secret thickets of palo verde and mesquite, they hung several sets of clothing: trousers, shirts, jackets, and shoes for men and boys, dresses and shoes for women and girls. A family needing to go to the city simply went first to a thicket, put on the Anglo clothing, then marched into Phoenix, not with Anglo dignity but with Indian pride at having beaten the system. Upon returning, they hung the clothes back in the trees for use by the next family.

I figured the best way to get to know the contemporary Pimas was to live on the reservation, and eventually I did. But during that first year, while I commuted between the Anglo and Indian worlds, the second-best way was to simply loiter, to talk to people, to try to become less of another curious outsider constantly asking questions and more of an oh-hell-he's-all-right participator in the local goings-on. Knowing many of the children was a start.

Soon I discovered that the east end of a large warehouse-type structure next to the rodeo grounds housed a café and game room known as the Bean Pot. Here, many of the kids gathered after school to play pinball, pool, and the first of the video games—Pong, Asteroids, Video Football. I began having lunches at the Bean Pot, then returning in the afternoons to talk and shoot pool with the students. On my first visit, I recognized the curled coif of one of the women behind the counter. It was Betty Perez, of the parent committee. She and her husband, Perry, owned and operated the place.

The Bean Pot was, for the Perezes' thirteen-year-old son, Joey, a second home. We fast became friends over missed shots at the pool table. I also spent long hours talking to Betty and Perry, sitting on a long wooden bench across from a candy counter. By the end of the school year, I was regularly returning with them to their home, a mobile located across the road from the Indian Hospital. Over dinner we discussed school matters, tribal politics, Indian health issues, our own lives. They were always excited about the plans I had for the creative-writing program. Sometimes the four of us relaxed by playing Scrabble or the card game Uno.

Betty was born and raised in the village of Blackwater. Perry, incongruous as at first it seemed, was Puerto Rican, born on the island and raised on red bananas and rice. He relocated as a youngster to New York City. As an industrious young man, he left the city to stake out a future in the western United States. The two met in Denver, where Betty worked for a clothing manufacturer and Perry made a comfortable living as a sewing-machine repairman. A dapper, pencil-mustached man, he caught the eyes of the female factory workers whenever he came to fix their machines. He introduced himself to Betty, but at first she showed reluctance in dating this smooth charmer. Perry persisted, and eventually they hit it off. After marriage, the couple moved to Nogales, Arizona. Then, after several years, desiring independence, they took Betty's one-acre reservation allotment, put a mobile home on it, and went into business for themselves in Sacaton. Besides the Bean Pot, they also operated a small factory across the village, near the schools, which produced vinyl duffel bags, briefcases, wallets, and such.

Their daughter, Sheri, had by now married and was living with her husband in Casa Grande, eighteen miles from Sacaton, leaving Joey as the only child in the home. An exceptionally bright boy, he appeared to be neither Pima nor Puerto Rican, but both, a true composite with his black curly hair and his distinctly Indian eyes. I spent much time with my new "little brother," and learned right off that he felt uncomfortable on the reservation. Being only half Pima as well as being accustomed to life in racially mixed Nogales, Joey was more at home trekking through the shopping malls of Mesa than cruising the dusty streets of Sacaton. He also loved hiking out into the desert, away from people, away from Sacaton, through mesquite groves or across cracked limestone flats. At times, he bore a playful self-consciousness about his dual heritage and appearance. When we drove to the city to catch a movie or to shop, he often delighted in looking around the crowds and saying, "These people must think I'm your shadow."

Ironically, as I became more and more immersed in the Pima world, Joey grew farther and farther away from it. The Perez family maintained little of the tribe's traditions. Indeed, few of the Pima's traditions remained intact. As a young "outsider," Joey scorned the alcoholism and violent behaviors he witnessed in many Pimas. He vowed that as soon as he could, he would leave the reservation. His father wanted him to join the military service when he graduated from high school. There, Perry said, he could "learn the discipline it takes to make it anywhere." Although Betty Perez always seemed torn between her Pima and assimilated identities, she nonetheless held much respect for the heritage of the O'odham. Once she told me that when she was four years old an elderly medicine man had warned her family that upon his death Betty would fall gravely ill. About ten years later, while the family was living in Denver, she became so sick she was thought to be close to death with fever and the resulting convulsions. Mysteriously, by the next morning, she was well again. Three days later, an aunt called from Sacaton with news of the old medicine man's death. He had passed away on the very day Betty had fallen ill. Deep inside, Betty knew about and believed in the old ways.

Although there exists no documentation, a story handed down in Betty's family purports that one of her grandmothers worked for the Ronstadt family of Tucson as a housekeeper, and that she became pregnant by the man of the house. To this day, Betty continued to refer to singer Linda Ronstadt as "my long-lost cousin."

The Perez family was the first to take me in. More acculturated into Anglo ways than most of Sacaton's population, they nonetheless provided me an entrance into the Pima world.

3
Cactus Fruit

BETTY PEREZ SAID, "Here's one. Just where it was last year. There should be another one a little farther up that way." I picked up the twenty-five-foot pole—two saguaro-cactus ribs wired together—and studied the small crosspiece wired about three inches from the tip. Still secure. Perfect for hooking the high cactus fruit and jerking it loose.

The second stick lay at the spot Betty had remembered. She said, "When we're finished, be sure to put the sticks back where they were. That's the way we do it. Everyone who comes here for fruit knows where they are." Immediately, Joey lifted one of the poles alongside a sturdy saguaro and began pulling down fruit. I caught them in a bucket.

Earlier we had loaded a gallon of water, ham sandwiches, and two plastic buckets in the back of my car and headed out of Sacaton and into the Sacaton Mountains. Between the craggy peaks, a narrow valley zigzagged its way for three miles through dense stands of saguaro. The June foliage of brilliant white flowers crowning the tops of the cacti had now given way to the maroon egg-shaped fruit, a prized delicacy of the Pima. The traditional harvesting of these represented the beginning of the new year.

I had been looking forward to this excursion. Our plan: to

gather enough fruit for Betty to make cactus candy. In the past, the fruit would have been used to make wine, as they still are among the Tohono O'odham to the south. To celebrate the new year, everyone would drink to the point of vomiting, drink some more, vomit again, and continue drinking. It was the one and only time during the year that these hardy people really cut loose. It was a festive time of sharing and laughter.

For half an hour, Betty, Joey, and I meandered through the little valley, searching out the ripest of the fruit. The best for immediate eating, I learned, were those that had split open less than twenty-four hours before. The rich, seedy pulp lay exposed just long enough for the sun to burn a delicate crust over the sweet morsels. At the next monsoon rain, they would perish. And if the killing wet didn't come within a day or two, the birds or the sun would finish them off in no time. As Joey and I knocked loose these gifts of a harsh land, Betty caught them in a bucket so they wouldn't smash to the ground and be ruined by gritty soil. Every few minutes, however, we succumbed to temptation and munched down a few. Delicious. A texture somewhat like a fig. A candied flavor unlike anything I had tasted before or since. The desert truly at its best.

When we had filled the first bucket, Betty looked toward the southeast and said, "Oh-oh, there's a storm coming. We better get back to the car." Above the sawtooth peaks, the sky hunched in a solid gray-brown vestment.

The Sonoran Desert experiences two rainy seasons. In winter, low clouds from the west bring occasional steady drizzles. In summer, starting usually at the beginning of July and lasting until the end of August, massive and spectacular thunderstorms get carried from the Gulf of Mexico across the desert in theatrical displays that may drop several inches of rain along a random path. These giants of nature are often preceded by merciless dust storms that can wreak havoc on a car's paint job.

As Betty retreated for the shelter of the car, Joey and I lingered, trying to collect as much fruit as possible before it became washed into uselessness. I called out, "We'll be there in a minute."

Betty shouted over her shoulder, "It's your lives!"

I should have trusted my friend's knowledge of the desert. I assumed we had another fifteen or twenty minutes before the storm hit, but within five minutes I was proved foolishly wrong.

Before Joey and I knew what hit us, the sky caved in, dropping a full cargo of dust and sand, filling the valley with blinding chaos. We ran in the direction of the car, tossing the saguaro ribs toward, we hoped, the spots where we had found them. The earth itself whipped around us in a furor. Billions of fine sand particles pinpricked our backs through our lightweight T-shirts, and we were forced to look down with tightly squinted eyes. I cupped a hand over my nose. Nothing helped. The dust was everywhere, assaulting us with mindless violence. It caked in the corners of our eyes; it entered our nostrils and lodged in our throats. It crept right down to the roots of our hair and clung to our skin.

Fortunately, we reached the safety of the car and made it through the valley to the paved road before a torrent of rain transformed the single-lane dirt pathway into a quagmire of impassible quicksand. All the way to Sacaton, Betty sat in the backseat, chuckling to herself.

Once inside the trailer, the three of us sat silently around the kitchen table, nibbling on cactus fruit and staring out the window at the steely monsoon storm. Rain swept across the land in opaque waves, and the sky flashed brilliantly at regular intervals. I watched tiny rivulets form and grow, coursing over ground that minutes before resembled bonemeal. Joey muttered one word: "Beautiful." At that moment, I became overwhelmed with a sense of well-being. Never had the word "beautiful" meant as much. The wind. The rain. The lightning. The darkened kitchen. The fruit. The sharing. The silence of three people mingling with the sounds of the storm. Beautiful, yes.

4

Desert Hike

ONE AFTERNOON IN August of 1980, as I drove along on my way to visit the Perezes, I felt the heat swirl through my non-air-conditioned Toyota as I had never felt it before. It made my head spin. As one who enjoys a bone-dry, hundred-degree day, I marveled that the desert could become *this* hot, making even me fantasize mounds of ice cubes and cool mountain waterfalls. I stepped harder on the gas to force more of a breeze through the car's vents. What I got was not relief but fingers of heat wrapping around me, burning my eyes, searing my flesh. Immediately, I slowed down and closed the vents. A sneak preview of hell, I thought.

I turned off the road onto the Perezes' dirt driveway and saw Joey in front of the trailer leaning over his seated "cousin," Jerry. Joey held up the younger boy's bare foot, and they both were excitedly examining it. Jerry, a Shoshone Indian, had been adopted as a baby by Joey's maternal grandparents. He suffered from fetal alcohol syndrome, and as a result was small for his eleven years. Also, because of his condition, he exhibited behavior problems and got constantly into one kind of trouble or another.

When Joey looked up and saw my approaching vehicle, he screamed as loud as he could, "Quick! Come here! Jerry's foot!"

Instantly, the thought rushed through my mind that Jerry had been stung by a scorpion. At that time of the year, the nasty crustaceans were all over. I accelerated. Joey hollered twice more, "Quick!"

"What is it?" I yelled as I jumped from the car and ran up to the boys. I knew Perry and Betty were not home; their car was gone.

Joey said, "Look!"

From the sole of Jerry's right foot, just beneath and between his first and second toes, protruded a gray-brown splinter the thickness of my own little finger. Its size startled me, and for a moment I just stared at it.

Jerry sobbed, tears streaking his thin face.

Joey looked at me. "How do we get it out?"

I said, "We don't. We take him to the hospital. That thing's too big for us to handle." I picked up Jerry and carried him to my car. During the short drive to the Indian hospital, Jerry became nearly hysterical, screaming, "They're going to give me a shot! No, no, I don't want no shot!"

In one of the hospital's emergency rooms, the boy lost all control and had to be held down by one of the nurses and me. It took nearly ten minutes for the doctor to remove most of the splinter, which kept breaking apart between the steel forceps. When Jerry noticed the needleless syringe, from which an antiseptic could be squirted into the gaping hole in his foot, he nonetheless concluded "shot" and became so wild he had to be sedated.

A short while later, this young, drowsy victim of his own incautious running over old plywood fell fast asleep on Betty and Perry's bed. At last, quiet. I flopped back on the sofa, and Joey turned on the television. Then, remembering the day's dreadful heat, I said, "Damn, it's wicked today. I wonder what the temperature is."

Without another word, we both rose to our feet and headed for the front door. Just outside, hanging in the shade of the trellised porch, the thermometer registered 118 degrees. Joey exclaimed, "Holy Cow!"

I blurted out, "Never has my body experienced this kind of heat. And in the shade, no less. And we're still alive!"

Joey's black eyes flashed. "Hey, we should take a hike and see what it feels like."

My instant reply: "No way."

"C'mon," he coaxed.

I asked, "What possible reason could we have for hiking in this heat? Besides, it's too dangerous."

"Just to see what it's like," Joey went on. "C'mon. We don't have to hike far. Just a little ways."

"You're crazy," I said, and started to go back inside for the relief of evaporative cooling. But then, in a moment's passing, the idea struck me as absurdly appealing. Joey's answer, "to see what it's like," tapped the rationale every mountain climber has expressed with the cliché "Because it's there." Forever afterward I would be able to announce to friend or foe, "I hiked on the desert through one-hundred-and-eighteen-degree heat and survived. I know what it's like," heedless that I might be regarded as a fool.

"Okay," I said to Joey. "But we're going to play it safe. First of all, we'll hike up the river. That way, if we get disoriented even slightly, we can turn about-face and head back. Second, we're not going far, maybe a couple hundred yards."

Like a whip snapping, Joey said, "Let's do it!"

We each drank down a quart of iced tea, donned baseball caps, and climbed into my Toyota. At the Gila River, I pulled off the road and parked the car facing east, shading the inside-front from the three o'clock sun. As we stepped onto the soft sand of the Gila's parched bed, the earth's heat instantly clawed through the rubber soles of my sneakers and ripped at the bottoms of my feet. Damn, I thought, I guess we're committed to this . . . just step high, and walk softly.

Joey broke off a rib from a dead saguaro to use as a walking stick. Then he confidently bounded on while poking the rib firmly and rhythmically into the riverbed. But I was worried. I knew how sneaky the heat could be. We might at first notice only a slight dizziness accompanying our thirst. Then the gradual disorientation. The world would start to blur. I imagined us turning around and around, wondering from which end of the river we had started our hike. I imagined us finding what we would falsely envision as lifesaving shade under a scruffy mesquite tree. I imagined us sitting down there in that shade. And that's where we would be found. Several times I muttered, "It's just too hot. This is *not* a good idea."

Joey's response each time: "C'mon."

We continued through the riverbed for several hundred yards. The heat crushed us. Even Joey began to slow down. We stepped over the bleached jawbone of a cow, or bull, or horse, its teeth still sparkling with enamel shine in the murderous sun, as though they retained some memory of chewing sagebrush or, perhaps, the poisonous locoweed.

I knew that Joey was now also beginning, at least in his thoughts, to concede the inevitable. So I suggested that we climb up the riverbank, walk another fifty feet or so to clear a dense thicket of dwarfed mesquite trees, then go to the left toward a gravel quarry that lay less than a quarter-mile away. From there we could go back out to the road, back to the car, back to the trailer, back to cool air, back to another quart of iced tea, Joey finally agreed. We left the Gila River walking side by side.

As we climbed to higher ground, I looked to the left and spotted the tops of the quarry's gravel hills, built up by steam shovels and bulldozers. Joey, head turned to the right, was first to see the dead man. He let out a sharp, grunted scream. Startled, I jerked my head around and caught his arms flying straight out in front of him; he appeared to be fending off some sort of attack. The walking stick rocketed from his hand, made a high arc in the limpid air, and dropped directly on top of the corpse. Joey completed the fastest one-eighty I had ever witnessed, then ran off through a tunnel of excited terror. I, on the other hand, was overcome by a numbing paralysis, exactly the kind one experiences in dreams: You want to run, you need to run, you *must* get away, but your legs won't work. My muscles had turned to jelly, and my feet had metamorphosed into concrete slabs.

At such a moment, everything is so still and so quiet that the moment itself seems to linger forever, as though a wedge out of some horrifying eternity had been sliced and placed before your eyes and was itself eternal. In the second moment, I became aware of my breathing, now labored and rapid. I was fighting for air.

The most striking feature of the death scene happened to be the prominent saguaro rib lying diagonally from the corpse's right shoulder to its left ankle, and I knew what had to happen next: I had to remove the walking stick. If we brought the tribal police back and they saw the stick lying on the heat-frozen body, they might infer a drama that had never taken place. The most innocuous of possible accusations: "So, you guys found this body and thought it would be fun to play 'Let's throw sticks at the dead man.' One of you's got a good aim."

I stepped forward, knees shaking, and glanced away as my fingers gripped the cactus rib. When I threw it, and I threw it as hard as I could, I felt some of the horror being released through my fingertips. Joey was now standing within fifteen feet. Seeing him, I said, "Look, he's got false teeth." I was trying my best to give a calm, controlled appearance, because what you want to do at intense moments like this is not only *get* control, but prove to those around you that you *have* control. Joey's quivering voice said, "How do you know?" Then he blurted, "Let's get the hell out of here!"

We did, and quickly, though not before gathering our senses and stopping to look around for obvious landmarks that would lead us, and the police, back. A saguaro to the left, deformed and fluted at its crest, would be a sure giveaway. Joey pointed to the curvature of the desert as it sloped to the left of the conspicuous cactus. "If we follow that hill down from the quarry," he said, "it'll take us back to the body."

We walked through the desert in silence. Then I hung my arm over Joey's shoulders, saying, "Damn, Joey, I'm sorry you had to see that." More silence. A bit farther on, I said, "I hope this doesn't ever give you nightmares." And then: "I hope it doesn't give *me* nightmares." We laughed, uneasily.

Later, we were to learn that the unfortunate man had probably succumbed to the wretched temperatures, perhaps a month before our discovery. Nothing had been found to indicate foul play. No empty bottles of beer or wine or hard liquor had been discovered in the vicinity, ruling out the possibility that he had gotten drunk and collapsed from what would have been accelerated dehydration. His clothing had told that he was a Mexican national, while the absence of any identification seemed to suggest that he had come across the border, 140 miles to the south, undocumented. One theory a tribal officer related to us: As an illegal alien, the poor fellow, walking through Sacaton toward Phoenix, may have become frightened at seeing the tribal police headquarters, which was in fact the last building he would have passed, coming to the north edge of town. To avoid notice, he may have detoured into the desert, attempting to walk a parallel line with the road until he was far away from the authorities. A fatal mistake.

That night, as I lay on my bed, I listened to the hot winds slashing across rock and sand. I was temporarily residing in the guest quarters at the home of the school's counselor, just at the edge of the reservation and *quite* in the middle of the desert that had claimed that man's life. For a while, I studied the dead scorpion caught in the ceiling light above my head: another victim of incautiousness. Then I flicked the switch and lay in darkness. It seemed the wind had become a kind of voice. The desert was speaking to me, though it spoke in tongues I couldn't decipher. I listened intently, trying to uncover meaning as earlier I had from the thick accents of the Pima children. The desert was speaking, or perhaps laughing. Was it trying to communicate, or was it simply ridiculing me? I was, in significant measure, agitated. I sprawled on the bed, looking up at the darkened ceiling where the dead scorpion lay in absolute stillness. A day or two ago, I thought, this scorpion in its struggles could have dropped, alive, on me. Could I yet be its victim, I wondered, since scorpions are deceivers, and have a reputation for a stillness that fools?

Before sleep took me, it seemed I understood at least something of what the desert told. The winds danced in a frenzy around the small guest house. In their unrelenting translation of the desert's intent, they seemed to say, "For a long time, you have flirted with me. I've been kind to you, showing until today only my beauty. Now, beware, there are many sides to me, and of those who would believe I am tame and generous, I may prove, at my whim, to be a killer."

5
The Whitmans

DURING MY FIRST years at Sacaton, I came to know several Pima families. I joined a volleyball team and met people at the games. Many Pimas find volleyball irresistible, and we played right through the summers, often in 110-degree heat. Coolers filled with water or Gatorade quickly drained as each of us consumed up to half a gallon at a single match. Our games sometimes got interrupted by spectacular monsoon lightning flashes and downpours that sent us bottlenecking through the front door of whomever's house or trailer we were at. On one such occasion, we fled into the shelter of the Perezes' trailer carrying food brought for a huge potluck after-game dinner. Nearly twenty-five people crammed shoulder to shoulder into the tight quarters. When it became apparent that the rain was not going to let up for a while, we stood in the gathering dark—the electricity had gone out—and passed over our heads plates loaded with tamales, chili stew, tortillas, potato salad, cold chicken, and cake, until everyone was served. And there we stood, and ate, and talked, and laughed—no room even for the cats to meander between our feet for fallen scraps.

On another evening, after a night match under floodlights, several of us milled about near the parked cars just off the court. Then Joey Perez let out a sudden shriek and hopped up onto a car's hood. Within an instant, the rest of us spotted the source of his disquiet: A hand-sized tarantula was racing for all its life directly toward us. Amazing how much of a crowd a car's hood can hold. The spider, frightened by the activity of our game, had apparently remained hidden in a nearby bush until things calmed down. It was now making a rather misguided attempt at a getaway.

On yet another boiling afternoon, we found ourselves momentarily hushed with fear as an enormous fireball rose from the western horizon, spewing behind it a plume of silver smoke, then flaring to the size of the sun before it was gone. Nuclear war, we joked. Or perhaps the initial staging of an alien invasion. We decided we had at least enough time to score a few more points, so we played on. Later we learned that the fireball was in fact a test missile shot from the Pacific Ocean, several hundred miles away.

Such gatherings were really more social than athletic events, and it was easy to make many friends at these outings. I continually wondered, however, about Pimas who remained generally removed from contact with outsiders. My teammates worked at the school, or for the reservation's legal-aid service, or for the tribal administration, or the Bureau of Indian Affairs. One player was a tribal judge. But what of the Pimas for whom contact with a *Mil-gahn* resulted only from the necessity for some sort of official business? Those who had never known an "Anglo" personally? I had heard stories from non-Indians about the unfriendly, standoffish nature of many desert natives. I was curious about them.

It was true that by now I had established contact with the parents of several of my best students, visiting them occasionally to sing the praises of their offspring's talents. But these visits were always short, and our meetings were invariably conducted outside. Typically, I would knock on a door and step back. Mother or father would open the door just wide enough to peer out. Then they would emerge from the house, closing the door behind them. Much of what was said was said by me. The parents would nod, thank me, say good-bye, and vanish back inside. An outsider might assume that such behavior translated to "unfriendly" and "standoffish." I decided I would assume nothing, and I continued my visits.

I'm glad I did. I learned, in this long process, a traditional

Indian value that seems, in retrospect, mere common sense, something we non-Indians seem to know deep down but often ignore. Simply put, friendship is not a condition that naturally arises because people are in contact with one another; rather, it is a bond of trust and love that must evolve according to mutually agreed-upon standards of interaction. Had I assumed that the Pimas I visited were downright unfriendly, had I not returned to visit again, and again, and again, then this startlingly elementary lesson might have been lost to me.

My visits were motivated by a genuine desire to let parents know, firsthand, how well their children were doing with their writing. And I felt pleased to be able to deliver good news rather than the anticipated bad news often brought by school personnel. But these contacts constituted a form of official business. I knew I had no right expecting to be welcomed with open arms. And I wasn't: a nod, a thank you, a good-bye. Over and over. Month after month. I was being sized up, though not secretly, and without pretense of friendship.

One of the students whose home I regularly visited lived in a tiny three-room board-and-batten house with his parents and a younger brother and sister. Brian Whitman had been singled out early in my second year at Sacaton for individualized writing instruction because of his nearly outrageous ability to produce masterly poems with lightning speed and without noticeable effort. He became a regular in our group of "readers," reciting his poetry at various conventions and luncheons.

I frequently stopped by Brian's house in the late afternoons to share with his mother or father his latest literary achievements, or to discuss with them the details of our next excursion and presentation. They read and enjoyed the poems he wrote, and we shared pleasantries. Once they saw their son reading one of his works on a Phoenix evening news broadcast, and another time I brought them a copy of a feature story from the *Arizona Republic* that prominently displayed a photograph of Brian under which a poem he had written was boldly printed.

To deliver this kind of tangible proof of the students' success made me ecstatic. The small crescent smiles that formed on the faces of proud mothers and fathers were no trivial part of the reward I felt. For four months, I continued these fairly regular visits to the Whitmans. Each time, though we conversed outside the home, standing in the desert sun, they became a little less tense, a little more talkative, although they punctuated my every departure with the habitual "Thank you."

Then one afternoon, near sunset, I stopped by the Whitman home to drop off a sheaf of Brian's latest writings. The door cracked open, and I saw his mother, Linda, peering out at me. Behind her, the kitchen half of the house's main room was brightly lit, and several men sat at a table laughing, drinking beer, and apparently playing some kind of board game. A voice boomed out from inside, "Who is it?" I recognized Nelbert Whitman's tenor. Linda turned and told him who it was, then turned back and started to open the door just wide enough for her to ease through sideways. My meeting, I knew, would be with Linda alone, outside as usual. I stepped back to allow room for Linda to emerge and heard Nelbert yell out again, "Hey. Tell him to come in." Linda caught herself in midstride.

I was genuinely startled. I realized instantly that I had become comfortable with the typical format of our encounters. It now occurred to me that entering the house, even though I had always wanted to, would complicate the very straightforward and simple nature of our relationship. Frankly, I wasn't sure if I was prepared for this new dimension. And besides, there were people in the house I didn't know. I was being invited into a group. How should this white man behave in front of Pimas who perhaps had never had a white man in their house before? Impulse told me to back off, hand Linda the folder of poems, and invent an excuse to leave. Logic, however, insisted that such a withdrawal might appear offensive, and at the least it would be mildly insulting to Nelbert. Linda backed into the house and held the door wide open. "Come in," she said.

Nelbert and three other men sat around the kitchen table. I wondered if the way I now felt had been the way both Nelbert and Linda felt when initially they walked through the same door, coming outside, at *my* invitation. The grounds for our previous contacts had always been dictated by me. We may have stood outside *their* home, in *their* yard, but we had certainly always stood inside the perimeters of *my* purposes for meeting.

"How ya doin'?" Nelbert was jolly but did not get up. He stretched a stiff arm toward me. I shook his hand, sensing that the gesture was something he merely acquiesced to. Then he

said, "I want you to meet some guys here." Their penetrating
black eyes comforted me not the slightest. "This is my brother,
Marshal . . . and another one of my brothers, Troy." We clasped
hands self-consciously. Nelbert then pointed to the third man,
saying, "And this guy ain't no brother to no one." The men and
Linda laughed as Nelbert went on, "His name's Spanky. At least
that's what we call him. And let me warn you right off, he can
be a big pain in the ass." More laughter.

Spanky offered a limp hand, which surprised me because
he was one of the largest men I had ever seen. Three hundred
pounds plus: a fat-muscle marriage that reminded me of a sumo
wrestler. Jesus, his ears were as large as oranges. "Don't believe
this asshole," said Spanky, pointing to Nelbert. "I'm gentle as
an angel." Spanky made his plea with the put-on air of a hurt
puppy and the voice of Bullwinkle the Moose. Somehow I believed him.

Marshal reached under the table and pulled out a luke-
warm Budweiser and handed it to me. Nelbert said, "You ever
play Battleship?"

"No."

"Sit down then. Watch a couple games. You'll pick it up,
then you can play."

I drew a chair up to the table, appreciating the opportunity
to sink back into the role of the observer. I pulled a long swig
from the beer and relaxed.

Nelbert Whitman, a short, round man with a pleasant face
and thick glasses, was fortunate enough to hold down a job as
a maintenance worker at the Indian Hospital in Sacaton. His
two sons, Brian and Dooncher, shared one of the tiny bed-
rooms, while his daughter, Alva, the youngest, slept in her
parents' room or sometimes on a sofa in the living area. Linda
Whitman, a small, lovely woman who looked so young I mistook
her for a daughter at our first meeting, maintained the house-
hold, which included the luxury of a washing machine set up
outside, behind the house. In the summers, when the nighttime
temperatures dipped only to a sweltering 98 or 99 degrees, the
Whitmans hauled their beds outdoors and slept under the stars,
between the house and the post-and-wire corral Nelbert had
built for their two horses. Nelbert made just enough money so
that the family always had plenty of food, the horses always had

plenty of hay, and he always had plenty of beer, which he admitted he drank too much of.

Nelbert and his brothers had, in their youth, a reputation as hard drinkers and fighters. They also had experienced modest success in the arenas, roping and bull riding at all-Indian rodeos, and young Brian was now keeping alive the family tradition by bull riding whenever he had the opportunity. His uncle Troy served as his coach and manager. The brothers Whitman also had savored a bizarre sense of the practical joke—not, I would discover, altogether uncommon among young Indian men. Once a family friend had passed out drunk outside of Nelbert's house, and the three pranksters superglued his fists closed and then stuffed a crumbled loaf of bread down his pants, knowing that when their friend awoke, he would be in great need of relieving himself, and would be unable to do so without severe embarrassment.

No one passed out that first night I was invited into the Whitman home. Four hours later, we said good-bye, after a dozen or so games of Battleship, a case and a half of Buds, bowls of chili stew with homemade tortillas, and plenty of laughter. Driving off, I felt lifted into a boozy euphoria. One of Nelbert's purposes had now become clear to me. I had been asked into his home to have fun. Simple as that. We joked, we ate, we played. Now, in my memory, the cluttered Whitman kitchen presented itself as a marvelously homey environment in which, I fathomed, I had been regarded as a potential friend all along. But friendship takes time. Tonight, after months of scrutiny, I had been invited into Nelbert's home in friendship.

Contemporary Indians remain wary of friendship with outsiders, a trait perhaps acquired after the countless deceptions they suffered under a government that broke most of its promises. But when the age-old bond of true friendship becomes fastened, one will not, cannot, find more loyal friends than Indians. Such was Nelbert's purpose for inviting me into his home. Such was his offering, and his love. From that day forward, I was part of the Whitman family.

6
Desert Dances

THE PIMA LAND is a place of many dances. Often, with friends or alone, I walked through the desert on warm days and listened to the dance of gentle winds weaving through the needles of saguaro cacti. A peaceful sound, the soft whizzing can be heard even in slight breezes. Not far from the half-dozen buildings called the village of Olberg, in the San Tan Mountains, there is a canyon of uncommon beauty, a stretch of which contains scores of magnificent petroglyphs. These ancient sketches of lizards and turtles and deer and people were carved on large boulders by the Hohokam. Their significance remains unknown. Did they serve a religious purpose? Were they merely the decorative art of the day? The Hohokam continue to keep their secrets. But these figures, frozen in rock for a thousand years, seem to come alive and dance if you watch them long enough; they shimmer and vibrate to the murmur of wind dancing through cactus thorns. I once saw a large chuckwalla scurry up and over its own ancestral image, then disappear into a crevice in the blink of an eye. It is easy to lose oneself for hours among the lively images in this ancient gallery.

There is also the dance of water. Not often, granted, but perhaps because of its scarcity all the more glorious. The crackling dance of steady winter rains or quick, pounding summer torrents. The churning dance of muddy water filling the arroyos. The graceful improvisations of mists rising off the scorched earth immediately after a storm has passed.

One winter the water dance became life-threatening. The Gila River filled, then flooded. The bridges crossing it disappeared, and all suffered structural damage except one, a sturdy old WPA-constructed span to Olberg. A taxicab from Phoenix, attempting to take a man home to Coolidge, was swept away as several of my students watched from horseback. Both occupants perished. Farther downstream, a pickup carrying a couple of young men from Scottsdale took a ride on the currents. The frightened passengers escaped and clung to tree branches until they were rescued. Later, that infamous rag the *National Enquirer* featured a story about this harrowing incident complete with ridiculous accounts of how the men wrestled off terrified rattlesnakes.

The waters of this flood rose so high they literally sliced the state of Arizona, along with the Gila River Reservation, in half. Anyone just south of the river in need of emergency treatment in Phoenix had to be airlifted by helicopter. Half of Sacaton's student body could not cross into town, so the school closed down for over a week. And this in the heart of a land that receives five or six inches of rain in an entire year.

And there's the dance of creatures. The reptilian flash of the whiptail lizard and the early morning scampering of the regal horned toad. The stingless wind scorpion's deliberate, stalking step. The darkling beetle's hopeless attempt to be graceful with its ass pointed skyward. The menacing glide of the tarantula hawk as she searches for her arthropod prey, which she will paralyze before depositing her eggs in the spider's nutritious body. The danse macabre of mating black widows. The coyote's wary steps, always leading him away as he turns his head over his shoulder to spot you. The ballet of wild horses zigzagging through mesquite trees and cacti. The rarely seen nighttime dartings of the kit fox. The nearly blind peccary grunting out its footfalls. Each and every creature choreographed by instincts adapted to the extremes of the desert. Each magnificent in its grand or minute way.

The most wondrous of all, however, is the dance of the people. The Pimas' sheer will to be here and to survive in the heart of the desert's challenging hostilities enacts a dance of the human spirit remote and unknown to most other groups of people. This spirit looks out on the desert and does not see barrenness; it sees a bountiful land of rich diversity. It does not regard the sawtooth mountain peak, the sun, the storm cloud, or the snake and coyote as enemies; rather, they are simply a part of the family. So, in truth, the Indian extended family goes far beyond biological or clan relatives. This spirit remains alive. It is the same spirit that is a part of the recent thrust of many tribes to retain or regain traditional values.

To watch old men at the Pimas' annual Mul-chu-tha fair stomping ancient dances in the dust to the rhythms beat on large cardboard boxes by other old men is to witness the dance of the wind, and of the water, and of the creatures, as well as of an enduring human spirit. The jingle of shells tied around the men's ankles shakes through one's muscles and into one's veins and arteries, never to be forgotten. And by this dance in the blood, the often-cited, little appreciated Indian relationship with the earth may be recognized.

And then there is Nelbert Whitman's strange dance, one that represents an evocation of his determination and agility. One evening I witnessed it. I had driven Linda and him to Casa Grande to grocery-shop. On the way out of town, I slowed the car when I noticed the long tan rope of a western diamondback just leaving the highway and coursing onto the gravelly right shoulder. Nelbert, sitting in front, also spotted the snake. He said, "Pull over, and keep your headlights on him. I need a skin like that for a hatband."

"What are you going to do?"

"Just watch. And don't come too close."

From the backseat, Linda mumbled with resignation, "Oooh, Nelbert."

Nelbert got out of the car and walked right up to the three-and-a-half-footer, now fully onto the loose gravel of the road's shoulder. I stood by the fender, intensely curious. When he got within a couple feet of the snake, he kicked some sand and pebbles straight into its face. The rattler coiled back and began to shake its tail. Nelbert stepped forward, saying, "Come on, baby. Come to me." He kicked more sand in its face.

Then the snake struck. But Nelbert, quick as lightning, jumped back, avoiding the angry fangs. He kicked more sand,

and then his dance began. He shuffled to the left, kicked sand, shuffled back to the right, kicked sand, then jumped back to the left. The snake valiantly aimed and repeatedly lashed out but never met its mark, for its Pima target never stilled; Nelbert danced left and right in unpredictable configurations. The snake's eyes soon became blinded by grains of sand and dust.

What happened next happened with such speed I don't remember seeing it. Nelbert's right leg came up, and with deadly accuracy his foot shot down and pinned the rattlesnake's head on the ground beneath his boot. The length of the reptile's brown body wriggled frantically to get loose. Nelbert reached down and gripped the snake's neck in his hand. Then he yanked hard, separating head from body. He then stepped back, dug a shallow hole with the point of his boot, and buried the snake's head so that no unsuspecting creature would stumble onto it and get accidentally fanged. I stood watching, my mouth agape. As Nelbert walked back toward me, he held his trophy in the air and said, "See, this way there ain't no bullet holes to ruin the skin." Indeed.

Nelbert Whitman had reason to be proud. He had speed and agility. He had confidence in the success of his odd snake dance. He had, in a very real sense, power.

7
Mul-chu-tha

EVERY MARCH I looked forward to the Mul-chu-tha, when the fairgrounds roared to life with a vengeance. Several thousand Pimas, as well as non-Indian tourists, gathered to celebrate, and the festivities transformed sleepy Sacaton into a miniature Indian Disneyland.

In the outdoor arena, an all-Indian rodeo drew ropers and riders from reservations throughout the West. Great clouds of dust rose into the air, enveloping the arena at all hours. Local Pima boys were hired to work the gates and prod the calves and bulls. They made enough money this way to enjoy the rest of the fair. A boxing tournament raged inside the exhibition hall next to an area jam-packed with booths selling Indian arts and crafts. In the northwest corner of the fairgrounds, a traveling carnival offered stomach-wrenching rides, dart games, bottle-ring games, basketball-hoop games, and teddy-bear prizes. Hot dogs and Polish sausages were consumed by the ton, and blue and pink puffs of cotton candy drifted along in front of contented faces.

In the center of the fairgrounds was a large ring of log and adobe ramadas, maybe ten in all. Each was leased by a community, church, or school group, and presented a menu of O'odham cooking at its best.

Each ramada had its specialty. While one was known for its exceptional popovers and chili, another had a reputation for its tamales. At still another booth, a Pima woman might announce that she had the best menudo—tripe and hominy soup—and she would be right. Next door, one might find the tastiest red or green chili burritos. The culinary experience at Mul-cha-tha required at least one stop at each ramada. Spreading this out over two or three days, one could expect to gain at least a few pounds. So what.

Each night the celebrations ended with an outdoor "chicken scratch" dance. A live band, consisting of drums, electric bass guitar, electric lead guitar, amplified accordion, and lead and background vocalists, thumped out its polka rhythms as the dancers bobbed up and down on a circular concrete dance floor. The music itself seemed born of the desert, and spread through the nighttime air like pure oxygen.

One March afternoon, the day before the 1982 Mul-chu-tha began, I went along on a sixth-grade class picnic at the picture canyon outside Olberg. Seventy-five kids devoured hot dogs and Coke and then fanned out in all directions to play among enormous boulders or to climb the steep rocky slopes. A short while later, young Brian Whitman returned through a small grove of palo verde trees holding his right hand up in the air. He had fallen down, and his hand had smashed full-force onto an oval teddy-bear cholla branch. Reflexively, his fingers had closed over the egg-sized cactus, and now the sharp spines pierced deeply into the flesh of his palm and fingers. Like a pitcher clutching a baseball, he held the cholla tightly, but, unlike a pitcher, he could not let go.

The teddy-bear cholla, a tree cactus with small, stubby branches densely loaded with pale golden spines that resemble, from a distance, the furry limbs of a stuffed teddy bear, is in fact one of the most treacherous of the cacti. At the tip of each spine is a tiny fishhook barb that makes extraction from flesh extremely difficult and painful. The small branches detach from the main stems with as little encouragement as offered by a breeze. This is a cactus you don't just walk *by*; it's one you walk *around*, keeping a wide, respectful distance.

Brian Whitman bravely fought back tears as he climbed into my car for the drive to the hospital. I stood next to him in the emergency room as a doctor pried his fingers apart with forceps. The cactus also came apart, and the doctor pulled out the pieces one at a time. Brian's left hand squeezed my hand every time the doctor yanked at the thorns. When the ordeal finally ended, Brian's right hand was bloodied and swollen and turning blue. A nurse cleaned it, then wrapped it in gauze.

Even more than the pain, Brian felt anger and disappointment. He was scheduled to fight in the Mul-chu-tha's boxing tournament the following day, and now had lost use of his punching hand. On the short ride back to his home, he kept mumbling, "Damnit."

"That's all right," I tried to console. "Next year you'll do it."

Brian's only response: "Damnit."

The next day I walked over to the fairgrounds with several students and some friends from Tucson. After passing through the entrance gate, the students headed for the carnival rides, while my friends and I ate, went to the rodeo arena to watch the saddle-bronc competition, ate again, strolled through the exhibit hall, then ate once more. Satiated, we ambled back to the exhibit area. We admired Tohono O'odham baskets, Hopi kachinas, and Navajo jewelry of silver and turquoise that none of us could afford. Then we found ourselves wandering in the direction of the boxing ring.

The area was surprisingly empty of life, and the ring itself had been dismantled. I assumed the tournament had been called off and felt happy for Brian; his disappointment might be mitigated. We took this opportunity to sit on the bleacher seats and relax—and digest. Every few minutes, however, kids appeared in the hall and, recognizing me, stopped to chat. During one of these casual conversations, one of my Tucson friends asked a couple of Pima boys if there would be any boxing this year. Said one, "Sure. It's outside, next to the chicken scratch."

I didn't know why the boxing event was moved outside, but I knew I was reluctant to go. All I'd think of, watching those kids slug it out, would be Brian Whitman's inability to compete because of his encounter with a teddy bear. I doubted that Brian would be there, even as a spectator. And I winced, picturing the young boy at home in anger and pain.

In the crowd around the outdoor boxing ring, I spotted

Nelbert and Linda Whitman. My friends and I sat down beside them.

I said to Nelbert, "Sorry Brian can't fight today. I know he was looking forward to it."

Nelbert looked at me with a broad grin, "That crazy boy's gonna fight anyway. He's over there gettin' ready."

"But he can't . . . with his hand the way it is . . . he won't be able to punch."

"Tell *him* that," Nelbert said with a chuckle.

Nelbert pushed his glasses higher on his face when the ring official announced Brian's name. Brian entered the ring and faced his opponent. Nelbert, never taking his eyes off his son, said, "That's my boy there." He shook his head proudly. "Maybe he ain't gonna win, but he's up there. Damn, he's up there."

The bout was scheduled for three rounds. The other boy was a Maricopa Indian from the tiny nearby reservation of Ak Chin. Tall and lean, he came out slugging at the bell. Brian fended him off with an outstretched left, and kept backing away. It was all he could do, but unfortunately it would get him no points from the judges. Linda Whitman mumbled, "I want to yell, 'Hit him,' but I don't really want him to."

Then Brian suddenly, and surprisingly, landed a solid right. His Maricopa opponent staggered, giving Brian a moment to back up and shake his gloved fist. I could feel the sting in Brian's hand; I'm sure Linda and Nelbert felt it, too. The boys resumed their combat. Brian landed another right, then backed up again, trying once more to shake the pain out of his hand. His mother caught her breath.

Nelbert yelled out, "All right, boy!"

The bell clanged. A respite. Brian sat in his corner, shaking his hand as he listened to instructions from his uncle Troy.

Nelbert turned to me. "He's something, ain't he?"

"Sure is," I said.

The bell sounded again. The two boys bounded toward each other. Immediately, Brian punched again with his right hand. The Maricopa boy weaved and dropped to his knees. Nelbert, Linda, my friends, and I were in a frenzy. We screamed, "Get him, Brian, get him!" The boy from Ak Chin came to his feet, and Brian stopped shaking his hand just long enough to score two more solid hooks. Again, the boy went to

his knees; the referee began counting: "One, two, three." Brian
hopped up and down on his feet and shook his hand violently.
"Four, five, six, seven." The boy was not recovering; he leaned
forward and held himself up by resting his gloves on the mat.
"Eight, nine, ten." We jumped to our feet, hollering our heads
off. Brian turned our way and raised his arms in victory.

For the rest of the day, for the rest of the week, we called
the determined pugilist "Rocky." And every time we did, he
modestly turned his head away and involuntarily smiled, still
shaking a blue hand.

Perhaps the only unique thing about this little drama is that
it is not unique at all; certainly not unique in either the Indian
or the non-Indian worlds. In movie scripts and in real life, such
scenes unfold all the time. Give Brian Whitman tousled red hair
and freckles over pale skin, and his victory stance could have
been a painting by Norman Rockwell. Make him a fictional
heavyweight loser-turned-winner, and you receive an Academy
Award for best motion picture.

Determination, perseverance, concentration, tenacity, and
performance in the face of almost certain defeat, not to mention parental pride, encouragement, and enthusiasm: These
are not ethnic characteristics. They are universal human traits
and values.

I have, since that day at the Mul-chu-tha, heard non-Indians, many working on reservations, say that Indians are completely different from non-Indians, and that any apparent
similarities are metaphorical. And thus the "noble savage" or
"romantic" image of the Indian is perpetuated. Conversely,
others have argued that all people are alike, and that there
exists no good reason to regard Indians differently from any
other group. Many people of this persuasion still believe that
Indians should be totally assimilated into mainstream society,
even against their will, and that reservation land—*Indian* land,
even by white law—should be taken away from them. *Both* of
these positions miss the truth, for Indians are *like and unlike*
other peoples at the same time.

Early in my years at Sacaton, I witnessed behaviors in the
Pima children that resulted from a cultural upbringing radically
different from my own. I also saw behaviors that reflected traits
common to all people. All too often the non-Indian, while look-

ing at the Indian world, chooses either to believe he should be looking at a mirror in which he sees essentially himself, or that he should be looking through a window, at a totally foreign landscape. Realistically, one sees, at various times and in various circumstances, both.

8
Arnold Allison

ARNOLD ALLISON REMEMBERED the old days. The days before the shift in government policy away from the educational objective of total assimilation of young Indian schoolchildren into mainstream society. That objective had, in fact, underscored the realm of Indian education ever since the first dark-skinned, shaven-headed little "savage" bewilderedly made his way across the threshold of the first Bureau of Indian Affairs boarding school. Through the 1950s, and into the sixties, the attempt to take the Indian out of the Indian persisted. Allison's "education" had begun in the 1930s. It was from him I first heard stories of life in a BIA boarding school.

Allison cut a striking figure. He was a fairly slender, thickly muscled man whose visage projected an angular, rugged handsomeness: good features coupled with lines of experience. He seemed to have grown into the look of wisdom. His skin was a rich manzanita umber, and the whites of his eyes, because of a lifelong condition, were always red, like small flames of sadness. His chromium-white hair, combed back from a sharp widow's peak, was as shocking as a solitary sun-drenched cloud floating over the desert, and it provided an uncommon contrast to his O'odham coloring. The general impression was mythic.

"In my day," he told me, "they didn't want us kids around

our families. Afraid we'd just keep bein' Indian. They figured
if they could keep you kinda like a prisoner for nine or ten
months each year, then you'd start actin' like them. Once you
was actin' like them, it's not too far to go until you're thinkin'
like them.

"If you was caught talkin' about your family or about your
tribe, you was punished—like no supper for that night. If you
was caught sayin' anything in your own language, or if they
found you was hidin' anything Indian, like a feather, then the
punishment was worse, like maybe a whippin' or solitary con-
finement for a few days.

"To make matters worse, when we finally got to go home
at the end of the school year, our parents was real suspicious
that maybe the education was workin' and we didn't fit in with
our people anymore. Those Navajos up north have some ceremonies they would put their kids through when they got home,
to purify them, to make them Navajo again. Hopis did that, too.
I guess other tribes did, but not us Pimas. I mean, not like
with ceremonies and such. If we was lucky, though, we would
sometimes get teased about actin' too Anglo. And the older
folks in the house would refuse to speak English, so you had to
keep up with the O'odham language."

Now, ironically, Arnold was employed by Sacaton School
District as the attendance officer. Each school day he was given
a list of absent students, and it was his job to track down the
truants. No outsider could have done the job more effectively.
The patterns of dirt roads crisscrossing the reservation were as
familiar to Arnold as his own palm prints. He understood the
complexities of O'odham family life, and thus knew not only
where the students resided, but also in which homes they likely
could be found on days they skipped school. And being a Pima
himself, he had no qualms about banging on doors, marching
in, and retrieving wayward youngsters.

Arnold Allison took his job seriously because he knew what
Indian education had been in the past, and he had seen the
beginnings of the positive changes it was now going through.
Assimilation of Indian people had not worked. In 1961, President John F. Kennedy's interior secretary, Stewart Udall, said
in a report by the Task Force on Indian Affairs, ". . . to ensure
the success of our endeavor we must solicit the collaboration of
those whom we hope to benefit—the Indians themselves." And,

strengthening this notion a decade later, President Richard Nixon stated, "The right of self-determination of the Indian people will be respected and their participation in planning their own destiny will actively be encouraged."

Planning one's destiny, of course, involves participating in the education of one's children. The way was now open for Indians to have a say in what and how their offspring were taught. This in turn made possible the development of education programs that were relevant to Indian students' identity *as Indians*. By the end of the 1970s, with the renewed pride in heritage that was spreading from reservation to reservation, and the government's continuing withdrawal from its former policy of assimilation, many schools, some now run by Indian school boards, were allowing previously taboo materials and teaching approaches into their classrooms. Sacaton was such a school. And Arnold Allison, an employee of that school, had witnessed over the last two decades perhaps the most significant long-standing change in government Indian policy ever to have taken place.

I must have struck Arnold as one of the new breed of educators coming out of this change in policy. In truth, at the time I began my work at Sacaton, I was not even vaguely aware of government policy or its effects on Indian education. I simply wanted to find the most effective way to get Pima students excited about writing. I followed my instincts and began to use the children's own experiences as a basis for their writing. Excluding their Indianness, in whatever forms it took, would have been to exclude their personal experience. It seemed to me only a matter of logic. That my approach conformed to a new concept of Indian education was a happy coincidence.

Arnold and I became friends. Occasionally, I enjoyed riding around the reservation with him. He pointed out landmarks—an abandoned adobe house, a slumped, long-dead palm tree, the rusted-out shell of an ancient car—by which I could find my way along the maze of dirt roads. He showed me where to find desert mistletoe, clumps of which he traditionally brought to school at Christmastime. And he began to teach me some of his language.

From Arnold's point of view, it must have been extraordinary. Years before, he had been punished at school for mentioning anything related to his tribe. Now, he regularly brought arrowheads, wild desert spinach, and old Pima legends into a school on his own reservation. Years before, he had been beaten for accidentally answering a teacher's question with "*heu'u*," the O'odham word for "yes." Now, he was teaching his language to an instructor at the Indian school for which he himself worked. Years before, he had been told that being "Indian" was something to be ashamed of. Now, he was telling Indian children to be proud of themselves and their heritage, to carry the past into the future with dignity and assertiveness.

I especially enjoyed listening to the old legends Arnold would tell. One of the first of these came in response to a question I had asked about the traditional O'odham tribal symbol. The pattern depicts a round maze; at the top a small human figure is entering the opening. The maze design is found all over O'odham territory: woven into baskets, sewn onto sweatshirts, glazed in pottery, displayed on tribal buildings, and used on letterheads.

"I'itoi—you could call him Elder Brother—he's the Creator. Well, he made this house for himself up on top of South Mountain near where Phoenix is. He made it in the shape of that maze so that if any enemies came after him, he could hide out at the center, and they would never be able to get to him.

"One day some enemy warriors came. They was gonna kill him. I'itoi hid right in the middle of the maze. Those warriors went right into his house. Soon they lost their way in the dark and began fallin' on top of each other, screamin' and suffocatin' the whole time. I'itoi was safe, and all those warriors died in the maze.

"So that's it. The maze is I'itoi's house, and the little man at the top, goin' into the maze, is I'itoi himself."

The story struck me as metaphorical. For over a hundred years, the missionary and BIA schools had sought to reach the core of Indian inner life and destroy that which made it ethnically and culturally unique. Somehow many Indians had managed to steal away into the center of a complex maze of minimal outward adaptation and maximal inward adherence to their particular vision of the world. It took a long time, but now the enemy forces were figuratively dying off; the government could not penetrate that essence that makes the Indian what he really is. The little man at the center of this maze is the spirit of hope and pride that often the conquered refuse to relinquish when all else has been lost.

The metaphor, of course, is too simple. Thousands of individual Indian people have had their Indianness stripped from them, have lost their identity. Some have been assimilated, and more have simply fallen into a spiritual limbo from which there appears no rescue. The resurgence of Indian pride in the last few decades may seem like a phoenix rising from its own ashes, but the truth is Indian heritage and vision were never fully snuffed out, even at the cruel hands of teachers who, for over a century, strove to eradicate the practices and lifestyles, the behaviors and beliefs, the very minute-by-minute thoughts of a free people who once looked with trepidation upon fair-skinned, invading foreigners. Arnold Allison had seen a lot in his years; he was a man who remembered the old days, *and* the old ways.

9
Culture Shock

FLIP A COIN. Chances are 50–50 you will come up with heads—
or tails. The same is true in much of the Indian world; flip the
coin of an ordinary day on a reservation, and chances are 50–50
you will come up with some startlingly beautiful reflection of
true, old Indian values, or some modern tragedy that baffles
and horrifies. My own white cultural orientation did nothing to
prepare me for this paradox; as a result, during my second year
at Sacaton, I experienced a culture shock that left me so numb
I considered leaving the reservation and the Indian world for
good.

The month of March came and left like a scorpion on
attack. The first of several stings was delivered the first week of
the month. Sacaton was abuzz with the whispers of a horrible
event that had taken place on the west side of the reservation.
A young mother, living alone with her baby, had not been heard
from for a week. Upon investigation, she was found in her
home holding a mute vigil over the dead body of her child,
which lay decomposing on the kitchen table. The girl was taken
to the psychiatric unit of the Indian hospital in Phoenix.

The day after hearing this, I stopped to visit the Perez
family. Betty was home alone. She was seated on the sofa, curled
over and weeping into a handful of tissues.

"What happened?" I asked.

She blew her nose and straightened her back. "A friend of mine got killed last night," she said.

I sat down, catching my breath. "How?"

"She was arguing with her husband. He was drunk and was gonna drive off in their pickup." Betty paused to wipe her eyes, then went on. "She grabbed the door handle, and he hit the gas. They said when the truck jerked forward, it pulled her down, and the back tire ran over her."

I sat in silence with Betty for quite some time; not the wonderful silence I remembered we had shared when we sat in her kitchen eating saguaro fruit, but the painful silence that rises for the dead. In my manicured upbringing, what had happened to Betty's friend did not occur except as headlines in newspapers or on television news broadcasts.

The next week still another sting was thrust deep into many of us. Lucille Thompson, wife of our school-board president and an active participant in the school's parent advisory committee, had been driving home from a visit to her Maricopa family on the west side. It was late on a Saturday night. The car that hit her head-on was said not to have had its lights on. The girl driving that car, who was intoxicated, died instantly. Lucille lingered unmercifully for four days, asking her husband in moments of consciousness if she was dying.

Lucille's wake was the first of several I would attend at Sacaton. Wailing alternated with a crushing silence; and when eight Indian women stood by the casket singing hymns, a profound sadness seemed to lift out of the very earth that was preparing to accept Lucille Thompson's mortal remains.

The following weekend, news of yet another death arrived. Tommy Sanchez had been a bus driver for Sacaton School District. Recently, the school board had dismissed him for having shown up at work drunk. The board was fully justified in its action. It is a terrible thing, however, to see a man's life sink deeper and deeper into an abyss of despair. Tommy Sanchez spiraled into constant drunkenness with blinding speed.

On Friday night, he had been drinking heavily at Last Chance Bar at the northern edge of the reservation. He left the bar intending to go home on foot. Weaving his way into the darkness, he wandered into the middle of the highway and was struck by a car and killed instantly.

I knew Tommy Sanchez. The previous year his son had

been a student of mine. In August, as I worked in my office at the school, Tommy had come by with several pieces of paper in his hand.

"I want you to have these," he had said. They were copies of three poems written by his son, all about the boy's grandfather. The older Sanchez had passed away that summer, and the boy had taken the death hard. Sanchez explained that his son had withdrawn into his bedroom after the funeral, refusing to come out for several days. During this intense time of grief, the boy had composed the poems. He finally had emerged from his room and shared his written thoughts with the family.

Sanchez had said to me, "I just want to thank you for teaching my boy how to express his feelings. It helped him." I felt deeply moved. Now, seven months later, the boy would be attending his father's funeral, and I wondered if his ability to express his feelings would help in the face of another devastating loss. Probably not, I thought. Maybe a little, I hoped. The tragic circumstances of Sanchez's death would not help.

During the following days and nights, a terrific depression swept over me. In the world of the eastern suburbs where I spent my childhood, the deaths of people we knew were facts that had to be dealt with perhaps every few years. Such common regularity of death as I now witnessed shocked the very tips of my nerves. The world, indeed the universe, seemed out of kilter. Time itself seemed to have speeded up in a cruel way.

At this time, I lived in an apartment on the reservation. A Tohono O'odham friend of mine who had worked for the school district was renting a room from me. Some months before, he had almost lost his own life in a single truck accident that had claimed two other lives. The rollover had also affected Greg's memory, which was now slowly returning in bits and pieces, like fragments of a puzzle that sometimes delighted and sometimes confused him. I had offered him a room so he would not have to live alone during his recovery. Initially, after visits from his friends, I would have to remind him who they were. Sometimes he looked bewildered; sometimes he grinned with a flash of recognition; the pieces of his life, one by one, were again coming together. Some pieces stayed in place, while others became dislodged and disappeared after a short time. But even these were starting to take hold. I was watching an entire life reconstructing itself before my eyes.

Greg told me that his first memory in the hospital was of

watching two orderlies attend to him—one white, the other Indian. He said he had become instantly overwhelmed with a sense of dreadful, soul-scorching fear, because he had lost his identity entirely; he did not know if he himself was white or Indian. Later, able to lift one of his arms to observe its color, he concluded he was Indian but felt no less panicked, for now he had no idea which tribe he belonged to.

Now, we sat at night talking about Betty Perez's friend, about Lucille Thompson, about Tommy Sanchez. Greg would say, in response to my stuporous questions, "You've just got to accept it. That's the way it is with many of my people. For a lot of them, there's no hope of a future, and without that there's no reason to accept the present." His memory of being Indian, and of the suffering of many of his brothers and sisters, was clearly back.

The following Saturday, Greg visited his sister and brother-in-law. They also lived in Sacaton and had picked him up for dinner. The day was breezy and warm, and the delicious odor of desert wildflowers wrapped itself around the reservation. Only the purr of a car pulling up to the front of the apartment broke the springtime quiet. I thought maybe Greg had come back early, but then the doorbell rang, so I knew it was someone else. As I walked through the living room, the sound of soft sobbing entered the open windows. I stopped in my tracks. Shit, I thought, this better not be more bad news. Opening the door, I didn't recognize the young women or the two children with her. All three were crying.

"Is Greg here?"

"No. He'll be back later." I waited.

"I'm sorry." The young woman wiped her nose with her sleeve. "Can you give him a message?"

"Of course."

"Tell him to come to the Martinezes' house as soon as he can. His friend Albert is dead."

My knees buckled. I leaned against the doorframe and asked the inevitable question, "What happened?"

"Last night, at Bapchule . . . he was at a party with his brother . . . he got stabbed."

"Who did it?"

"Some cholo guys."

The cholos on the reservation were young Indian males

who, having no Indian identity, emulated young Mexican-Americans in their dress style, musical taste, and compulsion to establish gangs.

I told her that as soon as Greg returned, I would drive him to the Martinez home. She thanked me; then she and the children drove off. I shut the door and fell back on the sofa.

Albert Martinez, Greg's friend, lived to the age of seventeen years. He prided himself on his reputation as a cowboy. Like Nelbert Whitman and his brothers, like Nelbert's own son, Brian, Albert Martinez traveled the rodeo circuit and lived the young, brave life of those who witness the arenas from the inside. Albert Martinez happened also to be the victim of mistaken identity, and it cost him his young life.

Albert Martinez was a confidant of the Whitmans and a close friend and supporter of Brian's bull-riding efforts. He was a lifelong friend of Greg's, and had frequently visited Greg at my apartment. Just three days before his murder, he sat in the living room as Greg attempted to give him an even haircut. Albert Martinez was a teenage father. His child would never know him.

Last night, Albert Martinez had nothing to do. He accepted a friend's invitation to climb into the cab of a pickup and head out to the village of Bapchule where a dance was being held. He and his friend got drunk. Albert knew little of the cholos who for some reason hated his friend. He began to feel ill and wanted nothing more than to sleep. He found his way back to the pickup, opened the door, climbed in, weakly pulled the door behind him, and drifted off into unconsciousness. No more than half an hour later, a group of cholos, looking for Albert's friend, spotted the pickup. They approached it and saw a young man sleeping in its cab. They flung open both doors and jabbed their knives forward. Albert Martinez died.

Albert's wake was in the carport of his family's home. After the funeral, a feast was held at the Catholic Mission in San Tan. As I sat over a bowl of chili without the will or appetite to eat, I thought about what the priest had said during the service: "When a young person dies, we often look for and find reasons that help comfort us. But the truth is, there was no reason for Albert to die. And we should not be comforted. Albert's death came from an act of mindless violence. There is no comfort in that. And no good will result from his death unless you, the parents of the young people who perpetrate such deeds and the young people who are the victims of such deeds, put a stop to the gangs, and the alcohol, and the drugs. If you do not do this, Albert died for absolutely no reason at all, and more will die."

The next week passed, and then the next, and the next, without a death, though I had braced myself. I had learned to expect the unexpected, but now I expected the worst. At night, I suffered dreadful nightmares. During the day, I felt hollow, as if all natural emotion had been drained out of me. I couldn't laugh and I couldn't cry, and I didn't care. I thought the only remedy would be to leave Sacaton, to go back to Tucson and a world I knew, a world I could handle. I knew that leaving would betray a personal weakness, but I didn't care. I considered handing in a letter of resignation, effective at the end of the school year.

But then, late in the evenings while I lay sleepless in my bed, the faces of the children with whom I had everyday contact began to haunt me. One by one I saw them and whispered their names. I wondered what the future held for them. I wondered how many and which ones would not survive until their twentieth birthdays. These were beautiful children, happy and alert. Yet within only a few years some of them would find no more reasons to smile; some would be gripped and shaken by the hands of anger and bitterness. Some would kill, and some would die.

But this, I concluded, was not reason enough to stay. Such hauntings, I had learned, often drove the non-Indian to assume the role of "missionary." Most of my Indian friends had no time for people who were out to save their tribe, while most non-Indians who devised such plans burned out quickly. Indians do not need to be saved; they need to be given more opportunities.

When it occurred to me that I had already touched a few individual lives, and that a few had touched mine, I began to have second thoughts about leaving. Not second thoughts about saving a tribe, but about my relationship with students and friends. There were young people here who through our being together discovered talents and abilities they had previously been unaware of. Perhaps one or two would someday use these talents in ways that would improve the quality of their lives. There were also Pima friends I saw nearly every day, who loved me and whom I loved. If I resigned and moved away, these were the people I would leave behind. I remembered the lesson about friendship and loyalty I had learned from Nelbert Whitman. Was I now to say good-bye and shut these friends out of my life? Was I to become just another white man who had gained true friendship only to disappear when things weren't going the way he thought they should?

I did not have to be a "missionary" to help children. An educational need existed in the community, a small part of which could be, indeed was being, addressed by my work. Although it was true I needed to be braced for anything, I also needed to consider my actions in the light of my duties as a responsible educator and a loyal friend.

There was no choice but to stay. With this new resolve, and with a clearer sense of my role in the community, I started to feel again, to feel the *grief*. And then I began to feel a little bit better.

10
Readings

Two of the most pleasurable as well as rewarding aspects of my role as writer-in-residence at Sacaton were bringing Pima children into contact with professional writers and providing them on occasion with the experience of sharing their own writings with audiences. From the start, I regularly drove three or four of my best students to Tucson to attend literary readings at the University of Arizona. On each excursion, I would brief the students on the writer they were about to see, and after the readings we discussed the work we had heard. We also attended the after-reading receptions, where the children were introduced to the writers. One group had the opportunity to meet the great Indian writer Leslie Marmon Silko. Another was fortunate enough to spend several minutes chatting with the legendary Robert Penn Warren.

I also arranged for writers to visit Sacaton and meet with students in their classrooms. Creek poet Joy Harjo and Seminole writer Cindy Wilson were among those who provided strong Indian role models during their visits. Some of the students were fortunate in getting to know poet Rita Dove, who would go on to win the 1987 Pulitzer Prize for poetry. Rita, her German novelist husband, Fred Viebahn, and I attended the University of Iowa together, and Rita now taught at Arizona State University in Tempe. They often came to Sacaton for desert picnics with my Pima friends and me. On several occasions, the well-known poet Norman Dubie visited—once for the Mul-chu-tha fair. One April, in fact, Dubie donated his typewriter, which was given to the winner of a schoolwide poetry contest. Richard Pedro, the young Pima junior high school student who won, now typed his poems and schoolwork on the very machine with which a nationally recognized poet had pounded out several of his books.

These visits by writers were not just one-way avenues of teaching/learning. Through classroom encounters, picnics, and just being in the community, the writers themselves learned much from the Pimas. The fabric of O'odham life and culture were gleaned and appreciated by the writers who came to this little village in the middle of the desert. Fiction writer Kit McIlroy, after a number of visits to the community, wound up writing a short story about a Pima family that was published in Houghton Mifflin's *Best American Short Stories of 1986*. Later, McIlroy and his wife, Karen, joined me in establishing a nonprofit organization whose purpose remains the teaching of expressive writing to young Indians. These exchanges at Sacaton benefited everyone, and in Kit and Karen's case resulted in long-term commitments to Indian education.

I wanted my best students not only to meet and interact with professional writers, but to experience a taste of the writer's life; I wanted them to get up before audiences and give poetry readings. With the support of the community and most of the school-board members, and the resulting support of an ever-changing school administration, I was able to arrange a number of "field trips" on which the students gave poetry readings to a wide variety of audiences.

The first off-reservation performance the students gave was at the 1982 National Indian Child Conference, an annual convention sponsored by Save the Children Federation and held that year in Phoenix. Our presentation was to be given in three parts. First, I would conduct a forty-five-minute workshop on the importance of teaching creative writing to Indian students. This would be followed by a demonstration lesson in which ten sixth-grade Pima students were to compose poems in front of the audience. In conclusion, three junior-high students would recite their works.

The conference was held in September, and we had three weeks to prepare. On the off-chance we might receive some publicity, I had written letters describing our presentation to the Phoenix television stations and the state's largest newspaper, the *Arizona Republic*. Ten sixth-graders were chosen for the demonstration lesson, and three of the best writers were selected to read their work. Of the three, only eighth-grader William Andrews had prior experience reading before crowds. The previous year he had participated in performances we had given locally to the school board and parent advisory committees. Eighth-grader Lorrie Johnson had never given a poetry reading, but she was outgoing and confident. Of more concern to me was seventh-grader Brian Whitman.

Brian was clearly a writer of enormous talent, but his painful shyness was matched by his thick O'odham accent. I approached him several times and asked if he would be willing to join us as one of the readers. He decided he would not and told me so. I decided he would and told him so. I knew by now that to hold high expectations of children meant making specific demands on them.

I scheduled nine training sessions for the readers, three each week. During the first week, I met with each of them in the gymnasium, where I taught them how to hear and control their voices. William and Lorrie required only one of these scheduled half-hour sessions; they quickly became comfortable modulating their voices to several volumes with and without a microphone. Brian, in his unwillingness, was another story.

I'd stand all the way at the back of the gym. Brian would stand on the stage at the other end. I'd yell, "I want you to say 'hello' to me, but I want you to scream it."

Over and over, I could barely discern his mumbling voice.

Over and over, I'd shout, "I can't hear you! Scream it! Scream it out the way you scream at a little kid who's got you angry!"

Finally, in sheer frustration and anger, Brian bellowed out, "I can't!"

"That's it!" I shrieked. "That's the voice I want you to learn about today! Yell at me again!"

Teaching Brian to articulate his words so that a non-Indian audience could understand him took longer. It seemed we spent an eternity on each of dozens of words, but each passing day found Brian growing more confident, and sounding better and better.

Then I got word that the feature writer for the *Arizona Republic*'s Sunday "Arts and Leisure" section was coming to Sacaton to do a story on us. On Friday morning at 10:00 A.M., three days before our presentation date at the conference, reporter Ed Montini, the students, and I sat down around a table in the school's music room as a photographer's flash exploded like continual lightning.

Montini said, "Why don't we start with the students reading me a couple of their poems. Then I have some questions for them."

I handed the kids the manila folders containing their poems and said, "Okay, let's begin with you, Brian. Read the poem you wrote called 'The Stallion.' "

He found the poem and laid it flat on the table. This was the first time he would read his work out loud to someone other than William, Lorrie, and me. He studied the words he had written. I said, "Go ahead, read it now."

Brian opened his mouth, and that was as far as he got. He simply froze up. "Go ahead," I said again. He giggled uneasily and once more froze solid. Good Lord, I thought, and he's supposed to read in front of scores of people on Monday. "Brian," I whispered, "I want you to take a few slow, deep breaths. Do it now." He shut his eyes and breathed deeply. Then I said, "Now, I want you to pretend that there's no one else in this room except me. You're going to read your poem to me, only me, the way you've read it for the last couple weeks. Go ahead, read the poem."

Brian cleared his throat. His voice cracked as he read the first few words, and then he stopped. He tried again. On his third attempt, either because of mounting courage or because of the fear of what I would do after the reporter left, his voice took on authority, and the poem rang out. A shiver ran down my spine.

In Sunday's paper, three quarters of the front page of the "Arts and Leisure" section was devoted to us. The story was titled "Seeking a Voice," and featured photographs of the students and me. Poems by the students were printed next to close-up photographs of them. The article, needless to say, became a point of pride for the Gila River Indian Community.

By Monday morning, I had developed a severe case of psychosomatic laryngitis. There were several good reasons for my terrific anxiety. For one thing, I myself had never spoken before a large group of adult strangers. For another, I had no idea if the ten sixth-graders would actually write poems in front of the crowd, much less good poems. We had never done anything like this before, and my high expectations were founded on faith, not experience. Third, would William, Lorrie, and Brian do as well at the conference as they had done in the gym? I didn't know. I bought some throat lozenges and spray, and then I prayed.

On Monday afternoon, as we were setting up in our designated conference room, a sudden icy wind blew through my bones when I saw news crews from two Phoenix television stations entering the room with cameras and klieg lights. Oh, shit—would any of us be able to go through with this while two cameras recorded our every word and gesture? With a trembling hand, I coated my throat with a thick layer of numbing spray. There was no backing out now. Nearly eighty people came in, sat down, looked at me, and waited for the show to begin.

During the first few minutes of my talk, I kept glancing at Norma Richardson—Sacaton's federal-grants writer and my mentor. She kept smiling and nodding. This had a calming effect on me, and it wasn't long before I relaxed and started to enjoy standing there, talking about things in which I believed so strongly. My voice regained its muscle as I went along.

When I finished, I introduced the ten sixth-graders. They came forward and sat behind a long table. I offered the demonstration lesson, then asked the students to write a poem in ten minutes. They all completed their poems with time to spare, and they wrote as well if not better than they usually did in the classroom. I was astonished. I read their poems aloud, and the audience applauded each one. I wanted to run behind the table and hug every one of those kids.

Then I called William, Lorrie, and Brian up to the front. One after the other, they delivered perfectly beautiful recitations. I was in heaven.

After our presentations, as the people drifted out of the conference room, a television news reporter asked if the students would read their poems again for some close-up shots.

The students breezed through the second reading. These three children, as well as the sixth-graders, had more than measured up to my faithful expectations; they gave their parents and everyone on the reservation reason to be proud.

Later, after a fine restaurant dinner, I took William, Lorrie, and Brian to Rita Dove's home to watch the early evening news. Sure enough, there we were. When William saw himself reading one of his poems, he became so overwhelmed he began to hyperventilate. Rita gave him a brown lunch bag to breathe into.

Over the next three years, I had students give presentations at a number of different functions. The children faced their largest audience at the Heard Museum Guild's annual luncheon, where they recited their work before five hundred people. We appeared at such diverse places as Northern Arizona University in Flagstaff and at another National Indian Child Conference in Spokane, Washington.

On one occasion, through the efforts of Rita Dove and Norman Dubie, we were invited to the Swarthout Literary Awards Ceremony at Arizona State University. There, the students appeared as the featured poets for the gathering's finale. Until that time, the university had always brought in a famous writer to conclude the event.

As we sat in the front row of the darkened auditorium, the students bent, twiddled, and broke the paper clips I had given them to work out their nervousness. I reminded them to take several deep breaths before climbing to the stage. Then I was called to the podium to explain who we were and introduce the young readers. As I had come to expect, the kids performed splendidly.

Malania Pasqual's composure was particularly remarkable. She had quietly risen to her feet as I introduced her. Then, as she climbed the stairs leading to the stage, she tripped and fell down. Without hesitation, the fourteen-year-old pulled herself up, gathered her poems, brushed off her beautiful Indian ribbon dress, then delivered a flawless recitation. When she finished, the audience gave her an extended, enthusiastic round of applause.

As I write this, years later, it's only days since I attended and presented Crow and Chippewa-Cree students at the annual

Montana Bilingual Education Convention. During one of the luncheons, a Sioux educational leader was introduced as a "genuine Indian celebrity." He began his address by saying, "I was just called a celebrity, but in truth I am not. Not a real celebrity, that is. The real celebrities—and we must never forget this—are the children, our Indian children. They are a reflection of us, and they are the future. We should be mindful and take care. Our children are the true celebrities, and they should always be treated with profound respect."

11
Peach Springs and the Hualapai

IN 1984, AFTER FIVE successful years at Sacaton, I decided to throw caution to the wind. I was interested in expanding the writing program I had developed, and wanted to try it out with children of other tribes. Several reservation schools in Arizona were interested, so I left the security of my position in Sacaton, financed a small pickup truck, threw my gear in the back, and took to the road as a free-lance education consultant with the aim of hopping from one reservation to another to work several weeks at each. Fortunately, I also had several contracts stuffed in the glove compartment, all signed by school superintendents.

On an early autumn day, I arrived in the remote town of Peach Springs. I had come to work with the Hualapai Indian children, but I was suddenly not at all confident that the Hualapai would respond to me as the Pimas had.

To make matters worse, when I pulled into Peach Springs, there seemed to be no physical center to the place. There seemed, in fact, to be very little *life* around.

Driving from Flagstaff, I had my first inkling of the Hualapai's remoteness when I exited Interstate 40 at Seligman, a strip of old fast-food joints, older gas stations, and a few motels whose sun-bleached exteriors resembled faded 1950s postcards. From

Seligman I pushed through forty miles of old Highway 66, traversing a colorless desert grassland flanked on the north by the Aubrey Cliffs. Stately as they were, the cliffs in their grayness seemed to have been drained of life. A few miles before Peach Springs, a sign announced the Grand Canyon Caverns— not the biggest attraction in Arizona—and just beyond was a small motel and a general store. Moments after this speck of civilization, the flat terrain became joltingly rolling, and I was headed steeply downhill into what at first appeared to be a ghost town.

Peach Springs. A motel, all right, but obviously closed for some time, its windows either broken out or boarded. And a barely standing, 1940ish gas station—closed, too, its pumps rusted into relics of a time before Interstate 40 took all the traffic away from old 66.

I had been over this road twice, years before, but back then Peach Springs and the Hualapai were not, for me, a reality. I had known they were there, but just passing through, I could not have testified to their existence.

Now, I followed the map Lucille Watahomigie, a school administrator, had sent me. A short distance off 66, I came to the apartment complex owned by the school. Number 3 was reserved for consultants. I parked in front and walked to the last unit, where one of the teachers and his family lived. Lucille had indicated on the map that this teacher would have the key to my quarters.

A short, thin white man with a mustache and a Beatles haircut opened the door. I introduced myself.

"Yeah. I'm Tom. I got the key for ya. Come on in."

His voice startled me; he spoke with a distinct New York City accent.

He said, "We're having dinner in about half an hour. Wanna join us?" I thanked him but excused myself. I was not hungry. All I felt was nervousness at suddenly being in this odd place.

After unpacking, I decided to take a walk; maybe I could burn off a little anxiety. The hills around Peach Springs didn't impress me. The stony earth was a drab beige and bore but one distinctive feature—lots of round juniper trees. In my unsettled mood, I thought the land looked like a measled body.

A number of disturbing thoughts crossed my mind. Maybe

the students wouldn't like me. Maybe the adults would think me presumptuous. Maybe I'd be laughed off the reservation. These people weren't going to look at me with the same indifferent eyes they cast toward a passing tourist. Rather, they'd be expecting some tangible results from my contact with their children. Maybe the Hualapais would soon be snickering—"Another ridiculous white man."

When I finally got around to scolding myself for entertaining doubts before I'd even started my work at Peach Springs, I began to relax a little. As a language-development consultant, I would be going into many new situations like this, on many different reservations, and I realized that I had better not anticipate them negatively. Maybe I wasn't going to be confident in each situation, but I could at least approach my responsibilities with an appreciation for these opportunities to work with and learn about Indian people.

It also occurred to me that the real traveler enjoys the excitement of new experience, the anticipation of the unexpected. And, further, I was now a traveler with a definite purpose.

As I walked back to the apartment, I looked around at the juniper-speckled hills, at the irregular geometry of ancient rock; they were really quite beautiful.

The Hualapai, I would learn, were one of several loosely connected bands, all of whom generally referred to themselves as the *Pai*—a name which in their Yuman language means "people." To this day, they remain relatively undiscovered by most non-Indian Americans. The old Pai, living in an area bordered on the south by the Bill Williams River and, to the north, by the Grand Canyon, had no extended, significant contact with outsiders until the nineteenth century. Even now, the only non-Indian settlement of any size located on Pai ancestral land is Kingman, a rolling fifty miles west of Peach Springs.

The old Pai, numbering nearly fifteen hundred, lived in local family groups that assembled—for discussions of mutual problems—into thirteen regional bands. Eventually, these flexible units came together under the names of two of the bands: the Havasupai, or Blue-green Water People, who still inhabit a gorge under the Grand Canyon's rims, and the Hualapai, or Pine Tree People, named for the forests of the Hualapai Mountains. Today, these two bands of the Pai occupy two reservations and are considered two separate tribes, though they share the same Bureau of Indian Affairs agency.

The Hualapai reservation was established in 1883, and although the tribe was essentially peaceful, it was nonetheless regarded by Anglo settlers as a nuisance to be disposed of. In 1887, the *Mojave County Miner*, an area newspaper, ran an editorial that suggested the Indians' rations be mixed with "a plentiful supply of arsenic." The "Indian problem" would thus be neatly solved.

The Hualapai survived such intentions. Today, they share many of the same problems that other tribes suffer, but they also retain their basketry, excel at beadwork, honor old religious ways—and their language still lives.

Indeed, one of the great recent achievements of the Hualapai has been the development of a nationally recognized bilingual-education program. Under the inspired and aggressive direction of Lucille Watahomigie, a genuine force in Indian education, the program was singled out by the federal government as one of the top bilingual curricula in the United States. The many publications produced by the program have been distributed throughout the nation and serve as models at numerous reservation schools. Through language, the old Pai are still around. And through revitalization of Hualapai culture, the new Pai are spreading their educational influence across the country.

12
The Canyon

MY INITIAL UNEASINESS in Peach Springs was unfounded. The Hualapai children and I took to each other immediately; they were open, willing, and talented, not to mention just plain fun to be around. And they were sensitive to the historical realities of Indian people. Darlene Sinyella, a seventh-grader, wrote this about the tenacity of the American Indian:

> . . . We fought, but many of us died.
> Our spirits now haunt
> the lands we walked on.
> Now we sing, laugh, dance, and lie
> under the bright blue sky. We are waiting
> for our enemies who killed us to pass by.
> We shall stay here and wait until
> we find them. Until then we shall wait
> in peace and harmony.

Malinda Powsky, a Hualapai and a sixth-grade teacher, shared with me a respect for and a sense of friendship with the students. Her understanding of them was evident in her high expectations, and her affection reflected itself in her gentle patience. Malinda and I began to talk to each other, usually in snippets, about our aspirations for Indian education. One afternoon I invited her to drop by Apartment 3 for coffee. We sat in the sun-drenched living room and found ourselves excitedly exchanging, for nearly two hours, similar hopes for Indian youths. I was discovering, as we talked, the warmth and generosity of spirit that Indian adults readily offer when they do not perceive themselves as being backed into a corner. With my background in Indian education, and with the apparent compatibility of my ideas with a lot of Indians' ideas, I was finding friendships developing more quickly than when I had started at Sacaton.

The next day, in the corridor outside her classroom, Malinda said to me, "What are you doing after school?"

"I don't have any plans. Why?"

"Do you want to go for a drive? There's something you should see while you're here."

"What is it?"

"Something you should see. But I'm not saying what until you see it. It's kind of a surprise."

"Definitely. When do we leave?"

"Right after school," Malinda said. Then she added, "My nephew Arnell's going with us . . ."

Of course—I understood; two unmarried people heading out for mysterious destinations would not think of doing so without a chaperon. The most reliable types: the honest young and the frank old. Arnell, a fourth-grader, fit the bill.

I fueled up my truck after school, then swung by the playground to get Malinda and Arnell.

"Go up that way," Malinda said. She pointed, as Indians do, with her pursed lips. We headed north, away from Highway 66, climbed a gentle slope, and crested the hill near the first homes of a large housing project. Ah, I thought, *here* was the life I had not seen upon my arrival in Peach Springs, tucked away on a sage flat above and out of view from the highway.

Hundreds lived here. I spotted the tribal-police headquarters, the BIA agency building, the health clinic, and a definite pattern of north-south and east-west streets lined with scores of houses. Here were children bicycling and skateboarding, teens playing driveway basketball, older folks strolling in afternoon sunlight. Here, at last, was a Hualapai community. A center.

"So this is where the people live," I said.

"Most," Malinda responded. "And some more on the other side of the highway, across the railroad tracks." Peach Springs was becoming larger by the second.

A few minutes later, we reached the end of the housing project—and the end of the paved road. My truck lurched from one side to the other and back again over deep pocks and ruts and washboards and rocks the size of grapefruits and footballs. It was as though the housing development we had just gone through, with its smooth roads, was nothing more than an illusion, a hologram projected on the cool desert air that surrounded us. A lunar rover would have done nicely here. I slowed the truck as Malinda said, "You better take it easy from here on."

Almost instantly there rose, on either side of us, steep cliff walls, though they were not terribly high. We had entered the upper end of a canyon. I asked Malinda, "Are we going to the Wahavo'?"

The Wahavo', a cave in Madwida Canyon from whose depths, the Hualapai say, Indian people came up to the earth, is the most sacred place on the reservation. Just inside its entrance are many burial sites, the disturbance of which is said to bring death to the perpetrator. One would never consider coming close to the Wahavo' without the deepest reverence.

Malinda turned to me and smiled. "No, we're not going to the Wahavo'. But you're sure curious now, aren't you?"

"I've been curious from the start." I laughed.

"Good," Malinda said with the brevity of a final punctuation mark.

I tried to put the puzzle together. We were descending, gradually. We were in a canyon. We were headed north. *North.* That was it!

Quietly, cautiously, I asked, "The Grand Canyon . . . are we going to the bottom of the Grand Canyon?"

Malinda turned to me and smiled. Nothing more.

I had heard of this road before—the only one to reach all the way to the Colorado River within the huge Grand Canyon complex. It spanned reservation land, and non-Hualapais were required to possess a tribal land–access permit to drive it, or at least be in the company of a tribal member. The road did not appear on some of the popular road atlases, while it showed up on others inaccurately charted. Most cartographers apparently were not endowed with a memory of the importance this road had held around the turn of the century.

Before the development of the South Rim area, which today is jam-packed with gawking, shutter-pushing sightseers from every part of the globe, this corrugated track of dust and granite was the preferred route of the few tourists lucky enough, and wealthy enough, to experience the grandest of all canyons. A rustic lodge near the bottom, at Diamond Creek, long since washed away with other sediment, provided a welcomed oasis for the desert-weary. When the influx of the curious shifted eastward to the South Rim area, this road was left to the Indians, who still cherished it.

Our descent proved much more gradual than I would have guessed. The twenty-seven-mile road didn't plummet into the canyon, and there was no teetering at the edge of treacherous drop-offs or switchbacking dangerously down 9 percent grades. We seemed, rather, to be slipping into the chasm little by little. Every now and then, alert jackrabbits suddenly bolted from statuelike stillness, and with each leap put another fifteen feet between themselves and my truck. The craggy cliffs steadily rose, blocking out more and more of the sky, illumined by every pastel shade from dirty yellow to burnt orange to flamingo pink. The canyon was gradually swallowing us.

"We're almost there, aren't we?" I said. I could *feel* the Colorado now.

"Almost," Malinda answered.

We came to a junction with a side canyon. I stopped the truck. Malinda, again pointing with her lips, said, "That's Diamond Creek Canyon. About a quarter-mile upstream is where the old hotel used to be. Nothing left of it. Hardly anyone goes up there anymore."

We drove on. Huge domes and spires towered above the cliffs, dominating the narrow skyline. Within minutes, the road ended on a broad, stony flat. I jumped out of the truck and stood as still as a rock. The Colorado River, which lay twenty-five yards ahead and around a bend, gave off a much, much bigger sound than I had imagined possible—deep, steady, full-bodied, grave, perceived not just with the ears but with the entire body, a sound that signified nothing else, that was its own magnificent meaning. I stood there not knowing which ran faster, the river water or the adrenaline surging through my

own arterial rivers: "Jeeeezus," I said, overwhelmed, unaware
of anything but the river. Then I began to run.

At the river's edge, I just stared, wide-eyed as a child. The
sight of the red-colored river astonished me; this was one of
those moments that remains ambered in memory until memory
itself is ended. Late afternoon light dripped down gargantuan
sandstone formations, and the water ran wild and thunderous.

The old Indian value of the importance of direct contact
and communication with the earth could never have been more
starkly felt than at this place. Metaphors may be made, but to
touch this landscape with the senses, and to feel the resultant
emotional charge, was to know a well-grounded euphoria.

Malinda knew what I was feeling; she gave me time to look,
time to walk around, time to wander off humming to myself,
time to think and reflect, time to sit with my feet soaking in the
silty water. All the while she sat on a boulder, silently watching
the river.

At last I approached her. "I don't know what to say."

"You don't have to say anything."

"I should at least thank you."

"What you've been doing the last fifteen minutes is thanks
enough. I told you I wanted to show you something you should
see. Now you've seen it. Those moments when you first saw the
river, right after you ran off from us, you were excited like a
little kid. I knew what it would mean to you. Why do you think
I held Arnell back? He wanted to run along with you to the
river. I held him back because you needed to see with only two
eyes, not four. You needed to see by yourself something that's
common to us Hualapais."

I sat down on the powdery sand near Malinda. She said,
"You might wonder if we take it for granted? Some of us do.
But not most. I've just been appreciating it now as much as I
ever have. This is our heaven on earth. This is it."

A while later, as we stood on the red beach, Malinda said,
"You know, even the most beautiful things can sometimes be
deadly; and when you least expect it, too." She pointed up the
beach with her lips. "About ten years ago, some relatives of
mine came down here for a picnic. They had a baby girl, about
one-and-a-half years old, who wandered off when everyone else
was busy with one thing or another. A few minutes later, they
saw something floating downstream. It looked like trash, like a

clump of white Styrofoam. Then, about when this thing was straight in front of them, the father realized that it was Pampers—the kind his little girl was wearing. He knew that there was no place upstream for Pampers to be coming from. He jumped into the water and caught up to his little girl before it was too late. In another thirty seconds, she would have been swept too far away to be rescued."

13
Reggae Inna Hopiland

THE PEACH SPRINGS New Yorker, Tom Nicas, also became a friend of mine. One of the things we had in common had nothing to do with Indian education at all—we both loved and collected reggae, the Jamaican music first popularized by the late Bob Marley and his Wailers. On this and my several subsequent visits to work with the students of Peach Springs, we would tape each other's rare recordings.

Tom had long been known in Peach Springs as a reggae middleman, making available to the general Indian public the latest island sounds. Reggae, as hard as it may be for some to believe, has been for years the music of choice among the younger Hualapai, as it has for the Havasupai, the Hopi, and the Tohono O'odham. The Indians no doubt identify with the lyrics of the Jamaican superstars, lyrics that constantly assert the themes of standing up for one's rights even under oppression; of holding fast to the ideals of love, hope, and peace; of stoutly defending one's religious point of view; and of steadfastly refusing to abandon true cultural roots. Add to these concerns a rhythm so irresistible that no living organism can remain inert in the midst of it, and you have a genre of music that many Indians—as well as non-Indians—find addictive.

On one of my visits to Peach Springs, Tom asked, "What are your plans this coming Friday."

"Well," I answered, "I'm due at a school in New Mexico Monday morning, so I'll take off after school and stay in Flagstaff for a night or two . . . or maybe Gallup."

"That's kind of on the way," Tom said.

"On the way to where?"

"There's a reggae concert over on the Hopi reservation Friday night. I'm thinking about going. You interested?"

"Well, probably. Who's playing?"

"The Wailers. Marley's old band."

I had loved reggae for years, but I had never attended a live reggae concert.

At three-thirty on Friday afternoon, we left Peach Springs. One of Tom's daughters, thirteen-year-old Terra, and a young male friend of hers, Red Bird, came with us. On the first leg of the long trip across northern Arizona, I followed Tom's truck. The late afternoon drive was superlative—cool October temperatures and cumulus puffs sailing through an azure sky. From Seligman to Ash Fork, Tom led me over an old stretch of Highway 66 that paralleled Interstate 40. This wonderful, weed-choked route was now used only by a handful of locals. The only vehicle we passed was a fifties pickup with an ill-fitted, tiny camper top. Protruding from a hole in this withering aluminum shelter, near the back of the truck's bed, was a black wood-stove chimney. A camper for all seasons. Silly-looking, perhaps, like something from *The Beverly Hillbillies*, but practical enough.

Along this forgotten road stood equally forgotten road signs. One old yellow warning read NO PASSING ACROSS YELLOW LINE YOUR SIDE. Ah, the verbosity of our Anglo grandparents. The sign had been cratered with a war's worth of bullets.

When we reached Ash Fork, we had no choice but to take I-40. From there, old 66 was unfit even for coyotes. An hour and a half later, at Flagstaff, we stopped and rented motel rooms, then we left in my truck. Evening's shadow soon spread out across the immense hundred miles of plateau country that lay between us and the Hopi village of Kykotsmovi. We passed through Leupp, a small Navajo town, and after nightfall we spotted the distant lights of Hotevilla, Second Mesa, and Kykotsmovi floating in an ocean of darkness.

The Hopi Reservation looks, on a map, like a doughnut hole in the center of the vast Navajo reservation. Its borders are still in dispute. At the center of Hopiland is Old Oraibi, continuously inhabited by humanfolk longer than any other community in North America.

For more years than anyone knows, the Hopis have coaxed blue corn, squash, melon, and beans from sun-blasted rock. The Hopi religion, tied to the crops and the sun and the rock, has remained essentially unchanged. Even Hopis who spend most of their time away from this center of their universe are never really far from home, at least spiritually.

I had met one such Hopi a year before. At that time, Hartman Lomawaima was assistant director of the renowned Lowie Anthropological Museum at the University of California, Berkeley. He said he was preparing to take a lengthy leave of absence in order to return to Hopiland for further religious instruction. A big man with a soft voice, and confident in his dealings with the non-Indian world, he was nonetheless—and above everything—a traditional Hopi. Had the museum not granted the six-month absence, Lomawaima would have resigned his position.

Now, Tom, Terra, Red Bird, and I were on a different pilgrimage. We climbed a hill, nearing the ancestral mesas, then turned right where the road ended at its intersection with Indian route 264.

Given the absolute desolation of the Hopi high desert, I was astonished by the community center at Kykotsmovi. Imagine a college-size gymnasium without the surrounding college, without a surrounding of any kind. The parking lot was bathed in soft blue mercury light that created an unreal effect, as though we had climbed right into a movie screen showing a night-lit crowd. Hundreds of Hopis, as well as smaller groups of Havasupais and Hualapais, milled about, waiting for the concert to begin. We met several Indian friends and acquaintances of Tom's who had also made the long drive from Peach Springs.

Inside, along one wall of the gym, hawkers sold T-shirts, buttons, and wristbands sporting the Jamaican Rasta colors of red, green, and yellow. I bought a shirt displaying a Hopi kachina mask surrounded by the six-point Rastafarian star and six eagle feathers. A striking, stirring, amazing blend of designs and cultures. The lettering over the pattern read:

REGGAE INNA
HOPILAND USA

At other tables, the hungry bought tamales or tissue-paper-thin ash-colored cylinders of *piki*—the traditional Hopi bread made with blue corn and, yes, ashes.

As the lights dimmed, the crowd shifted from the food and souvenir tables to the center of the gym. Many of the fans jammed as close to the stage as possible; others hung back where more oxygen circulated. The stage lights flared up, and the crowd shouted its enthusiasm as four Jamaicans walked onstage with their fists raised high. This warm-up band, Sounds of Jamaica, delivered a rousing set.

And then came the Wailers, all sporting long, tightly coiled ropes of hair called "dreadlocks." With a new front man sounding remarkably like Marley himself, they covered all the old classics that had become internationally known since the great singer-songwriter-musician was claimed by a brain tumor in early 1981. Off to one side of the gym, a cadre of two dozen or so young whites and a few blacks, presumably from Phoenix and Tucson, shook their bodies in the loose reggae style of dancing called "skanking." The band members themselves moved about the stage with the grace and fluidity of a fast Blue Mountain stream.

In sharp contrast, the hundreds of Hopis stood motionless, transfixed, barely breathing, and hanging on every beat, strum, and lyric. This didn't surprise me. At powwows and other cere-monial dances, most Indian observers do not move. Foot-and finger-tapping, head-bouncing, or body-swaying are virtually nonexistent among Indians. Yet they do dance to the rhythms they hear—"in our blood, in our hearts," as one young Indian friend had told me.

What really surprised me was that halfway through the Wailers' set, many of the Hopis did begin to bounce their heads and tap their feet. This I had never witnessed. And toward the end of the concert, scores of Indians were swaying—almost skanking. I was shocked.

At one point, the band's percussionist shouted into his microphone, "We love Indians!" The Hopis roared, throwing their fists skyward. They roared again when the lead singer altered the refrain of Marley's classic oppression-survival song, "No Woman, No Cry," and sang out, "No Hopi, no cry!" The Hopis take their reggae seriously, and many, I learned, are moved to uncharacteristic physical expression when they attend reggae concerts.

When the music ended and the houselights came up, the
Wailers remained onstage. A young man introduced Miss Hopi,
and she presented the band with an exquisite coiled basket—a
gift of Indian friendship to be taken back to the island. Then
the Wailers came downstage to shake hands with their fans.
Jamaican and Hopi hands clasping. So many differences, yet
so many similarities. The "Rootsmen"—as black Jamaicans call
themselves—pressing flesh with the rootsmen and rootswomen
of America.

Perhaps the most touching moment, however, came when
Miss Hopi stepped to the front of the stage and reached a hand
out. The Hopi fans grabbed and shook her hand as enthusiastically as they shook the hands of the world-famous musicians,
as though she, too, were world-famous. In a way, here at the
center of the universe, she was.

14

The Moccasin Telegraph

NEWS TRAVELS FAST among Indians. The grapevine stretches and winds from one reservation to another sometimes so quickly one can hardly believe it. The common Indian term for this is "the Moccasin Telegraph." A really hot item might travel from coast to coast in a matter of days or less. And news spread among tribes that share a common regional culture travels throughout a given area sometimes in minutes, thanks to Mr. Bell. I was to learn about the power of the Moccasin Telegraph through several events.

One day I received in the mail a call for presentations from the Montana Indian Education Association. I looked hard at the envelope several times; it *was* addressed to me, no mistake. But with this form letter came no note of explanation, no number to call with questions, not even a hastily scribbled missive telling me from whom, what, or where my name had been gotten. I pondered this for several minutes. Had someone in Montana attended one of the workshops I'd given at a national Indian education conference? Had someone up North happened to come across one of several newspaper articles about the program I had developed? Had my name gotten into a computerized mailing list? I didn't know, but the Moccasin Telegraph was clearly at work.

I pulled out a map of Montana and located the Indian reservations—seven in all. The names of several lit a fire in my imagination. Cheyenne, Blackfeet, Crow. These were the names of tribes that from my earliest childhood I had encountered in those dreadful old westerns that didn't seem so dreadful at the time. These were the legendary people of the Northern Plains who, for a time, reigned supreme over a vast, buffalo-peppered prairie, who rode bareback and wore buckskins and eagle feathers, and who spread their tepees out across the land in great nomadic villages. These were the Indians whom practically everyone thought of when they thought of Indians. In my mind, they were the very stuff of legend, the core and pith of rightful resistance, the grit of hard endurance. And they were among the tribes who now were sponsoring a conference for educators of Indian children, to be held in October in Butte. I wanted to go.

After a little arithmetic, I realized I couldn't fund the trip entirely by myself. So, on the day I mailed back my presentation outline, I also sent an application to the Arizona Commission on the Arts, requesting a travel grant. The ACA, which had always been good to me, had sent me to the Gila River Reservation in the first place. During my years at Sacaton, I had served as the liaison between the ACA and the Sacaton School District, coordinating visits from various artists. I kept my fingers crossed.

Within two weeks, I received word from Montana that my presentation would be included on the MIEA agenda. To my great relief, I also was notified that my travel grant had been approved by the arts commission. Montana, the Plains tribes, Butte, indeed all that was *North*, would be altogether new to me. I couldn't wait to climb into the cloudless Arizona sky and soar off toward a land that had always existed only in my imagination.

Butte, Montana. The jet came in over the Continental Divide at a sharp angle, and there, atop the ridge, stood a snow-white, fifty- or sixty-foot Jesus, or Mary, or Moses—I couldn't tell which—watching over the houses, markets, churches, bars, and brothels of Butte. I had half expected the pilot to point out gleaming mountain peaks; rather, he drew our attention to an equally obvious sight—a perfectly round, gargantuan copper pit that looked for all the world like a bronze target, waiting, perhaps, for some blazing bullet or arrow to be shot into its center by the Great Creator.

Once the plane landed, I threw my bags into the back of the Copper King Inn van, and settled down to gaze at the sights. Unfortunately, the hotel was just across the highway from the airport; we were there in less than a minute. I climbed out and looked back at the plane I had just flown in on, only several hundred yards off. I could have raced back to it on foot had I left something valuable in the overhead storage compartment. So much for the sights.

The conference itself began the next day and turned out to be disappointing for only one reason: There were not many people in attendance. I heard grumblings from several folks that the MIEA should not have held the conference in Butte, that no one likes to come to Butte, that many who would have attended the conference had it been held in Billings or Great Falls or Missoula or Kalispell had stayed away because they were not particularly fond of Butte.

Butte, for some reason, often falls in at the wrong end of many a Montanan's jokes. Why, I'm not sure. Maybe because of the once-enormous, now-failed copper economy and the industrial flavor it had brought to a town smack in the middle of one of the nation's most rural states. I guessed that perhaps seventy people had shown up for the conference.

Disappointing also was the attendance at the workshops I conducted. At the first, nine people sat scattered in a room with fifty chairs. And only six seats were occupied the following afternoon. I had flown all the way from Arizona to speak to a total of fifteen Indian educators. It seemed hardly worth it, except now I could say I'd seen Montana—well, Butte.

At the workshops, I nonetheless delivered my presentations with the same enthusiasm I would have showed at a gathering of two hundred, making my pitch for the benefits of easing Indian children into written English language through culturally relevant creative writing.

After the second, smaller session, half of the audience— three people—came up to talk to me. One was a school-board member from the Blackfeet reservation. Mr. Thompson introduced himself, then mumbled, "Good talk," and was gone. Indians rarely, if ever, put on effusive displays of congratulatory praise. Benign silence can indicate a warm, accepting response. A "good talk" comment, as I had just gotten, often translates to special recognition.

The two women who had come forward asked if I would sit down with them and talk some more. I was hastily bundling my papers, ready for a quick dash to the hotel pool, but their interest filled me with pleasure. As far as Indian responses go, silence with head-nodding is good; a two- or three-word comment is great; but a call to talk further means you've transformed curiosity into dialogue, the best-possible aftermath to any workshop.

Barbara Bacon and Sharon Peregoy were Crow Indians, teachers on the Crow Reservation in South Central Montana, and both were interested in using creative writing in their classrooms. We talked for another forty-five minutes.

After we said good-bye, I gathered my things and left for the pool. I felt elated. Okay, the conference was poorly attended. And only fifteen people had come to my two workshops. But if I had flown all the way from Arizona to Montana only for this contact with two Crow teachers, then it was worth it.

Back home in Arizona, I began to think seriously about the advice my friend from California, Kit Douglass, had given me: Why not expand my writing program by taking it to reservations throughout the nation. I had asked Kit how she thought I could accomplish this. She suggested I get a van and simply drive from one reservation to another and market the program, on the spot, to interested school administrators.

This of course sounded a little fanciful. But now I was sincerely wondering if, in fact, there might be some other way it could be done. The concerns I had heard voiced in Montana by Indian educators from tribes with whom I had had no previous contact proved strikingly similar to the concerns of Indian educators of the Southwest. The needs of northern Indian students were also much the same. But, try as I might, I couldn't figure out a logical course to take in establishing an effort to work on reservations scattered far and wide beyond the borders of Arizona.

Then, six weeks after my trip to Butte, I received an unexpected phone call. A soft female voice introduced herself as

Lynn Hinch, bilingual-education specialist for the Montana State Office of Public Instruction. "How can I help you?" I asked.

She said, "We've had a request for your services by a school here in Montana. They'd like you to visit for a week sometime this spring, to work with their students and talk to their staff about the work you've been doing in Arizona."

Shocked, all I could muster was: "Oh?"

"If you're interested, our office will pick up your fee and travel expenses. Just tell us when you can do it."

I was caught in one of those moments when your head spins around wondering how such a moment could ever have come about. I sputtered, "Of course. I can do it. I'll have to check my calendar and get back to you."

"Good. Once we set the dates, I'll have a contract drawn up."

My amazement now succumbed to curiosity. I asked, "What school are you talking about?"

Lynn Hinch said, "Crow Agency Elementary. Obviously, it's a Crow school. It's about sixty miles from Billings, on the reservation."

"Can you tell me who requested me?"

"The principal." Lynn Hinch gave me her name, but I didn't recognize it.

"I don't know her," I said. "How does she know about my work?"

Hinch continued, "Well, two of her teachers attended the MIEA last October. Apparently, they returned to Crow and told her that if it was possible, they wanted you to come to their school and work with their students; they had attended a workshop you gave. So the principal called me, and it turns out that this is the kind of technical assistance the state can provide the schools."

"I'm just curious," I said. "Do you know who the two teachers were?"

Hinch's reply: "Barbara Bacon and Sharon Peregoy."

Suddenly it looked as though, out of the blue, a possible course had been set for me to develop and expand my program for Indian children of an entirely different cultural and geographical region. I couldn't believe it—just as I was searching for a way to work on reservations outside of Arizona, a way came to me over the telephone. Now, I would have the opportunity to sit among Crow Indian students, to converse with them, and to attempt to motivate them into artistic expression.

I could not contain my excitement, nor could I shake from my mind two names: Barbara Bacon and Sharon Peregoy. The two Crow women in Butte who, out of an audience of six, had stayed to talk, who had wanted to know more about my program, who had enthusiastically agreed with my ideas, and who had requested my services.

I had come back to the desert from Montana satisfied with my contact with the two Crow teachers, but I had expected nothing more to come of it. Then came Lynn Hinch's telephone call, and suddenly I would be returning to Montana for a visit to the Crow Reservation. All because of Barbara Bacon and Sharon Peregoy. They, like so many other *individuals*, are part of the network that carries news so quickly among Indians. I didn't realize it at the time, but I would soon be more involved with the Northern Plains Indian tribes than I ever could have anticipated. Thanks to the Moccasin Telegraph.

15
Crow Agency and the Crows

THE CROW CALL themselves "Absalooke." The name means "children of the large-beaked bird," and may have referred to the raven. In sign language, the historical Absalooke would flap their hands in a motion resembling a bird's wings whenever asked who they were. The early whites decided they were "Crows."

Originally, the Crow were part of the Hidatsa tribe, splintering off as early as the 1300s. They arrived in Montana in the 1600s, migrating from the Upper Midwest, as did most of the Northern Plains tribes. They settled along the Tongue, Powder, and Yellowstone rivers, where they established their territory in battles with the Shoshone, Cheyenne, Sioux, and Blackfeet. Eventually, around 1830, the Crow split into two politically independent groups, the River Crow and the Mountain Crow. The River Crow lived in the river valleys while the Mountain Crow occupied lands near and in the Bighorn, Pryor, Beartooth, Crazy, and Absaroka mountains. The two groups frequently intermarried and came together for important tribal ceremonies such as the sun dance. They also continued to share a matrilineal clan system that to this day is strongly adhered to. The ten clans of the Crow are named Greasy Mouth, Peigan, Newly Made Lodge, Big Lodge, Ties the Bundle, Filth Eaters,

Bad War Deed, Whistling Water, Sorelip, and Bring Game Without Shooting. To this day, responsible Crows never make a major life decision without first consulting their clan uncles for advice.

Nowadays, the River and Mountain Crow live on the same reservation and are governed by a single tribal government, although they are geographically separated by fifty miles of gently rolling reservation land. The River Crow reside along the banks of the Bighorn and Little Bighorn rivers in towns that include Wyola, Lodge Grass, Garryowen, Saint Xavier, and the tribal capital, Crow Agency. The smaller Mountain Crow group lives on the west side of the reservation at the base of the Pryor Mountains in a village officially known as Pryor, but referred to by many Crows as Aluutaashe—Arrow Creek.

I arrived in Billings on a blustery day in March, picked up a rental car, and was blown onto Interstate 90. The winds were fierce, and luckily at my tail; had I been commandeering a schooner, I'd have made the forty-eight-mile trip to Hardin in half the time it took. Along the way I marveled at the high plains—my first encounter. Not at all the level nothingness I'd expected—the flat plains, in fact, sprawled out farther to the east. Here, the land rolled up and down and gave one a feeling of elevation, of being close to the sky. Nothing was level, and that amazing sky, with its racing cumulus flocks, was everywhere. Okay, I may as well get it over with and say it—the sky was *big*, or perhaps, through some sleight of land, it just looked that way. Whatever the case, I'd never seen a bigger sky.

Then I discovered how deceptive the grass hills can be. I spotted some tiny black dots on a nearby hill and squinted my eyes to identify them. Black rocks? Little dark bushes? No. Those specks turned out to be grazing cattle, and that small, nearby hill was in fact huge and very distant. Big sky and tricky perspectives. The Northern Plains. I fell in love with them.

Hardin, seat of Big Horn County, was home to three thousand people and was located at the edge of the Crow Reservation. Crow Agency lay another twelve miles into the reservation but did not have overnight accommodations. I checked into a nondescript motel, unpacked my bags, and got back into my truck for a tour of the town, hoping to find, as my hunger pangs grew, a place to eat. No McDonald's or Kentucky Fried here.

Hardin was just too small; there were too few stopping tourists for the mass-market chains. But I soon discovered that something else was missing: a good restaurant. A few cafés and a family dining affair called the Purple Cow summarized the eating situation. Oh, well, I thought, I can live with it for a week. I stopped at an overgrown cinder block named the Corner Pocket Bar to deliberate over a beer what I should do for supper. Sipping the foam off a mug of Coors, I noticed a menu on the wall that offered pizza and sandwiches. What the hell. French dip, please. I was hungry. The sandwich was not bad. I hadn't found Mother's kitchen, but this would do.

The next morning I drove to Crow Agency Elementary School. From Hardin to Crow, I-90 ran straight through the valley of the Little Bighorn River. Somewhere nearby, on a hill overlooking the river, Yellowhair saw his last day at the Battle of the Greasy Grass. To non-Indians, Yellowhair is known as George Armstrong Custer, and the encounter is called the Battle of the Little Bighorn. I looked forward to seeing the site of the Indians' last great victory.

At nine o'clock, I walked into a classroom of fourth-grade Crow students. They eyeballed me curiously as I pronounced my name in a whisper to the teacher so that he could introduce me, as he said, without screwing up that last name. Then Mr. Dittis turned his head toward a chatty student and snapped, "That's enough, Bull Chief, get quiet!" He turned back to me.

I was momentarily stunned. Why had this white teacher called the boy Bull Chief? Was he being deliberately condescending, blatantly racist? Did he mean to imply that the boy was the most audacious of bullshitters? I glanced at the boy and could find no negative reaction in him. Then I noticed the name card taped to the front of his desk: Michael Bull Chief. I scanned the name cards on other desks, and my eyebrows must have scooted up to the top of my forehead. Most of these children bore last names like that—not Anglo, or Spanish, or trading-post names, but Indian names, or rather English translations of Indian names. Plain Feather, Plenty Hawk, Big Man, Big Hair, Old Elk, Old Coyote, Old Dwarf, Pretty on Top, Bird in Ground, Real Bird, Walking Bear, Knows Gun, Takes Enemy, Kills Wolf, Wounded Face, Bull Over The Hill. What extraordinary, wonderful names, I thought.

There was much I needed to learn about the Northern

Plains tribes. Many everyday things to the Indians would at first surprise, and then delight, me. Sometimes my misunderstandings would betray themselves, and everyone would get a laugh. Just two months later, in May, on a return trip to Montana, I entered a sixth-grade classroom of Blackfeet children in Heart Butte. One child with long braids was at a sink, washing off some red paint or ink. I said to the class, "What did she get on her hands?" The kids roared with laughter. *She* turned out to be John Talks About. It was my first meeting with kids of a tribe whose men and boys still wore braids. The Crows, although they did not wear braids, provided me with many other surprises. There was no question: These northern Indians, even though they held many of the same values as tribes from other regions, were quite different from the Indians with whom I had grown familiar in Arizona.

On Wednesday, during lunch with the students, I asked for directions to the Little Bighorn Battlefield. Three sixth-grade boys, Richard Wolf Black and brothers Gary and Alden Big Man, offered to go along as guides. After school, we left for the boys' homes to get permission for them to join me.

The battlefield was no more than a mile and a half from Crow Agency. We drove through town, passed by a large rodeo arena, then climbed out of the river valley and up toward one of the most famous historical sites in the United States. A large concrete monument loomed at the crest of Custer Ridge. We drove by a military cemetery shaded by tall pines, passed the battlefield headquarters and museum, then finally made the top, where we got out of the car and walked over to the iron-fenced acre where the actual Last Stand took place. At least fifty stone markers rose like white ghosts from the grass, each indicating where a soldier had fallen. At the center of the largest cluster, one of the ghosts announced its identity with the engraving:

GEORGE A.
CUSTER
Lieut. Colonel
B.V.T. Major General
7 U.S. Cav.
Fell Here
June 25, 1876

Other markers, scattered over the prairie right down to the Little Bighorn River and as far as I could see to the south, outlined an irregular pattern of death that graphically attested to how badly broken apart the U.S. troops had become near the end. Custer's five companies, about 260 men, attempted to fend off up to 4,000 Indian warriors. His failure to do so has long been the stuff of myth and legend.

Conspicuously absent here was any kind of monument to the scores of Indians who had lost their lives fighting Yellowhair. It wouldn't be until 1990 that a plan for such a monument finally was developed. That same year, in a landmark appointment, a Ute woman became the battlefield's superintendent—the first Indian ever to hold the position, the first Indian in more than a hundred years to again be in charge of Custer Hill.

The view west from the ridge was immense. Running north and south was the Little Bighorn River Valley, where dense stands of huge cottonwood trees obscured portions of the river. Farther on, the prairie rolled away like a tawny, fossilized ocean, while miles off the Bighorn and Pryor mountains lifted from the grassland to form a purple-mountain-majesty horizon. The place was at once both physically beautiful and historically eerie. Here, Indian and non-Indian could share at least one thought: So this is where it happened.

The day was defined by wind and cold, and the three boys and I were the only *living* souls around. Gary Big Man announced, "Hey, right now it's kind of like it was when the battle went on."

"What do you mean?" I asked.

"Well, the Indians outnumber the whites."

"Three to one." I laughed.

"So you be Custer," Gary went on, "and we'll be the Indians."

"Yeh!" Richard Wolf Black and Gary's brother, Alden, shouted.

I said, "Okay. Besides, it's a good day to die."

The boys began to war-dance around me, letting out piercing whoops and shooting invisible arrows from air bows. I pretended to be shooting a rifle, then a pistol, then I yelled, "This is it! It's over, men! They've got us completely surrounded. I'll never be president now!"

Round and round me the boys danced. Then they drew

their circle in tighter until they got close enough to strike me with war clubs and jab me with feathered spears. I crumpled down into the brittle grass, and they lunged forward, piling on top of me, each fighting the other for my scalp.

As I got up and brushed bits of clinging grass and dirt from my jacket, I was suddenly seized by the ironic fact that over a hundred years ago thousands of Indians annihilated Custer and his men at this very spot, while today three Indian boys playfully reenacted the drama with a white man they could trust.

Another irony, of course, was that these kids were *Crow* Indians; in 1876, the Sioux and Cheyenne reigned victorious. Indeed, Custer's scouts were Crow. The Crows had never really resisted the white man. Instead, they made early treaties with him—treaties that the government soon, and not surprisingly, broke as often as it broke the treaties made with more hostile tribes.

But these Crow kids identified with the fighting Indians, and I would soon discover one of the important reasons why. In the 1970s, director Arthur Penn, actor Dustin Hoffman, and a crew from Hollywood swarmed onto the Crow Reservation to shoot the film *Little Big Man*. A good number of the local Indians were hired to work as extras. The local Indians, of course, were Crow. Some of them even got speaking parts.

As I visited Crow schools over the next few years, I occasionally took an unscientific survey, asking Crow students how many of them had relatives in *Little Big Man*. In every class I asked, nearly all of the students raised their hands. And these Crow kids had watched the movie over and over on videocassette recorders, looking for and finding mothers and fathers, aunts and uncles, older brothers and sisters. The Battle of the Little Bighorn had become, for Crow children, a kind of family affair. One student enthusiastically told me, "My dad ran right up to Custer!" During my first visit to the battlefield, my three young Crow companions were the first of dozens of Crow kids to tell me of their families' participation in the film. Said Gary Big Hair, "My father was attacking the army, but when he started to cross the river, he fell off his horse. Boy, was he embarrassed. I've seen it lots of times."

The boys and I also explored the Reno-Benteen Battlefield before I took them home. On my way back to Hardin, I watched the coppery sun drop behind the low brown hills. I thought of Custer and his men, and of the Indians who so long ago had claimed victory here. For several generations after the battle, it was believed by non-Indians that this victory was the red man's last hurrah, that Custer's death marked the beginning of the end of traditional Indian ways. How wrong this belief was. I had seen, since entering the Indian world in 1979, a persistent and ever-strengthening tendency among Indians to look back to their ancestors for wisdom and guidance. I thought of the words of the Duwamish chief Seattle: "The white man will never be alone. Let him be just and deal kindly with my people, for the dead are not altogether powerless."

On Friday afternoon, I conducted my last classes at Crow Agency and said good-bye to the students. During the week, however, it had been decided by school administrators that a yearly springtime visit by me would benefit both students and teachers. The door to my working on Plains Indian reservations had now been opened.

16

Globe and
San Carlos

FOR A COUPLE of years after leaving my full-time position at Sacaton, I spent a lot of time at the beginning of each school year working at the public elementary school on the San Carlos Apache Reservation in Arizona. Because no housing was available in the agency village of San Carlos, I hunkered down in a small apartment in the border town of Globe, a once-bustling mining community of no current distinction. The great copper mines had been strung up by the fiberglass ropes of laser technology and left to rot in the dry Arizona wind.

Globites, I quickly discovered, had to do most of their "big" shopping down in "the *Valley*"—that is, the Phoenix metropolitan area ninety tortuous miles to the west. On any Saturday, maybe half the town's population formed traffic lines on the mountainous road that dropped to the desert.

Globe was big enough for a Kentucky Fried Chicken, but too small for a really fine restaurant. One did well to stick to any of the three Mexican restaurants. Globe was a might-as-well-stop-for-gas-on-the-way-through kind of town.

Normally, I liked small towns, in fact preferred them, and shopping and dining were not among my most pressing priorities. But Globe lacked the essential ingredient that makes many hamlets so wonderful: character. Globalism in Globe meant that the town fathers had denied a rezoning permit to a new business that probably would have folded within a year anyway. In many little out-of-the-way towns, Indian *and* Anglo, the people busy themselves with the maintenance of a culture. In Globe, they seemed to be attending the wake of the subculture of copper mining.

Nothing in Globe was flat. Little, sloppy neighborhoods oozed down from the humps of steep hills. Everything was uninterestingly above or below something else: "My place is above the McDonald's." "I work in a garage below the high school." "The Elks Club is just below the Chinese restaurant . . . you know, the one that's closed up." I've heard it said that people in the Midwest develop squinty eyes because there's nothing to see on the prairie but a continuous line of horizon, and so they always appear to be thinking hard. In the roller-coaster hills of Globe, I could see why the locals always appeared to be checking you over, from head to foot and back again.

Fortunately, in Globe's immediate vicinity, there were several delightful things, the most amazing of which was the Pinal Mountain Range. Pinal Peak, less than twenty miles from the southern edge of town, shrouded you with eight-thousand-foot cool air and a forest of pine and aspen as enchanted as any.

Because the Pinals form such a long solid wall, the nineteenth-century miners of Globe had to wagon their copper up and over the mountains on its way to Tucson. From the peak, looking south, you can still trace this battered road down through the desert scrub. And you can still spot the clearing, miles away, where the mining companies operated a rest camp complete with Old West–style ladies of the night.

From Globe, State 70 winds east along the base of the Pinal Mountains, and then leads directly into Apache territory. The mountains give way, and the topography switches to rolling desert hills and flat-topped mesas sliced by deep ravines and dotted with scraggly creosote bush and wispy desert broom. All reservation land. In the distance, three-peaked Triplets Mountain, sacred to the Apache, rises off the desert floor, while farther on looms eight-thousand-foot Mount Turnbull. Turnbull's heights, the Apache say, are home to the mountain spirits, or *Gan*. About ten miles into the reservation, at the site of an abandoned lumber mill, a side road heads north for another ten miles, then pierces into the heart of Apacheland—the town of San Carlos. When I worked at the elementary school, I commuted this route five days a week, and sometimes six or seven because of weekend activities on the reservation.

The center of this busy Indian community was made up of tribal and BIA offices, the Indian hospital, a public and a Catholic school, a Laundromat, a café, a closed bowling alley, a cable-TV business, a service station, and a trading post. Every day at lunchtime, women wearing long, colorful Apache camp dresses set up tables outside the trading post and sold fry bread, burritos, acorn soup, and Apache tamales (a heavy dumpling surrounding a core of minced jerky meat). San Carlos, a third the size of Globe, always seemed to be bustling.

The San Carlos Apache Tribe is, in reality, the San Carlos Apache band, or subtribal group. Over five hundred years ago, Athabaskan Indians migrated from the far north of Canada to what is now the American Southwest. A loose, nomadic tribe, the Athabaskans continually broke up into smaller bands that wandered in one direction or another until each band more or less settled in a definite area. Those homing down in the Four Corners area, where Arizona, New Mexico, Utah, and Colorado converge at a single point, took on some of the cultural traits of their Pueblo neighbors and became known as the Navajos. Other bands, settling in New Mexico, were the Mescalero and Jicarilla Apaches. In eastern, central, and southeastern Arizona, the Apache bands included the Chiricahua and the Western, the latter being further broken into subtribal groups known as the White Mountain, Cibecue, Tonto, and San Carlos. Currently, all these "tribes" share a common language and, with the exception of the Navajo, a common culture.

San Carlos Apacheland is roughly half desert, half forest. From the town of San Carlos, the visitor with a tribal permit can drive east and north over a dirt road that climbs first onto a grassland plateau that resembles parts of the Wyoming prairie. This land serves as open range for Apache cattle. From here the road climbs again, this time into cool alpine forests. After a total of about sixty miles, at a fire-fighting station known as Point of Pines, there rests in solitude what is probably the least crowded lake in all of Arizona. I wound up spending more than a few afternoons with friends at this exquisite site, fishing trout and trapping crawdads.

Through the 1980s, there existed an uneasy truce between

the San Carlos Apaches and the Globites. The Apaches had been the last of the Southwestern Indians to surrender during the Indian Wars of more than a century ago, and they still don't trust Anglos in general. The people of Globe tended to look down their noses at the Apaches and avoided all but necessary contact with them. And yet the Indians and whites were codependent. Businesses in Globe could not survive without Apache patronage, while the Apaches couldn't survive without the goods and services to be had in Globe. Because my work was with the Indians, and because most of my hours were spent with them, I felt like an outsider in Globe.

After extensive time in San Carlos, and after working with the Indian bilingual program at Globe High School, I would be grateful to the Apaches for having taught me a lot about the nature of *trust*—from the Apache point of view.

17
Mrs. Cassadore and Apache Students

ELENORE CASSADORE, AN elder of the San Carlos Apache, was employed in the bilingual program at the high school in Globe. Because she didn't drive, she rode with a fellow aide each school day from San Carlos to Globe and back, a round trip of over forty miles. I met Mrs. Cassadore at the beginning of a four-week stint working with the Apache high school students. Because there was no high school on the reservation, the students were bused to Globe. Sometimes, when Mrs. Cassadore's ride was unavailable, she joined the kids on the bus.

I knew from the moment I met her that I wanted to spend time talking with her; I could learn much about the San Carlos Apaches from this intelligent and wise woman. Mrs. Cassadore was of medium height and build, with salt-and-pepper hair. Her weathered face looked quiet, firm, sad. I never saw her in anything but traditional, ankle-length Apache camp dresses.

When I was first introduced to her, I explained what I hoped to accomplish with the students. We would, I said, put together a manuscript of poems, stories, articles, and drawings about Apache life, past and present—all composed by the students. I would also conduct several sessions on "survival skills"—that is, comfortable or at least practical ways for young Indian adults to get by in the non-Indian world. I added that it would be an honor if she sat in on some of the classes.

Mrs. Cassadore nodded and said, "Sounds good."

I pressed: "I hope you *will* be able to attend."

"In the morning classes," she answered. "Afternoons I'm busy in the office. But the mornings are okay. Those two classes are the ones I sometimes teach anyway."

In my enthusiasm to develop an acquaintanceship, I said, "I would really enjoy your company at dinner some evening. Maybe we could go to a restaurant. I'd like to talk to you about the students and the bilingual program here. My treat." What I really wanted was to talk to Mrs. Cassadore about her and her tribe. I had lied. A *white* lie.

Mrs. Cassadore nodded and said nothing. I sensed that I had been too abrupt.

The following day, I saw Mrs. Cassadore walking down the hallway toward the bilingual office. All the students were in class, and we were the only two people in the oak-floored, echoey corridor.

"Excuse me, Mrs. Cassadore," I said. "Have you thought about that dinner? Is any particular night best for you?"

"I've thought about it," she said. "There's nothing I can tell you over dinner that I can't just as well tell you here at the school."

I staggered under the weight of this rejection. Forget it, she had told me. And with a voice as soft and sweet as a mother's. If that quiet voice didn't echo in the hallway, it more than bounced around inside my skull.

"Oh," I said. Then, trying to regain my composure: "You're right, but the offer still holds."

My own Anglo need to be immediately accepted had been thumped on, and, ridiculously, it hurt. I spent that night repeatedly reliving the corridor scene, and winced every time Mrs. Cassadore's words replayed in my mind.

The next morning I almost said to Mrs. Cassadore, "Another thing I'd like to talk to you about is . . . well, I'd like to share some of my ideas about Indian education. And I'd like to learn about your tribe. I'd like to learn about you." That's how I sort of planned my words. But in the end I held my tongue. I had already been pushy enough. And now I was remembering what I had learned in Sacaton from the Whitmans and other Pimas about friendship. Observe the other person. Be patient. Assume nothing. Determine if there are common grounds. Open up only when the time is appropriate. And once you've

decided to open up, and only then, commit yourself to an understanding of relationship—maybe of friendship.

I was trying to see things from Mrs. Cassadore's point of
view, from an Indian point of view. Malinda Powsky, the Hualapai with whom I had developed a friendship rather quickly,
had known about me and my work before I met her. She had
seen me work with the Hualapai children, and we had spent
hours talking to each other before she invited me for the drive
into the Grand Canyon. Mrs. Cassadore, on the other hand,
had never set eyes on me until yesterday; she didn't know where
I had come from, or anything about my work, and we had never
spent a moment talking to each other.

This elder from the San Carlos Apache tribe had been
introduced to (had to shake the hand of) a tall (intimidating)
white man who wore a sports jacket over a sweatshirt (dressed
like a businessman *and* a hippie), and whose face was covered
with a beard (unnatural growth). Before she knew it, this man
had invited (cornered) her into making a decision about spending time alone with him so he could learn about (exploit) Globe's
bilingual program and the Apaches. Thinking of it from Mrs.
Cassadore's point of view, I was suddenly and definitely put off
by this image of myself.

"Good morning," I said to Mrs. Cassadore. This time I
spoke with the quiet respect I knew should be given a person
older than I was. At our first meeting, I had acted disrespect-
fully, forgetting the rules of Indian friendship and acquaintanceship. It's not easy, after all, to unlearn social habits that
have been practiced over a lifetime. I was now behaving toward
Mrs. Cassadore not from instinct, as I had yesterday, but from
the knowledge I had gained about appropriate social inter-
course in the Indian world. I was consciously unlearning, and
relearning. I had no right to assume that this Apache woman
should be comfortable with, or even aware of, the twists and
turns of my Anglo forwardness. I would merely do my best to
behave in a way that demonstrated the genuine respect I felt
for her, and I hoped that she had not already completely shut
out the possibility of some kind of relationship.

I offered, as I said good morning to Mrs. Cassadore, another show of respect by avoiding eye contact with her, instead
glancing down at the floor. Among many Indians, quickly establishing direct eye contact is regarded as rude and aggressive, if
not downright confrontational.

Mrs. Cassadore's sweet, motherly voice answered, "Good morning." Then we passed each other and walked in opposite directions through the cement corridor.

Be patient, I told myself. Patient and respectful. If it is meant for the two of us to know each other better, it will happen—when the time is appropriate.

My classes with the Apache students were both exciting and rewarding. Particularly interesting were the survival-skills sessions, since they involved more open discussion. Each group I saw was composed of students from all four high school grades, pooled from their English classes. Half of the students already knew and were comfortable with me, since I had worked with them when they were seventh-and eighth-graders at the elementary school on the reservation. At our initial meetings, as I entered the classrooms, the freshmen and sophomores exclaimed, "It's Mick!" "All right!" "You followed us to the high school!" The juniors and seniors, never having seen me before, were quietly curious and suspicious of this white man's presence.

In the first class I conducted, Mrs. Cassadore sat at the back of the room on an old pine chair pressed against the back wall, as far away from me as possible. In the following weeks, she would attend most of my morning classes sitting in the same distant spot. I was especially pleased, however, that she showed up at the beginning of the classes and witnessed the students' welcoming cheers. If nothing else, this would indicate to her the kind of rapport I developed with Indian students—with *Apache* students.

I waited until the third week to begin the survival-skills sessions, giving the older students time to become relaxed in my presence. The first and most important rule of these classes was that, aside from me, no non-Indians were allowed in the classroom. I wanted the Apache students to be open and honest about the problems they perceived in their encounters with the Anglo world. I felt that my established relationship with the younger students would make the discussions not only possible but productive.

And I tried to keep realistic expectations. There was no way I could make survival in two different cultures easy. These Apache students, as well as Indian students in general, had two major tasks challenging them: the maintenance of their own

Indian culture and the acquisition of skills that would enable them to function, when they had to, in mainstream non-Indian society. What separated them from other minorities, and made their task more difficult, was the fact that the nature of the differences between their culture and Anglo culture was so extreme. So, coping in the Anglo world meant, as it does today, not a *reconciliation* of opposites, but an *adjustment* to the very existence of profound opposites—an adjustment that must include the development of behaviors that often seem strange to the young Indian. True biculturalism also includes the maintenance of basic Indian cultural patterns and deep-rooted beliefs. As difficult as this may be to accomplish, it remains for Indians a realistic, attainable goal.

Not all the Apache students at Globe High School would become Hartman Lomawaimas, the assistant director of the Lowie Museum in Berkeley, but in our classes we could at least discuss specific problems and various ways to handle them.

Subjects for our discussions ranged from Anglo "time" as a concept different from Indian "time," to the analysis of Anglo behaviors the Apache students found odd or intimidating. I constantly reinforced the idea that the students, in learning survival skills, did not have to give up being Indian; they did not have to become *assimilated*.

The irony, of course, was that at the same time that I was conducting these classes, I was also adjusting my own behaviors to conform to acceptable Indian ways in my encounters with Mrs. Cassadore. Cross-cultural understanding is a two-way street. The non-Indian in contact with Indians has a responsibility to learn about their world and make the same adjustment to profound opposites that is expected of the Indian in reverse situations. When I talked to Mrs. Cassadore, usually in the bilingual office, I kept my side of the conversations brief and to the point, spoke in a soft voice, and never tried to establish prolonged eye contact.

On Wednesday of the second week, I began the morning class by saying, "Today we're going to talk a little bit about racial prejudice toward Indians, toward you guys. Can anyone define what the word 'prejudice' means?"

Tom, a sophomore, said, "It's like when white people look at you funny 'cause they don't like Indians."

Marie, also a sophomore, chimed in, "They get suspicious of you, and some of them just hate us."

"Okay. Why don't we talk about ways that some white people act toward Indians that might show prejudice, and how you can try to tell if those actions really do show prejudice. And we should talk about the ways you respond, and other possible responses. Someone tell me something that some whites do that might show prejudice."

"When they stare at us real long," offered an eleventh-grader named Sean. "You look away, but every time you look back, they're still staring." The class stirred, the students nodding and mumbling in agreement.

Sean added, "It's like they don't even blink their eyes, kinda like snakes or somethin'." Everyone chuckled.

This was a perfect start, I thought. The students had opened up quickly, and even some humor had been injected; a relaxed but honest tone had been set. I said, "Staring. How about their expressions when they stare? Can you tell what they're feeling, like anger or hatred or, as Marie pointed out, suspicion?"

"Sometimes they look like they're mad."

"Or like they think you're gonna steal something."

"Usually just a stare, kinda blanklike."

More students were joining in. I said, "Okay, so let's talk about the situations in which staring occurs. When and where do whites stare?"

"Like last week," a tall, muscular senior said. "Me and my family were at a restaurant here in Globe. We was real quiet, like good Indians." He snickered as he said this, and the class laughed again, acutely aware of the image many Indians believe they should project when in non-Indian public. "But this old white man and his wife just kept starin' at us. He even had to look partway over his shoulder to get a good view." More chuckles.

I said, "Let me tell you right off. Some white people like to stare, even though it may be rude. Many times it *is* from prejudice. Sometimes it's not. Staring itself doesn't *always* indicate prejudice. Do you think those old people were staring because they were prejudiced, or could there have been some other reason?" This idea had obviously not occurred to most of the students. Several moments of silence passed as they considered it. Then I said, "Can you think of any kind of staring that's really not prejudice?"

The muscular boy pulled his sunglasses down from the top of his head and over his eyes as he said, "Yeah. On the street, if it's a woman who's starin', it's 'cause she thinks I'm sexy." The whole class roared.

"Are you all laughing because white women get turned on when they see him, or because so many white women are blind?" The volume of the laughter increased.

When the students settled, I said, "But there you have it. There's a reason why some whites stare at an Indian that's kind of the opposite of prejudice." I pointed to the boy; he was smiling from behind his sunglasses. "Just look at him," I said. "He's a handsome, sexy dude." The kids laughed again, but I knew they were getting the point. "I'll bet every one of you has seen a white kid here at school that you thought was attractive. Maybe you even kind of stared at him or her. Maybe secretly. Maybe not so secretly." Little waves of giggles spread through the classroom. "Give me one good reason why a woman, any woman, wouldn't find this young man attractive. He may have been joking, but he was also right."

Our discussion lasted the full hour and would have to be continued the next day. The students had identified other situations in which staring clearly represented racial prejudice. The fierce, suspicion-filled glare of a store proprietor the minute a young Indian walks into a store—"It makes you feel like a criminal even though you wasn't gonna do nothin' wrong in the first place." The venomous stares of a group of young whites on a street corner challenging a young Indian to some form of perverted, one-sided combat—"They scared the shit outta me." Concerning the old couple in the restaurant, the students concluded it was impossible to determine the motive for their rudeness. They might have been locals who disliked Indians, or they might as easily have been tourists from the hinterlands of the Midwest who had never laid eyes on a real-honest-to-goodness "Injun."

During that first hour we had discussed the students' responses to their own individual situations; they had decided no *single* way of dealing with someone whose eyes are fixed on you suits every such encounter. In some cases, the students decided, it was better to ignore the stares. In others, they felt that staring back was justified, if only to embarrass guilty eyes enough to turn them away. A few situations seemed to call for actual verbal or physical responses. One brassy young man told of an experience at a hardware store in which, when the clerk leveled her sights on her Apache target, he pulled out his wallet, raised his arms, looked back into the clerk's eyes, and said, "I got money, lady. I got money." This uncharacteristic response had been applauded by the other students, but most of them, especially the young women, said they personally preferred to ignore stares altogether. We had also discussed at length the fact that different individuals, even of the same tribe, may react differently to similar situations. The important thing, we concluded, was to respond in a manner that felt as comfortable as possible, and at the same time maintain a sense of personal and tribal dignity.

After the bell had sounded its old-fashioned clang, I stood at the doorway saying good-bye to the students individually as they filed out. We all looked forward to the next day's session. It was good, and rare, for these Apache students to have shared such personal experiences with an Anglo who was sympathetic and who could offer legitimate, sometimes new, perspectives. It was good for *this* Anglo as well.

After the last student passed into the corridor, I took a deep breath, at once savoring the moment, giving the moment up, and readying myself to start the whole process over again with another group of kids. I felt exhilarated.

Then Mrs. Cassadore came from her usual spot at the back of the room. "That was good," she said. "We need more of that kind of thing."

"Thank you," I said, looking down.

Mrs. Cassadore had watched me interact with the Apache students for two-and-a-half weeks now. She had read their poems and articles. And she had just offered a compliment. I wondered if the time might be right to ask her to dinner again. If she accepted, I would be delighted; if she turned me down, well, I could handle it gracefully and resign myself to knowing her only within the context of our high school meetings.

Looking down at the floor, I said, "You know, I would still enjoy your company for dinner some evening." I braced myself.

Mrs. Cassadore thought for a moment. I readied myself to say something like, "That's okay. It's not that important." Then I glanced up.

Mrs. Cassadore raised her head. In the same sweet voice she used with everyone, she said, "How about tonight?"

18
Dinner with Mrs. Cassadore

THE STEREOTYPE OF the silent, stoic Indian was created by non-Indians who had never gotten to the first stage of the Indian manner of coming to an understanding of relationship. Had those non-Indians used the Indian approach of quiet, patient, cautious observation, and finally been accepted with trust and friendship, they would have experienced quite a different Indian, one who joked and laughed much of the time, one who loved to talk and share stories with an obsessive attention to detail, one who valued loyalty.

Over dinner, I witnessed a different Mrs. Cassadore, one who had decided I was okay and could be trusted. We had gone to a Mexican restaurant near the high school and sat down in a window booth next to a neon Coors sign that glowed like an electric-stove burner. Brightly colored piñatas hung from the ceiling, and south-of-the-border serapes covered the stucco walls. I ordered chicken enchiladas, rice, beans, and a Dos Equis beer. Mrs. Cassadore asked for combination number one—the basic taco, tamale, and enchilada served with beans and rice—and an iced tea.

We talked for a while about Indian education. I told her about the poetry books and calendars I had edited at Sacaton, the calendar of Apache student writings we had produced at the elementary school in San Carlos, and expressed my hope that the bilingual program at Globe High School would be able to publish the manuscript we were now putting together. The point, I said, was to demonstrate to the students the importance of sharing with the community their written creations while giving them the sense of pride that comes with seeing one's writing in published form.

Mrs. Cassadore said, "But there's a problem with that for some Apaches." I had no idea what she was talking about. Publishing student work and distributing it among the children's parents and throughout the community had always seemed an essential part of my writing program.

"What do you mean?" I asked.

"Well, some Apaches don't think books are important." My face must have registered the same kind of surprise that earlier I had seen on the faces of the high school students when I had said that not all staring by Anglos reflected racial prejudice. Mrs. Cassadore went on, "Some think that written words are kind of evil."

I stared at Mrs. Cassadore, confused and curious. My own experience in San Carlos had indicated the opposite. In fact, after we had published the poetry calendar, I had learned of a wonderful example of the benefit of written communication. An eighth-grader named Dawn Casuse had written a simple and elegant description of herself waiting to go through the Sunrise Dance Ceremony, the traditional puberty rite held for young Apache women. The poem appeared on the calendar. I assumed at the time that the girl had already gone through the ritual. A year later, when I returned to San Carlos, I was told by one of her aunts that before writing her poem, Dawn had never expressed an interest in the Sunrise Ceremony, and that whenever her parents had asked her about it, she had told them she didn't want one. Then they saw the poem on the calendar and wondered why she would write about the ceremony if she had no interest in it. They confronted her. Dawn then confessed to them the real reason she had acted indifferent—she feared that they could not afford the expense and didn't want them to feel guilty. Part of the ceremony involves the parents conducting a giveaway in which those in attendance receive blankets and food costing the family hundreds of dollars. Once her parents knew what Dawn was really thinking and feeling, they immediately arranged for her to have a Sunrise Dance Ceremony. Had Dawn not written that poem, and had it not been published, her parents would never have known that she secretly wanted the ritual. Dawn Casuse would have gone through life having never been initiated into adulthood in a way she believed important.

The Dawn Casuse story was one example of the positive side of printing students' work, but now Mrs. Cassadore was telling me that some Apaches viewed printed materials not only as unimportant, but as evil. "I'm lost," I said to her. "Can you explain?"

"Yes." Mrs. Cassadore sipped at her iced tea. I took a long pull from my Dos Equis, squinting into the orange neon glow to my left. "You know a lot of young Apaches," she said. "And you know some of their parents. But there's a lot of parents and grandparents you don't know, and they probably wouldn't want to know you, unless maybe they saw how you are with their kids. They been to school in their day, and what that usually meant was a bad BIA boarding school. And all they remember about school is that there were all these Anglos trying to make them forget they were Apaches; trying to make them turn against their parents, telling them that Indian ways were evil.

"Well, a lot of those kids came to believe that their teachers were the evil ones, and so anything that had to do with 'education' was also evil—like books. Those kids came back to the reservation, got married, and had their own kids. And now they don't want anything to do with the white man's education. The only reason they send their kids to school is because it's the law. But they tell their kids not to take school seriously. So, to them, printed stuff is white-man stuff."

"But Indian education is changing," I said. "Assimilation is not official policy anymore. The school in San Carlos has an Apache school board."

"Doesn't matter. Education for some Apache adults means what it always meant. *They* haven't changed. They shut education out a long time ago, and they don't want to hear anything about it. So of course they don't see the changes in the schools. And they don't read a poetry calendar from the school, either."

I said, "That means that we—I mean people working in Indian education, people working for change—have got to get

out there and talk to those parents. We've got to show them
how things like writing can be important, how education can be
used in a positive way."

"You're right. The more Indians you talk to, the more
that'll change. But it won't happen all at once. One or two
families at a time. A lot probably still won't trust you. Us
Apaches don't trust too many outsiders. Too much bad blood
between us and Anglos. And it doesn't just go back to Geron-
imo's day. Things still happen, even today."

"I'm sure," I said. "I know that's true at Gila River. Could
you give me an example, though?"

"I'll give you a good one. It's one of the reasons I really
didn't like you for a couple days."

"Oh," I said, again startled. "I knew you weren't sure of
me, but I didn't know you actually didn't like me."

Mrs. Cassadore continued, "Well, I didn't. You see, something happened to me a long time ago that I never forgot." She
hesitated.

"Yeah?"

"When I was raising my family, one time I got sick. Like
the flu. I coughed a lot, and my lungs hurt. And I was really
tired. For a couple weeks, I stayed in bed most of the time. I
didn't want to go to the clinic; I didn't trust Anglo medicine.
But I got worse. Finally, I figured I had no choice, so I went to
see a doctor.

"He was a young man, just outta school. Those young doctors that borrowed money from the government could pay their
loans off by going out to an Indian reservation and working for
the Indian Health Service for a couple years. That's how they
staffed Indian hospitals.

"Well, he told me they had to do some tests, so I stayed at
the hospital most of the day. Then he told me to go home, rest,
and come back a few days later. When I went back, he took me
into an office and closed the door. I didn't like that. Then he
told me I had tuberculosis.

"I knew about that disease; I knew it was bad. That doctor
said he was sorry, but I couldn't go home, I might spread it
around to my children and my husband and other people. He
said there was a place in Tucson called a sanatorium, and that
I had to go there right away and stay till I got better. But I knew
there was more to it than he was saying; I knew he really meant

I'd stay there till I got better *or* till I died. I got really upset. Not about dying, but about not seeing my children and husband, not even being able to say good-bye. That same day they took me to Tucson.

"That sanatorium was awful. All these poor Indians just sitting there, or lying there, some of them dying. Coughing and coughing, that's what I remember. I thought if tuberculosis didn't kill me, being in that place would.

"Soon I felt better. I thought I was getting over it. But they kept telling me I couldn't leave. I couldn't understand why I had to stay if I wasn't coughing no more, if I didn't feel sick like all those people around me.

"Then one day someone told me to go to one of the doctors' offices. When I got there, the doctor said, very politely, 'Please sit down.' I was thinking, *What now?*

"He told me that something had gone wrong, that some tests they took showed I didn't have tuberculosis after all, and that the tests they took last week, to make sure, proved it. I wasn't sick."

"I was so happy I cried. I thought of my children and my husband; now I could be with them again. I asked the doctor when I could go home."

"Just like that first doctor in San Carlos, he said, 'I'm sorry.' I knew something wasn't right. Then he told me that there was a chance I had picked up tuberculosis while I was there. I had to stay at least a few more weeks, in another ward, just to make sure I hadn't caught it.

"Every day and every night, all I could think about was that they had sent me away from home, to this terrible place, because of a disease I never had but might have gotten while I was there. If I got it and died, then the IHS killed me. Some white person had made a mistake that killed an Indian, and I'd be buried, and whoever it was that killed me wouldn't have to answer to anyone. I kept thinking about that young doctor in San Carlos. He should have checked. He should have made sure. It was his fault, really."

Mrs. Cassadore fell silent. She stared at the twisted napkin in her hand, visibly upset.

Shocked into numbness, I could muster no more than a few words. "How long were you in that sanatorium?"

Mrs. Cassadore mumbled, "Half my life." Though she had

been incarcerated for at least weeks, at most months, I knew
what she meant.

"When did this happen?"

"In 1973."

I knew that things like that had happened in the 1800s,
and maybe in the early part of this century, but I never would
have imagined that they were still occurring as late as 1973.
How wrong I had been in my supposition. Perhaps things like
this happened yet.

Mrs. Cassadore glanced up. "You see, that's why I didn't
like you when I first saw you."

I still didn't get it.

"Well, that doctor at the hospital in San Carlos—he looked
just like *you*. Tall, curly hair, beard. When I saw you, I saw him.
All my memories flooded back. You were that young doctor.
You were the one who almost killed me."

After a long silence, I whispered, "And now?"

"Now, I think you're okay."

"What changed?"

"That doctor couldn't be trusted. But you—I've watched
you awhile. I think you can be trusted."

"I hope I'm worthy of your trust," I said, again looking
down.

Mrs. Cassadore chuckled. "Well, let me put it this way, I've
lived long enough, as of tonight, to know I shouldn't judge a
white man by his face hair. That's a first for me."

19
A Trip with Apache Students

LATE AFTERNOON, OCTOBER 1985. I was restless as I sat on the sofa in the home of Martin Talgo and scanned the checklist I had given Martin's mother a week before. The Talgos lived in a housing development locally known as "Moon Base," in the Apache community of Peridot about six or seven miles from San Carlos. On the way over from the elementary school, I had stopped at another home to pick up eleven-year-old Carl Nolene and his luggage. Carl, a heavyset kid with mischievous eyes, now sat next to me on the sofa twiddling his thumbs.

Martin, a thirteen-year-old eighth-grader, darted from room to room searching for last-minute items such as cassette tapes of rock-and-roll music, fashionable bandannas, and sunglasses. I called out the essential items on the list.

"Toothbrush," I yelled.

Martin shot back, "Toothbrush?"

"Packed!" his mother hollered from the kitchen table. Noticeably anxious, she smiled much more, much wider, than was natural.

"Shampoo!"

"Shampoo?"

"Packed!"

"Heavy jacket!"

"Heavy jacket?"

"Packed!" Mrs. Talgo had used her savings to get Martin a new, fleece-lined herringbone for the trip.

"Underwear!"

"I got it on!" Martin laughed.

"Packed," his mother snorted.

Martin's brother, now in high school, paced back and forth from the living room to the kitchen. Fortunately, Mrs. Talgo had organized most of Martin's things the night before.

Our flight from Phoenix to Spokane, Washington, and to the National Indian Education Association Convention, was scheduled to leave at eight the next morning. Martin and Carl would spend the night at my apartment in Globe, where we'd review our busy weeklong itinerary before going to sleep. The two boys had been chosen for the trip on the basis of their writing excellence, their general academic achievement, and the essays they had written on why they should be selected. Within fourteen hours, the three of us would be on the winding, mountainous road to the Valley, well before the sun knew we were gone.

I had been through this kind of frenzy before, with Pima kids and their parents in Sacaton. In fact, on one of those trips I had taken four young Pimas to Spokane—to a National Indian Child Conference—so I knew a little about our destination: where the airport was in relation to the city, where our hotel and the convention center were located, how to get around town.

Knowing Spokane made me a little steadier as I sat in the Talgo living room, but I still felt the surge of anticipation and pretravel jitters that accompany taking reservation Indian kids from home to a place so far away. I still worried, as a parent does, about every detail of the trip. But, I confess, I still loved every minute of it; I knew that for these children this would be an experience like no other.

Martin finally said, "That's it. I'm ready."

We packed his bags into the back of my truck, then he hugged his mother good-bye. Mrs. Talgo didn't hold her boy tightly, but tears mapped her cheeks. I looked away, knowing she'd be embarrassed if she saw me watching her.

The one thing that increased my own anxiety was the thought that at the airport we would be meeting two other

Apache kids from the White Mountain Reservation—Cibecue Apaches, whom I had never met and who would be our companions for the next week. Our companions—*my* charges.

The Cibecue Apaches occupied the most remote village on either the White Mountain or San Carlos reservations, and were well known as the most fiercely traditional of any Apache group, maintaining their native language, customs, and religion—truly living in the "Apache Way."

The only business in the Cibecue community was the trading post, where shoppers paid $8.25 for a twenty-five-pound sack of flour. The nearest grocery market lay fifty miles distant, in the Anglo town of Show Low, and many Cibecue Apaches who didn't own vehicles paid thirty dollars for rides to get there and back. Many of the young people in Cibecue had experienced very little of the outside world.

When the bilingual-education director of the local tribal contract school had learned that I was taking two San Carlos Apache kids to Spokane for the NIEA, she phoned and asked if I'd be willing to take along two of their students. The school could pay for the two youngsters, but had no funding for a chaperon. Of course I had said yes.

At seven in the morning on the day of our flight, Martin, Carl, and I waited in the cavernous main terminal at Sky Harbor Airport in Phoenix. The boys were tired but excited. Then I noticed a white woman and two Indian kids coming up the escalator. When they reached our level, the woman introduced herself. Then she introduced the children, Jimmy and Linda, both eighth-graders. They remained silent and avoided eye contact. It would take a little time, I knew, for us to get to be at ease with each other. Before long, the four children and I were roaring north through cloudless skies.

We had to change planes at Salt Lake City. Inside the terminal we rendezvoused with a friend of mine from California, a longtime patron of Indian education who had helped fund this trip and who would join us for the flight to Spokane. Katherine Douglass, a small, attractive woman in her sixties, was delighted she would be, for the next week, Linda's roommate and companion, sparing the Apache girl the embarrassment of spending so much time in the company of three boys and a white man.

As we approached an escalator that led down to the ice-cream shop, Jimmy stopped in his tracks. I had been walking behind the kids—my usual habit—to make my job as shepherd easier. Jimmy was right in front of me. Now, he stood there as rigid as a statue, gazing at the floor. I stopped, too, and touched his elbow as I whispered, "Is there a problem?" Something was obviously wrong, though I hadn't an inkling what it could be.

Jimmy didn't answer, and he didn't look up. He started to walk again, hesitantly. I followed close behind, keeping my eyes on the boy, looking for any clue.

At the escalator's top, he again halted. He extended his right foot toward the moving stairs, then withdrew it. Instantly, I became aware of the problem—Jimmy was at a loss as to how to negotiate himself onto the sliding staircase. And he had to be painfully aware of my presence right behind him. His foot wobbled out again, then back. In a desperate effort to save face, he grabbed on to the hand rails and was pulled forward, almost falling onto the escalator. He let go and took a step backward.

I remembered that in Phoenix Jimmy had ridden an escalator, but that one was going up. He didn't have to confront a dizzying, narrow drop. I immediately stepped to his side, grabbed his shoulders, and silently forced him onto the first stair. Once he gained a steady, upright sense of himself, I let go and stepped back. We never said a word to each other. At the bottom, the boy practically leaped off the escalator. Fortunately, the other kids hadn't seen the incident.

After ice-cream cones, we headed for our boarding gate, going *up* the escalator. If this was a problem for Jimmy, it was at least one he could handle on his own. Then, as we walked through the corridor, I pulled up alongside the boy and placed a hand over his shoulder. We slowed down enough to put a little distance between us and the rest of the group. Jimmy cast his eyes toward the floor but synchronized his steps with mine.

"Jimmy," I said in a low voice, "I want you to do me a favor." As I had anticipated, Jimmy remained silent, but his footfalls were still timed with mine—that was response enough. "Jimmy, there's going to be a lot of things on this trip that will be very new to you. Very strange, maybe. And very confusing. I want you to know one thing. If you're not sure about something and you want to know about it, I'll tell you as much as I can." I knew Jimmy wouldn't want the other kids to learn about this, so I said, "Listen, Jimmy, any time you want me to tell you about something, just hang back, get behind everyone else, and that'll be a signal to me. When you do that, I'll come back to you and answer your questions. Okay?"

Jimmy said nothing, but I knew he could at least breathe a little easier now.

That evening, after checking into our rooms, Katherine and I took the children for a stroll around downtown Spokane. We walked through Riverfront Park, then down to the falls, and back through darkened concrete canyons. Not New York perhaps, but, especially for the two Cibecue kids, something to behold. Katherine and Linda occasionally conversed in hushed tones. Martin and Carl joked with each other and talked to Jimmy, but his responses were minimal.

Then Jimmy began to lag behind. At first I walked on past him. Then, without the others noticing, I ambled back and stood at his side. In the metallic glow of the streetlights, the boy's black eyes sparkled. "What are those things?" he mumbled. It was the very first time I heard his voice distinctly.

"What things?"

"Those things." He pointed toward the street with his pursed lips.

I looked hard and saw only a thousand different details of city, all blending together, all familiar to me. Which one had caught Jimmy's attention and piqued his curiosity? I asked, "What things are you looking at, Jimmy?"

"Those things." With an outstretched hand, he made quick up-and-down strokes in a kind of zigzag pattern. I followed the motion, then looked out to see what it might indicate.

There they were, like evenly spaced sentries guarding the sidewalks. Jimmy may have seen them in Phoenix, but if so he hadn't known what they were.

I said, "Those are called parking meters. In big cities, people have to pay money to park their cars along the sidewalks. That's where they put the money—they put dimes and quarters in those things. If they don't, they get a ticket."

Jimmy looked even more confused. I could imagine the questions swirling in his mind: Pay money to park? Why? Where does the money go? How would one of those things know if you paid it or not? How much do you pay? What is a ticket when it's not something you use to get into a movie?

I took him over to one of the meters and began to explain.

It was some time before we caught up with the others, and by then a rapport was already developing between the boy and me.

The next night we took the kids to the Ridpath Hotel's restaurant, where we had our one expensive, classy meal. The children had dressed in their best clothes—the boys in sports shirts and slacks, Linda in a striking green dress her mother had made for her. After only a moment's deliberation, the boys decided to order the biggest steaks they could get, while Linda followed Katherine's example by deciding to try the chicken Kiev.

Having a thoroughly enjoyable supper was one of the purposes of our eating at the Ridpath. Another was to give the students the opportunity to practice the table etiquette Katherine and I had taught them earlier in the evening.

Teaching the kids such manners was not a way of taking them a step further toward assimilation, as it would have been in the past. We hadn't told them that other ways of conducting oneself at a meal were wrong; to the contrary, we had discussed all kinds of manners appropriate to different situations. We had even talked about appropriate reservation manners, such as those expected at an Indian feast, where the children and other adults must refrain from approaching the tables until all the elders have been served. We had explained to the children that the manners we were teaching them applied to restaurant situations—they were not absolute rules. We simply were teaching them a few behaviors that would help them feel a little more comfortable in such a non-Indian setting. Indeed, restaurant etiquette was one of the sets of survival skills I had discussed with the older Apache students at Globe High School. Only now, these younger students were practicing the skills at a restaurant fifteen hundred miles from the reservation, without being told that their Indian ways at home were wrong.

Our days in Spokane were filled with activity. I had assigned specific workshops and presentations for each of the students to attend and report on. The subjects of the workshops ranged from drug and alcohol abuse to self-esteem, from coping in a broken home to learning how to pick one's friends. The students also spent time preparing reports about their general impressions of the airline flight, the hotel, the meals, the city, and the conference powwow and dances. Each evening they spent an hour doing schoolwork their teachers had sent along.

One of the kids' favorite activities was riding the hotel's elevators, an activity that had to be restricted to a few minutes at a time and confined to hours when there was little traffic.

On one afternoon, Katherine and I, along with several Indian friends of mine from California, drove the students to Coeur d'Alene, Idaho, for a picnic by the lake. There, they romped in piles of fallen autumn leaves—something they had never done back home on the desert. By week's end, Katherine and I were pretty well exhausted. Our four charges, however, were more energized than on the day we had arrived in Spokane.

Jimmy and I had become good friends. Our secret sessions had covered many things about which he was curious—taxicabs, buses, storm gutters, manholes, turnstiles, revolving doors, doormen. At first, Jimmy thought the doormen were courteous policemen. Each day, and with each new thing he learned, he grew more confident and outgoing. By the end of the week, his behavior was no more timid than Martin's or Carl's. Linda never became less quiet, which was proper according to her upbringing, but she did become much, much more relaxed.

Most important of all, the four children learned to interact with the people they met at the convention. They conversed with other Indian kids and exchanged cultural information about their respective tribes. They became particularly attached to a group of Chippewa-Cree kids from Rocky Boy, Montana, and spent much time hanging out with them. And they became well acquainted with my California friends. Linda later kept up a correspondence with Katherine Douglass.

On our return flight, I felt the same sadness I had experienced at the end of other trips with Indian kids. We had become a kind of family, close-knit and trusting. I knew I'd never forget any one of them. Martin, the stylish and peppy teenage leader. Carl, the short, plump boy who giggled at everything. Linda, the girl approaching her Apache womanhood with a quiet and stately grace. Jimmy, seemingly the youngest of the four kids, though in fact the oldest, who needed guidance and soft encouragement. And Katherine, who had the stamina of a woman half her age, and who had been an outstanding mother for the week.

Back in San Carlos, Martin and Carl wrote summarizing reports and gave a presentation about the trip at a school-board meeting. And then it was all over. But not really. The memories of the fun we had, of the things we learned, of the time we shared, would never be erased.

20
Rocky Boy and the Crees

NOT LONG AFTER my first visit to the Crow Reservation, I made the first of what would be numerous visits to the Rocky Boy reservation in the north-central part of Montana. From Billings (I'd flown up by jet from Phoenix), I took one of those eight-seat prop planes that simulates, on windy days, the motion of a roller coaster. Landing in Havre, a town of fifteen thousand people twenty-five miles north of the reservation, I felt as though I had reached the very edge of the earth. Flat plains stretched out in all directions.

My feeling of displacement was deepened by the absence of Louise Stump, director of the Rocky Boy schools' bilingual program, and presumably my ride out to the agency town of Rocky Boy. Several other things, as well, were absent at the tiny Havre International (Canada was just fifty miles away) Airport. My luggage, for one. The Big Sky Airlines clerk told me my bags could only be in one place—Billings—and that they would arrive in Havre on the next flight, the next afternoon. She gave me forms for an essential clothing allotment, shut down her counter post, said good-bye, and went home.

The two other passengers had already left, and except for me and a weather-bureau meteorologist, there were no people at the airport. I phoned Louise Stump's home several times and got no answer. In the weather station, the kindly weatherman proudly showed off his array of barometers, thermometers, and wind gauges. After half an hour, he took mercy and offered to drive me to the mall before it closed, so I could buy a shirt, pants, and underwear. A rural Good Samaritan he was, the kind common in the outer reaches. We taped a note for Louise Stump on the airport's front door and drove into town. Unfortunately, the little mall had closed five minutes before we pulled into the parking lot, and no other clothing store in town was open. Back to the airport to stare at weather equipment again.

My new friend had taken pity on me and kept the airport open well past the hour his professional duties had concluded for that day. I was grateful. I bought him a can of soda pop from the only active nonweather machine in the airport. And all the while I kept trying to reach Louise Stump and maintain a smiling facade.

Finally, Louise Stump answered her phone. She was genuinely shocked I was in Havre. Through some miscommunication between Arizona, the Montana State Bilingual Office in Helena, and Rocky Boy, she had come to believe my flight would take me into Great Falls, ninety miles south of Rocky Boy. The schools superintendent, she said, had driven down there to pick up another consultant and me. She assured me that help—a ride—would instantaneously be on the way. I told her we'd have to stop somewhere so I could get a toothbrush, hairbrush, and a razor, and that tomorrow, during my first presentations in the land of the Chippewa-Cree, I would be wearing a pair of ragged blue jeans with a knee peeking through a conspicuous hole. "No problem," Louise Stump said. "Oh, and by the way, you'll be staying at the home of Dorothy Small. She's president of the school board."

"That's fine," I said. What I was thinking, though, was, Oh, no—the president of the school board. The Supreme Boss of the place. I'd never relax tonight, or the next three nights of my stay. This Dorothy Small, whoever she was, would watch me like a hawk, not only at school but at breakfast and dinner in her own home.

The drive out of Havre took us due south over the plains, and then, surprisingly, we began climbing grassy hills. Ahead, the blue outline of a small mountain range washed across the horizon. "I didn't know there were mountains in this part of Montana," I said to Louise Stump.

"Oh, yes," she said. "They're the Bear Paws. That's where Rocky Boy is, up in the pines."

For some miles, we twisted parallel to Beaver Creek, and the foliage grew denser; spotty clumps of red-barked willow at first, then stands of aspen and ponderosa pine. In the blush of a rosy evening sky, the landscape looked lovely. We left the creek when Louise turned right onto a dirt road; the forest thickened, and the slopes of the hills grew steeper. Suddenly, we were back on paved road. "We've just come onto the reservation," Louise said. Then, passing scattered houses, we ascended a big hill and started down the other side. Straight ahead, about a mile away, were several fairly large buildings. The schools, I assumed. And I was right. This was the heart of Rocky Boy. Just past the high school, Louise drove up a dirt driveway and stopped in front of a neat white house. She pointed to it with her lips and chin. "This is Dorothy's," she said. "The family's expecting you."

I walked into the enclosed porch, and the front door opened wide before I reached it. Standing just inside the living room were a man and a short woman with a wide smile. The woman said warmly, "Come in. Come in. We've been waiting for you. We thought maybe your plane got lost in the clouds."

"No," I said. "But my luggage did."

"I'm Dorothy," the woman said, extending her hand. "And this is my husband, Andy."

Lean, leather-faced Andy said, "Welcome to our home. We hope you have a good time in Rocky Boy."

Dorothy said, "Junior, come over and meet our guest."

Junior Small had opened the door and now stood just behind me. We shook hands. In his late teens, Junior was a heavy-set boy with long, thick braids. "Hello," he said with a slight stammer, shyly and respectfully casting his eyes toward the floor. I don't remember him saying another word in my presence over the next three days.

Dorothy instructed her son to take my bag full of toiletries and show me my room. "We'll eat dinner in about ten minutes," she said.

I walked behind Junior down a long hallway and into a small bedroom. He laid the paper bag on the bed, turned, and left. I found a bathroom, washed up, then joined the family at the dinner table.

As Dorothy handed me a plate of boiled potatoes, she said,

"We want to hear all about you while we eat. I understand you've done a lot of good work for Indian children."

When everyone's plate was piled high with food, Dorothy, Andy, and Junior, without a word, bowed their heads silently and lifted their dinner plates an inch or two off the table. I later learned this was the traditional Cree way of blessing the meal and offering some of it to the spirits of the departed.

I must have appeared as tense as I felt. As she poured some evaporated milk into her coffee, Dorothy glanced at me and said, "You can relax here. We're friendly Indians. We won't scalp you while you're sleeping. Besides, we've had white men stay here before. We're used to it."

Andy covered his mouth with his napkin and laughed. Junior giggled. So did I. I loosened up some and began telling the family about my work.

After dinner we sat in the wonderfully cheerful, brightly lit living room, whose walls and shelves were cluttered with hundreds of family photographs. The place was a living monument to a very large and very loving family.

The next day, at the school, the students responded enthusiastically in the classes I conducted. What I experienced on every new reservation I visited proved more and more that Indian children were respectful, loving, and affectionate. Toward those they like, that is. I knew that my own experience ran contrary to the experiences of some non-Indians who taught in reservation classrooms. It is perfectly true that Indian kids are capable of leveling ruthless assaults on outsiders they don't like. I've heard of entire classes breaking into absolute anarchy. I've been in a few classes where the kids at first began to go wild, having grown accustomed to such behavior in the company of teachers they didn't respect. Restoring calm in such a class takes great energy and patience, believe me.

Disrespect, however, is not always shown openly by Indian kids. I knew of a teacher who had just come from the East to work at a Navajo school. He had trouble relating to the kids. His name, which many of the students never seemed to be able to correctly pronounce, was Mr. Martinson. He felt sorry for the junior-high kids who tried but could not get his name right. They'd stare at the floor when they addressed him, mumbling, "Mr. Maii bicho." "Mart-in-son," he'd correct them. "Maii bicho," they'd repeat. He had no idea, and I suppose still does not, that in the Navajo language *maii bicho* means "coyote penis."

Those students had invented a gloriously sneaky way of jabbing Mr. Martinson. I knew of this because the Navajo students told me, and they didn't swear me to secrecy because they trusted me. The way to receive respect from Indian youngsters, I understood, was simple—respect them and their culture, and let them know it both in words and actions. Indian kids recognize right away if an outsider respects them, trusts them, loves them, wants to be with them, and has no hidden agendas. And they will respond in kind.

That evening I was tired. Dorothy Small invited me to join the family for dinner in Havre, but I declined, electing to stay at the house, rest, and go to bed early. "But what will you eat for supper?" Dorothy asked. "There's nothing in the refrigerator."

"I'll be fine," I assured her. "I ate a big lunch, and I'm not really in the mood for dinner tonight."

I was wrong. By nine o'clock, I was hungry. Dorothy had been right. There was nothing to eat in the refrigerator. Nothing, that is, but four squares of Kraft American Cheese Singles, which I devoured. Then I went to bed.

Through the night, I kept surfacing from periods of deep sleep into a semiconscious twilight state dominated by intense hunger pangs and the imaginary odor of cheeseburgers. Finally, about 3:00 A.M., I stirred to full consciousness and decided to get up and drink several glasses of water; maybe that would quiet the hunger for a while. I reached over to the bed stand and flipped on the lamp, and my eyes opened wide with shock at what lay before them. The imaginary odor had not been imaginary at all. There on the little table, waiting for me, were a Big Mac, large fries, and a root beer. Anticipating my hunger, the Smalls had brought the food back from town, and one of them had placed it right next to me, so I wouldn't have to wander the house like a hungry ghost. I was so grateful I could have awakened them all with a hug.

The thoughtful, caring, and giving spirit of the Indian was certainly nothing new to me. The Plains Indians possessed it as strongly as the Southwestern tribes. I thought about how so many of my Indian friends went to great pains to show me this spirit by giving gifts and attending so carefully to my creature comforts when I stayed with them. Now, here in Rocky Boy, a family I didn't even know had graciously taken care to attend to an anticipated need.

I leaned back against the headboard and looked around

the room. The walls were covered with life. More family photos. Graduation diplomas. Prints of old Indian chiefs. Eagle feathers. The room, like the whole house, silently confessed to being a reflection of this family's pride in itself and its tribal heritage. I stretched and yawned. It was a comfortable place to be. I felt no farther away from home than the hearts of my Cree hosts would allow—in other words, I felt at home. After a while, before plunging into sleep, I chuckled; tonight, I would not be scalped.

Until 1916, several bands of Chippewas under the leadership of Chief Stone Child (Rocky Boy to the whites) and Crees following Chief Little Bear roamed Montana in hopeless, landless poverty. The bands, rejected alike by whites and Indians—who wanted them forced back to Canada—and officially unrecognized by the federal government, wandered the towns and reservations of the state looking for work, or handouts. They were just about the most destitute and despised group of people anywhere in the West.

Little Bear, along with his father and another leader, Wandering Spirit, had been involved in an 1885 armed rebellion against the Canadian government. It lasted two months. Big Bear went to prison, Wandering Spirit was hanged, and Little Bear escaped with about two hundred Crees to the United States. Little Bear was not about to go back to Canada, where thousands of other Crees made up the country's largest tribe. Besides, the bands under Big Bear and Little Bear had long come down to hunt buffalo in Montana Territory, so in their eyes the plains and mountains south of the border were part of their home.

The Chippewa bands originally came from the Great Lakes area. They drifted west and, like the Crees, became buffalo hunters. Stone Child's people settled for a while around Turtle Mountain in North Dakota, but came to Montana after being left out of an 1892 treaty that included the selling of a million acres of reservation land for a mere ninety thousand dollars.

In 1889, Little Bear held a sun dance near Helena, despite a law forbidding the ceremony. His band was deported to Canada but walked right back to Montana within a year. It became clear that the Chippewa-Cree bands were here to stay. Various proposals by the whites would have confined them to the Flathead, Blackfeet, or Crow reservations. But nothing was done; and the bands continued to roam Montana, even living for a year on the military reservation of Fort Assiniboine.

It was finally proposed that about fifty-five thousand acres of land south of Havre be declared the Rocky Boy Indian Reservation. The residents of Havre went along with the plan only after designating a nine-thousand-acre park between their town and the edge of the reservation, thus assuring a wide separation between white and Indian. The impoverished tribes would hardly be able to get into town easily on quick round trips, and there would be no Indian camping allowed in the park. Besides, many establishments in Havre refused service to Indians, a practice that continued through the 1950s.

On September 17, 1916, the Chippewa-Cree at last had a home. Stone Child, who for years had worked so hard to get a reservation, had passed away the previous April. The reservation was named for him, and he rests there still.

Though the Chippewa-Cree now had their own land, the land itself held no resources. The pathetic poverty of the Indians continued for decades, and many of them continued wandering off the reservation to look for work. Their very existence as a unique people had come to depend on government rations. Then, in the 1960s, a new pride gripped the Chippewa-Cree. Or maybe it really was new opportunities gripped by an old pride. Things began to change.

I had no idea, during this first visit to Rocky Boy, that Dorothy Small had played an important part in the educational changes the last few decades had seen in Rocky Boy. I would hear her story later. She was a part of the history of these tribes, an important part. A Crow friend of mine once said of the Crees, "They're real good scrappers." He had meant that they could face and fight just about anything. To have survived the life they had lived over the last century or so was an exultant victory of the will. Eventually, I'd learn more about the Chippewa-Cree tribes. And I'd learn more about Dorothy Small. Yes, she was a generous, loving matriarch. And yes, she was a scrapper, like most of her people.

My visit coincided with, and was part of, the annual weeklong Rocky Boy Education Conference and Powwow. I attended the powwow, a buffalo-roast luncheon, and on Tuesday night went along with Louise Stump and some of her friends to a country-western bar in Havre that featured a live band. I had already heard stories about how even through the 1950s some businesses in Montana kept signs in their windows declaring NO DOGS OR INDIANS ALLOWED. It was good, now, to see the Indians in what had once been an exclusively white club. And I felt good, and honored, to be in the company of Indians in such a place.

Dorothy Small had reminded me at the buffalo luncheon, in no few words, that the ugly realities of racial prejudice take a long time to change, and the Indian struggle against those who look down on them is still far from over. She had said that relations with the white community had improved greatly but added, "Here at our schools, we don't put up with anything. If we see any prejudice in a non-Indian teacher, out he goes."

I thoroughly enjoyed my stay in Rocky Boy. On Wednesday afternoon, it was time to say good-bye to Andy, Dorothy, and Junior. I wished I could have stayed longer. Enos Johnson, the schools' printer, was to drive me due west to Browning, on the Blackfeet Reservation. There, I would be met by the assistant principal of Heart Butte School, and he'd drive me the remaining forty-five miles south to Heart Butte, where I was scheduled to teach classes on Thursday and Friday. I thanked the Smalls again for the late-night Big Mac meal and climbed into Enos Johnson's car. Andy called out, "Come back and see us again!" Dorothy yelled, "You're always welcome in our home!"

Enos drove out of the Bear Paw Mountains and just outside Havre turned left on Highway 2. Better known as the Highline, it is the northernmost east-west highway in the contiguous states, and traverses mile after lonely, monotonous mile of flat, windblown plains. After hours of road had passed under us, I finally saw, far off in the distance, the jagged silhouette of the mountains of Glacier National Park. Ten miles or so east of the mountains, still in the grasslands, we came to Browning.

My thoughts, however, were still in Rocky Boy. What had initially seemed like the most remote spot on the earth actually turned out to be a place of bustling activity and warm friendship. Sooner or later, I thought, I'll return to Rocky Boy.

21
Crow Dinner

THE FOLLOWING MARCH I was again in Crow Agency. This visit would last four weeks. It had also been arranged by the school administration for me to take four Crow students to Missoula to present their poetry during a luncheon at that year's Montana Indian Education Association Conference. Toward the end of my first week at Crow Agency, Janice Singer, the counselor at the school, had invited me to her home for dinner.

In a housing development just west of the railroad tracks, I found the Singers' small house. Janice said, as I entered, "We're having an Indian meal. We want you to try some of the traditional food northern Indians eat."

"Sounds wonderful," I said.

"But don't expect any of that hot, spicy chili stuff that you're used to," she added.

I said, "It'll be an adventure, and I love adventures."

The Singer home was cozy with the warm clutter of family photos, Indian art, and houseplants. Although Janice was an Assiniboine Indian from northern Montana, she had married a Crow, Victor. Their daughter, Annie, was in the fourth grade. Their son, Richard, a sixth-grader, had been selected as one of the students to travel with me to Missoula.

Janice said, "Sit down. We're waiting for Hugh Little Owl.

He's a Crow elder and a relative of ours. We invited him to eat with us and play some traditional flute music."

Janice, Victor, and I chatted in the living room until Little Owl arrived. Then Janice called the kids, and we all sat down around a large dining table. Before we ate, Little Owl offered a blessing in Crow. He uttered his prayer in a respectful mumble, pausing frequently to take deep breaths between his words.

As is customary among many Indians, Little Owl, being an elder, was served first. The respect Indian people give to elders is one of the first values Indian children learn. Older folks are revered, attended to, and sincerely *listened* to. Their words are considered to carry the weight of wisdom.

Once Little Owl began to eat, the bowls and platters were passed around. The vegetables were standard—potatoes, corn, broccoli—but everything else resembled nothing I had seen. Victor handed me a bowl containing a dry purple-brown mixture. He said, "This was the Plains Indians' staple. It's called pemmican. Put some on your plate, and when you want to eat it, just pinch some between your fingers."

"What's it made from?"

"It's made by wrapping a bunch of dry meat in a cloth and banging the heck out of it with a club or hammer until it's pulverized. Then it's mixed with crushed wild berries. It lasts for months, so it was an important food for the Indians during the long winters when game was scarce. This batch was made with deer meat and Juneberries." Juneberries, I discovered, are a delicately sweet species of huckleberry. I immediately tried some of the pemmican; it had a mild, meaty, and distinctly nutty flavor.

Victor then passed me a platter covered with big slabs of dried meat. As I picked out two pieces, he said, "We still like to eat dry meat by itself, like our ancestors did." The Indians of today continue to refer to jerky as "dry meat."

He next placed a small bowl containing a whitish, greasy substance near my plate, explaining, "The meat's dry and chewy, so we use this. It's just animal fat. First you take a bite of meat, then you scoop up some fat with your finger—you don't need a lot—and chew it in with the meat. It softens it and adds some flavoring."

I did as he instructed. The slightly gamy deer, mixing with the fat, became softer and more flavorful with each chew.

Janice said, "I cooked a roast beef, too, just in case you didn't like the dry meat."

Then Victor said, "Try some bannock. It's a traditional bread of the tribes up north that us Crows never really got into. Janice makes it, though." He gave me a chunk of the bread the size of my fist.

"How's this made?" I asked.

"With baking soda," Janice said. "It's made right in a frying pan on the stove." The bread had a definitely bitter character.

Finally, Victor gave me a bowl filled with Juneberry pudding. "Some people," he said, "make this real sweet by adding a lot of sugar, and others don't sweeten it at all, letting the berries do their own work. Janice makes it somewhere in between. You can have it with your meal, or wait to have it for dessert."

I took a bite. The purple pudding was loaded with plump, juicy berries. It tasted so delicately sweet, so refreshingly moist, that I decided to save the rest for dessert.

Over dinner, Hugh Little Owl didn't say much. The Singers wanted to know about my travels to other reservations, and I told them stories about Pimas and Apaches and Hualapais. Near the end of dinner, Little Owl looked at me and said, "You're an odd white man. Sounds like you're really tryin' to *help* us In'dins. I like that."

After Janice and Annie cleared the table, we went into the living room and made ourselves comfortable. The kids sat on the floor, and no one said a word for maybe four or five minutes. Hugh Little Owl had taken out his flute and was fingering it and meditating at the same time. The flute, made of box elder wood, was smooth with years of use.

Then Little Owl began a song. In the northern tradition of flute playing, the notes had a coarse, breathy quality. The music filled the room with an ancient voice, and I imagined Crow campfires of long ago, before the white man, around which sat the old Absalooke listening to this same voice speak the same language. Here was yet another way, I thought, that the Indian ancestors continued to communicate with the modern Indian. And everyone in this room, including the children, listened with a reverent silence.

Today's Indians may drive pickup trucks, work in an office, and enjoy a Saturday matinee. They may appear to outsiders to be assimilated into the mainstream culture. But they may also dance at powwows, use Indian medicine, speak a native tongue at home, and envision the earth and the cosmos quite differently from the white man.

I would soon learn, in developing close friendships among the Plains Indians, that many of them at first appear almost totally acculturated—they have learned to survive in the white man's world—but in truth, on their reservations, in their homes, they continue to listen to the old voices. And, more and more, they do so openly, as their determination to remain a unique people strengthens.

This evening, I suddenly realized, had been planned for me. I was being both honored and scrutinized at the same time. And, once more, I was being offered friendship.

Little Owl played nine or ten songs. Then he rested the flute on his lap and said, "That's it."

Victor and Janice said, "*Ah-ho.*" The Plains Indian thank-you. As was proper, I followed suit: "*Ah-ho.*"

Indeed, the ancestors had spoken several times tonight: through a prayer delivered in the Absalooke language; through the dry meat, pemmican, bannock, and Juneberry pudding; through the flute-playing; and through a family huddled together in physical and spiritual closeness in a small living room on the Crow Reservation. *Ah-ho.*

22
A Trip with Crow Students

THE PLANE RIDE from Billings to Missoula was turbulent, and everyone had been instructed to keep their seat belts fastened. Rich Singer, Cindy Bull Chief, Chris Parrish, Lavern Old Elk, and Kevin Howe were scheduled to recite their poetry the next day at the Montana Association of Bilingual Education Convention's luncheon. The two girls, unfazed by the rocking and rolling, chatted and giggled excitedly, their eyes peeled out the window. The three boys all got sick and threw up. Cabin attendants busily paced back and forth, retrieving used airsickness bags and offering plastic cups of Seven-Up and fresh bags to the boys. Their faces had turned gray, and they appeared close to death. It was their first flight, and not a very good first impression. I hoped it wouldn't leave a permanent mark and dissuade them from future air travel.

Being sixth-grade children, the boys recovered immediately upon landing, while the girls' excitement rose in pitch and timbre. These five kids had been chosen for this trip because of the excellence of their writing as well as the easy, natural delivery they displayed in reading their works aloud (I had earlier produced a videotape of over thirty Crow students individually reciting their poems). Now, here we were in Missoula, and I knew we'd be lucky if the kids got even a couple hours of sleep tonight. But I was confident in their ability to spring to life and perform the next day—and my confidence now came from experience with Indian kids, not faith.

Cheryl Crawley was the seventh member of our group. As programs director for the Hardin School District—which included Crow Agency Elementary—she had arranged the funding as well as the details of our trip. A small, blond white woman, Crawley had put much effort into making sure the two Crow schools under Hardin's authority hadn't been neglected when it came to special services and programs. Cheryl and I would grow to be close friends. Her unwavering commitment to Indian education was only hinted at by her complete involvement in our present trip.

We all spent the afternoon at the Sheraton's indoor pool. Then, at dinnertime, I instructed the kids to dress in their best; we would be having a fancy dinner right there at the Sheraton's fancy restaurant. The kids were thrilled.

On trips with Indian children, I have always wanted them to experience new things. Tonight, the menu gave me an idea. The first item under the appetizer heading was *escargots*. I was sure none of them had ever tried this dish. I also knew that if I told them right off that *escargots* happened to be snails, none of them would so much as come within ten feet of such a thing. I asked the waiter, "How many *escargots* in an order?"

"Five, sir."

"Perfect," I said. One for each kid, I thought. Cheryl and I could share a second order. I told the waiter: "We'll start with two orders of *escargots*."

Once the waiter left, Cindy Bull Chief said to me, "What's that first thing you ordered?"

I said, "It's something I want all of you to try. It's just a little something you have before the main meal—you know, an appetizer, something to get your taste buds moving."

Kevin Howe said, "Yeah, but what is it?"

Trying to avoid the obvious, I said, "It's a French something-or-other. I think you'll like it."

Laverne Old Elk spoke up. "What's it made of?"

I put on my best Anglo-style polite talk when I said, "Laverne, *escargots* is considered one of the best appetizers in the world. You'll enjoy it. It's French. I don't know how they make it. It's French. You know, like what they eat in Paris."

I suspected the kids didn't quite trust me. Kevin Howe asked again, "But what is it?"

I said, firmly, "It's French. It's good. Trust me."

When the appetizers arrived, I immediately ate one and made a great show of how much I loved it. The kids were skeptical. I passed their order down the table, and one by one they plopped an *escargot* into their mouths. Cindy asked, "What's that flavor?"

"Garlic," Cheryl said.

Kevin commented, "It's kind of squeaky, like rubber."

As they chewed and swallowed, I asked, "Now, tell me, what's your honest opinion? How did they taste to you?"

Lavern answered first. "I don't like garlic, so I didn't like it too much."

Rich said, "It wasn't so good, and it wasn't so bad. Just kinda in between." The others nodded and grunted their agreement. That was the consensus—not so good, not so bad.

Then Rich spoke up: "Are you ever going to tell us what they were made out of?"

"Well, okay," I said. "They were snails." The children's eyes popped wide. I went on, "Now, if you guys had known they were snails, you wouldn't have tried them, right? And even if you had, you would have said they tasted terrible, right?" The children agreed. I continued, "At least now you know what *escargots* taste like from firsthand experience."

"First-*tongue* experience," Kevin shot back before wiping his tongue off with his napkin.

About five minutes into our entrées, I noticed that Chris, the smallest of our group, hadn't touched his food. I asked, "Is something wrong, Chris? Why aren't you eating?"

The boy mumbled through the side of his mouth, "I still got a snail in my mouth."

Good Lord, I thought, he hadn't swallowed the thing when I told them what they had eaten, and he felt it would be impolite to spit it out. He told me later that he intended to keep the snail under his tongue until he got to either the men's room or outside.

"Chris," I said, "it's perfectly all right for you to spit it into your napkin." Relieved, he did so, and then heartily ate his meal.

The next morning, at eleven, we went into the ballroom

where the luncheon would be held. We had an hour to practice. The room was huge; there would be several hundred people attending. I wanted the kids to learn to become each other's coaches, so I had four of them sit at the four corners of the ballroom while the fifth stood at the podium. Cheryl and I sat at the back center of the ballroom.

One by one the kids recited their work, then rotated around into the other positions. As each read his or her poems, the other students, Cheryl, and I would interrupt if necessary to offer immediate feedback. "I can't hear you!" I would yell. "Me neither!" one of the kids in a back corner would shout. "Get closer to the microphone," Cheryl would suggest. We kept the rotation going until all of the kids had their presentations just right. They were ready for anything. Rich swaggered: "Bring on the people!"

And the people came. Hundreds of them. The kids grew nervous, but an inner confidence helped them retain their composure. After lunch, I walked to the podium to introduce the young entertainment. Just as kids from other tribes had never disappointed me at a recitation, neither did these Crow kids. They performed magnificently. People sitting around me were moved to tears as they listened to the thoughts, feelings, and images of these young Indians. Little Chris Parrish was especially touching; he was so short we had to place a cinder block behind the podium so he could be seen, yet he read with a natural grace that left everyone stunned. Chris would later be invited by the Mountain West Educational Equity Center of Ogden, Utah, to join me at a school on the Sisseton-Wahpeton Sioux Reservation in South Dakota to again present his writings. Today, the last poem he read brought a spontaneous roar of applause. It was about his powwow dancing and his Indian pride. Unfortunately, I can't convey his assured voice, but here are his words:

When I Dance

I love to dance with my
feathers flying freely. I dance
because I am a Crow. I dance
with the beat of the drum. It's like
my heart pounding.

When I dance I feel like
never stopping. I look at

the drummers going faster and
my heart goes wild.

I may lose a contest but
I am very proud. I look
at the singers screaming
like the wind. I am proud
to be a Crow.

The next morning we packed our bags. In the hotel lobby, people kept stopping the children to congratulate them. Their smiles gave away the pride they felt. The flight back to Billings was smooth. No one got sick, and everyone relaxed and enjoyed watching the mountains and prairies roll by underneath us. The five kids felt a sense of achievement at having scored a real success. And I was proud to be with them.

23
Frank Takes The Gun

THE FIRST TIME I met Frank Takes The Gun was at the Billings airport, when the five Crow students, Cheryl Crawley, and I returned from our trip to Missoula. As our group approached the baggage area, I noticed an old man standing alongside Chris Parrish's mother, Agnes, and his brother, Tony. Chris, seeing them, broke into a trot. The boy got to his family and embraced each of them. When I joined the quartet of happy faces, Agnes said to me, "I want you to meet my father, Frank Takes The Gun. He wanted to be here to greet Chris."

The old man and I shook hands, and from his loose grip I figured him to be a traditional Indian. The hard-clasping handshake is a white gesture, and Indians, especially older ones who live and practice the old ways, who still predominately listen to the voices of the ancestors, acquiesce to handshaking, but without the macho fervor to which non-Indians are accustomed.

The most striking features of Takes The Gun were the etched wisdom lines darkly streaking his face, and his eyes, deep and rich with that amazing combination of profound happiness and sadness that comes with so many years of life—a look that the young find inscrutable. Widowed, he lived with Agnes, Chris, and Tony. He was obviously a man of much experience, of much inner reconciliation to the facts, fates, and cycles of life. He seemed to hold no grudges, and had long since given up any resistance to inevitabilities. As with the faces of others so blessed, his countenance appeared hard while it radiated a peaceable softness.

He stepped behind Chris, gently placed his large hands on the boy's shoulders, and said, "This is my grandson. Right here." He shook Chris lightly. "My own grandson, and I'm so proud of him. He's a good boy—a good, good boy."

Chris beamed, but his modesty had taught him to turn his head aside at such moments. Then Takes The Gun added, "I want to thank you from deep within my heart for helping my good boy here. Thank you so much for your help. When you help one, you help the whole family, and I want to thank you so much for that."

I will never forget that moment, a moment of gratitude offered to a white man in the wake of an outpouring of the deepest love and pride a man can feel for one of his own.

My subsequent meetings with Frank Takes The Gun all occurred at Agnes's house, during visits with the family. Every meeting with him ended exactly the same way. He would extend his hand, give a loose shake, and say, "Thank you so much for helping my boy. He's a good boy, and I'm proud of him. He's my own grandson."

Agnes's sister, Mary Frances Flat Lip, lived across the reservation in the village of Pryor, where the Mountain Crow resided. She worked as secretary at the little Catholic school, Saint Charles, one of several schools I was now visiting in Montana. A frail-looking woman, she was, I soon learned, made of iron. She pulled no punches, was relentlessly honest, and could handle any conflicts needing a cool-headed, strong-armed liaison between school and community. She also possessed another quality common to Indians—a genuine modesty when it came to talking about herself or her family.

One morning, as I sat in the office chatting with Mary Frances Flat Lip, the topic turned to Chris, of whom she, too, was proud. Just outside the window, newly returned robins bobbed up and down in green grass as though they also were filled with pride. "He's a good boy," Mary Frances said. Her father's daughter, I thought.

Then, for a minute or two, our conversation shifted to
Frank Takes The Gun. This is what she said: "When he was
younger, he was active in the Native American Church. Our
family spent some time down in the Southwest because of his
involvement. That's how I know Albuquerque . . . and some of
the Navajo reservation."

And that was *all* she said.

The Native American Church (NAC) was formed as a coun-
termeasure against attempts to make the use of peyote illegal,
even in native religious rituals. The peyote religion was actually
spreading among the Plains tribes as early as the late nineteenth
century. A blend of Christian symbolism and peyote visionary
beliefs, an NAC meeting is held in a tepee and begins in the
evening and lasts through to the following morning. Participants chew peyote "buttons," and thus receive revelatory vi-
sions.

Some time after my conversation with Mary Frances, as I
was idly paging through Volume 10 of the Smithsonian's thirty-
one-volume *American Indian Handbook*, I came to a chapter on
the spread, among Navajos, of the Native American Church.
Mildly interested, I started scanning, but within a few moments
my eyes nearly dropped out of my head. I couldn't move them
from the name they spied: Frank Takes The Gun. Suddenly, I
forgot about Navajos; I forgot about the Native American
Church; I forgot all but two things: This *was* a recognized history of Indian tribes of America, and that *was* the name of
Frank Takes The Gun. Could it be the Frank Takes The Gun
I knew as grandfather to Chris Parrish? In another millisecond,
another thought came crashing. Native American Church?
Hadn't Mary Frances mentioned that her father had, in his
earlier years, been active in that church? Hadn't she tossed out,
with casual modesty, that she and her family had spent time in
Albuquerque, and in the *Navajo Nation*, because of her father's
activities in the church? Yes. And, yes, it had to be the same man.
The same Takes The Gun. The next words I read confirmed it:
"a Crow Indian from Montana."

Frank Takes The Gun had been active in NAC, to say the
least. In the 1950s and into the sixties, he had been *president* of
the church. During his family's years in the Southwest, he was
taking the NAC to the Navajos, and eventually nearly 20 percent of that tribe could be counted as members. In 1956, 1958,

and 1960, Takes The Gun led major battles to have peyote legalized. And to this day, his name is legendary in the Native American Church.

The next time I saw Mary Frances, I mentioned my discovery. She turned her face slightly aside and averted her eyes in characteristic Indian modesty.

"I had no idea," I said. "He was active all right, but I'd never have guessed *how active* from what you said."

Mary Frances responded with total unpretentiousness, "Well . . . we don't like to brag about things. That's not the way Indians are."

But now that the truth was out, Mary Frances was willing to talk about her father and their time in New Mexico. Her memories were fond; she had loved the high desert and the constant sunshine and the Navajos she had befriended. She retained, however, one uneasy memory.

"I was just a kid," Mary Frances told me, "so I didn't know much about the world outside our family or our tribe. I didn't know much about prejudice and things like that. Well, one time I went with my father to Santa Fe, to the state legislature, where he had to give testimony about the church and try to get them to make peyote legal. Afterward, we were standing out in a hallway, and one of the legislators came up to us. He said he wanted to ask my father something. Then he said, 'You Indians still howl at the moon like coyotes?'

"I was so humiliated. Why did he say that? I couldn't figure it out. It was just mean. I thought that this big white man must really hate Indians. But why?

"I looked up at my father. I guess I was hoping he would say something back that would be real good, something that would put that man in his place. But, instead, he just smiled and kind of shrugged his shoulders. I was thinking, Why don't you say something?

"I felt so hurt and ashamed. When that man left, I asked my father why he didn't defend himself and the rest of us Indians. Then he said to me, in Crow, 'Nothing I say is going to change the way that man thinks. There's lots of non-Indians like that. Might as well just let them believe what they want. We know who we are, and we know that Indians are good people. That's what counts.'"

Mary Frances sighed. "I never forgot those words," she said. "I learned a lot from them."

Frank Takes The Gun passed away in March 1988. I attended a memorial for him in the cafeteria at Saint Charles School. The Crow women wore black clothes and black head scarves. One man delivered a long prayer in the Crow language, and then everyone ate. Beef, chicken, dry meat, potato salad, macaroni salad, fry bread, Juneberry pudding, Jell-O, soda pop, and coffee. A feast for the old man.

A telegram of sympathy had come from then–vice president and presidential candidate George Bush. Now, the same Frank Takes The Gun who had been ridiculed by a New Mexican state legislator in front of his young daughter so many years ago had received the respect of a future president of the United States. Frank Takes The Gun probably would have smiled and shrugged his shoulders.

Such history the man's life made. All of the battles he waged for his church were hard-fought, and he was, in his prime, a national leader; yet he had never even mentioned to me that he was "active" in the Native American Church. For me, the name of Frank Takes The Gun will remain synonymous with Indian modesty and a sincere desire to do what is right for the right reasons, not for fame or glory or riches.

24
Diné and Dinetah

IN NORTHEASTERN ARIZONA and into southern Utah and northwestern New Mexico, there is a land unlike any other on the face of the earth. Gouged by dizzying canyons, peppered with bizarre spikes and spires that sometimes rise up over a thousand feet, smoothed over in places with solid sandstone plateaus that look like stone icing, splashed with an infinite variety of colors, and topped off with a mountain range that wears a crown of dense ponderosa pines, it is the Dinetah—or, Land of the Navajo. Scattered throughout this otherworldly landscape, in family camps often miles apart, live the Diné, two hundred thousand strong and counting. Though the reservation, larger than the state of West Virginia, has towns—Kayenta, Chinle, Tuba City, Shiprock, Shonto, Crownpoint, Window Rock—built by and large around BIA agencies, tribal-government centers, and health clinics, most Navajos prefer to live "out, away from things," as they always have. The Navajo remain to this day united as one of the most traditionally "Indian" tribes in America, more likely to seek treatment from a Navajo medicine man than from a white doctor, and not at all likely to use English when conversing among themselves. Many Navajo children, in fact, don't speak *any* English until they begin to learn it in school.

Diné and Dinetah, the People and the People's Land, are

inseparable. One young man told me, "Us Navajos are just an extension of the land; we are a form of it." Add to this concept two things brought to the Navajo by the Spanish—sheep and horses—and you have, as the young man said, "a perfect harmony of earth, animal, and human." He then amended, wryly, "I think you could say we've added machinery as a fourth part of this harmony—you know, the pickup truck." Practically everyone in the Navajo Nation who owns a vehicle has a pickup, often a four-wheel-drive.

The Diné living in their six-sided hogans, the land stretching away to impossible horizons, the sheep grazing sparse grasses, the horses clopping over high mesas, and the pickups threading great distances closer together—that's the simple Navajo picture. What visitor to the Southwest hasn't seen the romantic Indian postcards: Navajo women, clothed in colorful blouses and ankle-length velveteen skirts, decked out in silver-and-turquoise necklaces and bracelets, herding their sheep over Martian landscapes painted with iron oxide, or sitting in front of outdoor looms. Or Navajo men, in black, high-domed, flat-brimmed reservation hats and gleaming conch belts, dashing across the high desert on horses that appear intent on some invisible yet urgent destination, with the monoliths of Monument Valley rising in the background.

But just as the Navajo land itself does not immediately make apparent the abundance of coal, oil, and precious metals just under its surface, so, too, these simple images of the Navajo people do not betray the rich cultural complexity just beneath the postcard image. Since 1985, I have spent considerable time in Navajoland with Navajo children and adults, in places like Red Mesa, Round Rock, Many Farms, and Fort Wingate. I have enjoyed the beautiful images, and I have been instructed by what lies beneath.

The Navajo, besides being the largest tribe on the largest reservation in the country, are also the most studied and written-about native people in the Western Hemisphere. From anthropology to fiction, the Navajo form the focus of more books than they themselves would care to count. While some Navajos live a more contemporary mainstream lifestyle, thousands enjoy the "Navajo Way," herding their sheep and weaving their famous rugs, planting the sacred corn, branching their families into the future in accord with a strict clan system, speaking their own language, and maintaining deep traditional beliefs and tribal practices. Yei-be-chei and squaw dances continue to be commonplace, and medicine men perform healing ceremonies, or "sings," all the time. Navajos who have acquired modern homes or trailers still keep their hogans as part of the family camp and spend much of their time in the clay, stone, or log-built structures whose doors open to the east in reverence to the sacred rising sun. Many family camps have no electricity or running water; pickups are used to carry firewood and coal and to haul huge plastic drums of groundwater pumped up at scattered locations. After the first snow, and only then, elders narrate to the young the enduring and venerable stories of creation and of that age-old trickster Coyote. Traditional Navajos still revere daylight and abhor darkness; once, while walking with a Navajo woman in Fort Wingate, New Mexico, I pointed out a magnificent sunset. When I looked back at the woman, I wondered why her head was turned away. "I was taught," she said, "never to look at the sun going down. The sunset is the beginning of the darkness, and darkness is like death." On the other hand, this woman pointed out that she never missed watching a sunrise, the time of new life.

"Navajos," she said, "always look to the light."

25
Navajo
Boarding School

JUST AS THE vast, spectacular Navajo landscape continually opens out, the life of many Navajo children is, much of the time, closed in—inside the walls of BIA boarding schools. These schools, once the citadels of the official United States government policy of assimilation, have changed radically since the unsuccessful policy was abandoned. From 1934 to 1945, a different policy, part of Roosevelt's New Deal, attempted to bring some new and positive ideas to Indian education. The effort, however, was largely stalled by the national priorities of World War II. Then, during the years of the termination policy, from about 1945 to 1960, many of the new ideas were lost under the effort to completely cut off any kind of support for Indians—even that which was spelled out in treaties—and to push America's natives into assimilation. Change came again with the Kennedy administration, when government policy shifted toward self-determination and self-rule, with federal recognition of the responsibilities the government had itself laid out in the treaties. More recently, under the Reagan administration, there was another shift back, albeit sly, toward termination. During these years, the executive branch maintained a facade of official support for self-determination by not recommending the abandonment of Indian programs. All in the same breath, however, in budget after budget, it recommended the allocation of zero dollars for Indian programs, including educational ones. In other words, the government was saying, "We'll support the programs that we agreed to fund, but we won't fund them." Cutbacks under President Reagan were severe, random, and, in many cases, devastating to Indians. The cuts, fortunately, were not complete, since Congress never accepted a total reduction.

Such continual shifting of official government policy toward the Indian, and toward the BIA's role in Indian education, has led, not surprisingly, to great confusion within BIA schools, as well as to a horrible lack of consistency in the quality of education from one government school to another. As of 1989, Bureau schools continued to have a national reputation as being the worst in the country, and this reputation was not improved by the government's efforts to terminate all BIA schools. Rather than make an effort to fix the schools that needed fixing and to allow the unimpeded continuance of the schools that didn't, the government wanted to throw the whole kit and caboodle out the window—to shut down all BIA schools. Such a policy would have left at least several thousand Navajo children educationally stranded hundreds of miles from the nearest off-reservation *or* reservation public schools, since, into the 1980s, there were over forty Bureau boarding schools operating on the Navajo Reservation. To shut them all down would have been unforgivable, since some of the BIA schools in Navajoland were, and still are, as I would discover, good schools.

It is always a sad thing to see children, especially younger ones, separated from their families. And it is disgraceful that a child should have to spend years, indeed any time at all, in an ineffective boarding school, where little teaching and even less learning go on, where drugs are rampant, and where fistfights and casual sex are common.

At some Bureau schools, those are the conditions, as indeed they are at some public schools. But a child attending a decent school with a good, caring staff, who is learning not only academic but social skills—even if it means periods of family separation—is arguably better off than a child who grows up illiterate.

Before my first visit to a Bureau school, I had heard the horror stories. But, I wondered, were these schools all the same?

How had current policies affected them? What was life like for contemporary Indian children behind those iron doors?

One way to learn, indeed the best way, was to go to a boarding school and live among the students and staff, to conduct classes there, and to spend time visiting the kids in their dormitories. When the opportunity arose, I took it.

Chinle Boarding School, locally known as CBS, was not in Chinle at all, but fifteen miles north, in the village of Many Farms. Many Farms Lake, a mile or so east of town, was not terribly inviting, with its brown waters and barren shores. But farther east rose the beautiful long hump of the Chuska Mountain Range. To the west of Many Farms ran a steep red ridge, several hundred feet high. To the north, two landmarks were prominent, Round Rock and Little Round Rock. Many Farms itself, at least the part of it that hugged Highway 191, consisted of a café-cum-Radio-Shack-cum-post-office, a trading post, a Thriftway convenience market, a Seven-to-Eleven convenience market, a public elementary school, and a service station. Just north of this hub, a side road headed toward the red ridge. A mile or so later, one came to a development of government houses and apartments, all single-story, all a faded peach color. Just after the last house, a large sign warned:

PROPERTY OF
THE UNITED STATES GOVERNMENT
DEPARTMENT OF THE INTERIOR
BUREAU OF INDIAN AFFAIRS
NO WATER HAULING
NO TRESPASSING AFTER 5 PM

Past this sign were two BIA boarding schools—Many Farms High School and CBS. These schools, which looked like small army bases, were spread out at the base of the red ridge.

My first visit to CBS lasted eight weeks. During that and three subsequent lengthy visits, I took up quarters twice in an apartment in the government housing compound, and twice in a dormitory isolation room just off a large recreation and TV area.

As I drove up to the complex of buildings for the first time, I read the government warning sign and swallowed hard. In the front office, I found the staff congenial and laid-back. The principal was a big man with white hair at the sides of his head and a cigarette dangling from his lips. After he introduced himself, he smoothed the front of his wrinkled shirt over a bulging hemisphere of belly, tucked it under a silver-and-turquoise belt buckle, sat down at a table, and lit another cigarette. Of Oklahoma stock, he spoke with a southwestern twang. What usually came out of his mouth, I quickly discovered, were not commands or discussions of school business but jokes. I never met a man who knew or told more jokes.

The operations of the school were pretty much left to the assistant principal, Art Hobson, and the head teacher, Wayne King. Both men were married to Navajos and had been on the reservation for years. Both were committed to Indian education and had the expertise to keep things running smoothly at CBS. Art Hobson came into the office and said, "You must be Mick. We've been looking forward to your visit."

We exchanged small talk for a few minutes, then Hobson said, "I'll take you around the school and introduce you to the teachers. We'll get you scheduled with the fourth, fifth, and sixth grades. You can start tomorrow. The cafeteria serves lunch from eleven-thirty to twelve-thirty. I've told the staff to expect you. If you want to eat dinner there, they serve from five to six."

The students in each classroom sat perfectly still as Hobson, the teachers, and I discussed scheduling. These children looked nothing like Pimas. Their skin was a bit lighter. They had high cheekbones and thin lips that turned down at the corners. Their hair, dark brown to black, was finer than the blue-black hair of the O'odham. Quite handsome—as were the Navajo adults. They didn't suffer the problem of obesity that plagued other tribes, and usually stayed in good physical condition through adulthood.

The next day, I began each class by telling the students about myself. I also told them the story about Joey and me finding the dead man in the desert. I had come to use this story with new students, and still do, for a specific reason. While I tell it, kids are enthralled. They are also learning something about my personality. And I am learning something about them by observing their responses to different parts of the story. What I learn determines the approach I will take in teaching them.

Years before, I had picked up a crucial fact from a Sioux counselor at an Indian education convention: There are no reservation Indians who are *totally* acculturated into mainstream society, and there are no Indians who are *totally* traditional. Every Indian falls somewhere between these two extremes. The more traditional child cannot be dealt with the same way as the child who is more assimilated, and vice versa. A teacher of Indian children, in order to be effective with all the students, must have at least several sets of teaching styles, and be sensitive enough to known which style works with which students.

When I tell the story about finding the dead man, I use humor, suspense, shock, and questions. When I reach these parts of the story, I make a mental note of the students' responses. The more acculturated students tend to laugh out loud at the funny parts; the more traditional kids tend to remain quiet, perhaps showing only a slight smile. In suspenseful moments, acculturated kids lean forward, their bodies more open than traditional kids, who seem to close in on themselves. At the point where I shock them, acculturated children jump, even shriek, while traditional kids sometimes show no physical response at all, though they certainly experience the rush of adrenaline. And when I ask questions, I know that those students who answer verbally tend toward the acculturated side. Traditional children often answer in their minds only.

These two sets of responses to the same situations are basic. There are others. But these tell me what I need to know to start off a class. Traditional Indian children are brought up to be respectfully quiet in the company of older people, especially those they don't personally know. Laughing too loud, moving around too much, speaking up, are all viewed as inappropriate behavior. Traditional kids also avoid prolonged eye contact. Staring into another's eyes can mean you are trying to know too much about him, perhaps even trying to do him harm—at the least, it is considered disrespectful. Acculturated kids just look back at you. This difference has led to the now-famous example of the insensitive non-Indian teacher who disciplines a traditional Indian child by first saying, "Look me in the eye when I talk to you." From the Indian kid's point of view, this is almost the same as saying, "Give me the finger when I talk to you."

While it is fine to single out an acculturated student for praise—this will encourage the student to further success—it is not appropriate to do so with a traditional Indian child who has been taught that one should not stand out from one's peers—cooperativeness over competitiveness is the rule. It is, however, proper to praise the traditional child privately. I've lost count of the times I have pulled kids aside in hallways or cafeterias or classrooms to offer whispered words of praise.

When I tell the dead-man story, I try to discover two things: first, if the majority of the students go to one side or the other, or are about evenly split. This will determine the general style I take. Second, I pinpoint the students individually. This will determine how I deal with them one-on-one.

On my first day of teaching classes at CBS, as I proceeded through the dead-man story, I got my first surprise. It seemed that virtually *all* of the students were on the traditional side of the scale—*way* over on that side. When I came to the humorous parts of the story, all the kids sat there like statues, not even smiling. When I narrated the suspenseful parts, all the kids sat there, yes, like statues again. I tried to see if their eyes blinked. When I attempted to startle them—my God, statues again. I tried two questions, both of which met with thunderous silence.

These were the most traditionally behaving kids I had ever encountered. I received from them absolutely no indication that they had even heard what I said, much less enjoyed it. Did they think I was funny, or crazy? Did they think I was friendly, or overbearing? Were they taken with my stories, or merely bored? Did they like this flamboyant white man, or consider him a corny, irrelevant outsider? I had no answers to these questions. Not a single student had made the slightest gesture that might have helped me figure it out.

At lunchtime I didn't feel like eating; instead, I went off to a secluded corner in the teachers' lounge and thought. I was sure of only two things: The students' total unresponsiveness had caused me to feel great frustration, and I intended to do everything in my power to conceal that frustration from them. I knew that if I was going to be successful with Navajo children, I would have to resist my own Anglo impulses to demand even minimally acculturated responses. I knew I had to adjust to the children's way of being comfortable in a classroom.

In my first three classes the following morning, I forced myself to project an even greater cheerful friendliness than I had the previous day. I joked around even more, still enveloped in the students' stony silence. After handing out a couple of

photocopied poems and reading them aloud, I asked a few
questions about them. I didn't expect verbal answers; instead,
I allowed the students time to consider the possibilities, and
then I gave them the answers. A few of the students, in response
to some of the simplest questions, actually shaped their lips
into voiceless responses. This encouraged me. Other traditional
Indian students I had taught had become more open as they
relaxed in my presence, accepting my overtures of friendship.
These shadowy Navajo dances of the lips indicated an explicit
and positive development.

I decided to have lunch. During the night, a light snow had
fallen, and now the mid-January sun shotgunned a half-dozen
brilliant rays through scattered clouds. The air was bitter-cold
as I made the long walk across campus to the cafeteria, leaving
a wake of visible breath. The red ridge and the red ground
contrasted wondrously with the broken puzzle of white snow.

I entered the cafeteria, stomped the snow from my boots,
and walked into my next surprise at CBS. As I made my way
through the dining hall, small pockets of students—those whose
classes I had visited—began calling my name from where they
sat at long tables. "Sit over here!" they yelled, or, "Eat with us!"
This sudden effusion of friendliness from all directions caught
me off guard. Were these the same statues I had been in-
structing, now miraculously brought to life?

Recovering from my shock, I pointed at one cluster of
students and said to the others, "I'll sit with these guys today,
and with a different group tomorrow, and a different group
the next day—like that. That way, I'll have a chance to sit with
all of you." The fifth-graders I had chosen cheered. The others
accepted my plan with mild groans. It then occurred to me that
all the students who had been calling out were boys; right off,
I understood that it would have been culturally inappropriate
for the girls to have demonstrated in such a way.

I sat down with a tray of fried-chicken legs, mashed potatoes, corn, and Jell-O, rolled up my sleeves, picked up the fork,
and then the barrage of questions from the children began:
"Where were you born?" "How old are you?" "Do you go to the
movies?" "Why is your hair curly?" "Do you have any brothers
and sisters?" "Did you ever fly on an airplane?" "Is it scary?"
"Are you married?" "Do you have a girlfriend?" "Do you have
any children?" "What's your favorite food?" "Do you like Nava-

jos?" "Where are you staying?" "Did you ever see the ocean?" "How big is it?" "Will you come watch TV with us in the dorm sometime?" "What kind of truck do you have?" Of course they assumed that everyone had a truck. I didn't disappoint them.

Then I felt four little fingers mousing up and down my forearm, and heard a voice whisper, "Ooh, he has hair on his arms!" Other fingers reached out from either side and from across the table. Indian men generally don't have body hair, and these kids were fascinated by it. I put my arms on the table and said, "Okay, you can touch them if you want, but not all of you at once." I reckoned it best to quench their interest before I attempted to use my arms to eat. Kids from other tables were now coming over and surrounding me with more questions and more fingers. Not wanting bedlam to break out, I asked those students to return to their tables, telling them I would sit with them another day. Without a fuss, they retreated.

The boy next to me asked, "Can I touch your beard?"

"Okay," I said, "let's get it over with. Anyone who wants to see what my beard feels like, now's the time." The kids took turns jabbing or stroking or just laying their fingertips on my face hair. It occurred to me that I could take this opportunity to introduce the students to similes, a technique I would be teaching them. I asked each one to tell me, after he touched my beard, what it felt *like*. "Like wire!" "Like grass!" "Like my saddle blanket!" And, most commonly, "Like sheep!" I could use these responses later, in the classroom.

I would soon find that this intense curiosity was no less manifest in the seventh-and eight-graders; during their later turns with me at lunch, they would likewise deliver their own fusillades: "Did you ever go to Paris?"—I had been there twice, and they wanted to know every detail of the city I could remember. "What tribe are your parents?"—I told them my father was Italian, and my mother was German. "Can they speak White?"—I explained that English was the first, and usually only, language of European-Americans. One boy, a seventh-grader, slyly tested me when he asked, "Do you know who discovered America?" The kids around him grinned. I told the boy that a lot of history books claimed the discoverer was Columbus, but that it was Indians who really discovered America. The boy and his friends were satisfied.

The single most shocking question I was ever asked by an

Indian kid came from a sixth-grade Navajo boy during a visit I subsequently made to Red Mesa School District. The youngster sat next to me on the bleachers one evening during a school basketball game. At one point, he tugged on my shoulder. I leaned over to hear him. Then he whispered in my ear, "How long is yours?"

I couldn't believe I had heard him right. "What?" I asked. He repeated, "How long is yours?"

I nearly toppled off the bleachers. My impulse was to berate the boy for asking such a thing. But at the same moment I understood that the question came from nothing more than simple, natural curiosity about a race of people with whom the boy had had very little contact. He obviously had never felt close enough to a white man to ask this question. He wasn't being intentionally vulgar; he was just wondering how people of different races compared to each other. Given his pubescent age, the focus of his question was normal and innocent.

I hoped my answer suitable: "I think you're curious not just about me, but about all white men. Well, it doesn't matter if a man is white or black or Indian. Men come in different sizes, whatever their color. There's not one size for whites and another for Indians. There's small, big, and in-between in every group of people."

The boy said, "Is it?" using a common and widespread Indian idiom for "Really?" or "Is that true?"

"Yeah," I said. The boy seemed content. We went back to watching the basketball game.

The Navajo children who sat around me as I had my first meal at CBS were anything but statues. They continued, however, to be quiet during our classes. This reserve, I learned, did not indicate boredom or disinterest. These kids had always been taught to be respectful of teachers—of anyone older than they—and to be mannerly in the classroom. They extended their respect and demonstrated their manners with behaviors they had learned within the Navajo way of doing so. Having Navajo teachers reinforced this.

As days, then weeks, went by, the students did begin to laugh when I told jokes. They started to move about a little more freely. And they began to answer, if under their breaths, my questions. But they remained generally quiet, all the while writing first-rate poems that exhibited how deeply they thought and felt and imagined. After I had adjusted to their way of behaving in class, I came to regard these Navajo students as among the most hardworking, and certainly the most polite, children with whom I had ever worked.

The Navajo students, however, did not regard the cafeteria, the hallways, or the playground as synonymous with the classroom. Away from their desks, they felt no need to conceal their enthusiasm for the things, and people, they liked. Every day, after that first lunch, I was continually encircled by curious and affectionate magpies. Little had I known that during those initial classes, when the Navajo children sat there like slabs of concrete, a great deal was going on inside their heads. They were, in fact, enjoying my stories, and developing a fondness for this strange white man. They would show him how they felt, but always later, outside the classroom. While at their desks, they could do no better than to let him know they respected him.

26
Navajo Kids and John Wayne

EVERY FRIDAY AFTERNOON, the boarding-school students would gather their clothes into duffel bags and wait for their parents or other family members to check them out for the weekend.

I always felt sorry for those few kids who, for whatever reasons, had to stay at school. They knew no one was coming for them, and it had to be painful as they watched the other kids leave for home. I often spent part of the weekends with these students, treating them to soda pop and chips, telling them a few stories. Sometimes I had them teach me Navajo words. Often, in the evenings, we played pool or card games, or just watched television in the lounge.

Like kids everywhere, they loved to watch "professional" wrestling; they became glued to their chairs whenever a match was broadcast. These Navajo youngsters seemed to know that the contests were staged, but this didn't dampen their enthusiasm. They'd ooh and ah or laugh at every body-slam and neck-twist, engrossed in both the prefab drama and the slapstick comedy.

They also enjoyed watching rodeos and cartoons and fast-action movies. Surprisingly, they liked old westerns—the kind that portrayed the Indian as a ruthless savage and the cavalry as the savior of civilized white settlers. I witnessed, several times, a bizarre tableau: Navajo kids lounging in front of a television screen, watching images of John Wayne and his men "heroically" pumping bullets into the last of a band of cutthroat renegades. And the Navajo children always cheered with each red man's dying gasp or horse-fall.

The obvious question always came to my mind: Why would full-blood Indian youths applaud the portrayal of historical Indians being roundly defeated and left for the buzzards? The answer, I found, lay in understanding how young Navajos envisioned themselves as individuals *and* as part of a cultural group. The following episode abruptly threw this into perspective for me:

I was in a classroom of fourth-graders. The day before, in preparation for the writing lesson I was giving, I had narrated the Franz Kafka story "The Metamorphosis." The students' eyes had grown twice their normal size as I acted out this tale of a man who'd been mysteriously transformed into a giant insect. The whole presentation had taken the full forty-five-minute class period—a bit of bad Broadway in the middle of the Navajo Nation, but the kids loved it.

Then I announced to the students that today they would write their own metamorphoses—in the first person. They would have to imagine what it would be like to wake up in the morning and discover that overnight they had been transformed into something wholly different from what they were. I told the students they could choose to turn into any animal or plant, or even into some object. I gave them a few minutes to consider the possibilities and make a choice.

They began clutching their pencils, eager to pursue this imaginative opportunity to become something *other*. Then a boy in the back row raised his hand.

I fumbled about for his name. "Yes . . . Eric?"

"Can I become a truck?"

"Sure. That'll be interesting."

Now, the other students wanted to tell me what they had chosen. Jolene Benally wanted to change into a river. Terrance Begay into a wild stallion. Mervin Kee into a comet. Julian Yazzie into a jumping spider. Thomasina Phillips into a lizard. Then, little Geraldson Begay thrust an arm skyward. "Yes, Geraldson," I said. "What do you want to become?"

"Can I change into an Indian?" I paused, then looked around at the teacher and her aide, both Navajo, and both hiding grins with their fingers. I looked at Geraldson again.

"An Indian?"

"Yes," the boy said. He had absolutely no idea that *he* was an Indian.

I thought for a moment about how I should handle this. "Geraldson," I finally said, "you're Diné, right?"

He answered in Navajo since I had used the Navajo word for the tribe: "*Ou.*"

"And you know that *Diné*, in English, is 'Navajo'?"

"Yess." He switched to the English affirmation, drawing out the *s*, in typical Navajo fashion.

"Do you know the word 'tribe'?"

"Yess."

"And you've heard that Navajo people are called the Navajo tribe?"

"Yess."

"People of the Navajo tribe are different from whites or blacks or Mexicans or Chinese, right?"

"Yess."

"But there are *other* tribes. There are over three hundred other tribes just in the United States. All the people of all these tribes are called 'Indians'—'American Indians.' Navajo is one of these tribes. So, *you* are an Indian. Everyone in this classroom except me is an Indian."

Geraldson thought hard about all of this, trying to incorporate it into his world. Up until now, he had only considered himself Diné, or Navajo, and had not connected his identity to a race.

"Okay," I said. "So, you are an Indian. In the story you write today, you have to change into something that you're not. You can't change into an *Indian*, because you already are an Indian. Now, can you think of something different that you could change into?"

Geraldson twisted his face into a thoughtful grimace—that charming, exaggerated mug so common to children. Then his eyes jumped wide open, and he sat straight up. "I know," he yelled out. "Can I turn into a Hopi?"

The teacher and the aide laughed out loud. I said to the boy, "Why don't you just pick some kind of animal?"

I would take time some other day to attempt a different explanation of what an Indian was.

Some months later, at the beginning of the next school year, I was working with Navajo students at Wingate Boarding School in New Mexico. One Saturday evening, I sat down with the weekend kids in a dormitory lounge. Seven boys and three girls were watching a John Ford production of a John Wayne western.

I'd seen this same thing happen at CBS, and the Wingate kids were reacting to John Wayne just as the Chinle kids had—they rooted for him as he and his horse soldiers tracked down a band of evil "Comanch'."

Oddly, and typically, the only landscape in Ford's film was Monument Valley. From the Mississippi to southern Arizona, the towering Three Sisters, the Mittens, the Fingers, and long stretches of sand dunes had been multiplied tenfold. Some of the Navajo kids must have thought that most of America looked just like Navajoland.

The movie Indians, roaming what in reality was sacred Navajo ground, wore moccasins, warbonnets, face and body paint, and rode bareback—distinctly an amalgam of several Plains tribes. When Captain Wayne entered their camp of te-pees carrying a white flag, he and the Indian chief faced each other and said, "*Yah-ta-hay.*" The Navajo kids watching this instantly exploded into laughter, repeating, "*Yah-ta-hay, yah-ta-hay.*" The words mean, in Navajo, "How are you?" The effect of hearing John Wayne and a painted Italian actor speak them was, for Navajo youngsters, pure comedy.

As the concluding battle between red man and white man raged, the kids cheered as one Indian after another succumbed to John Wayne's eternally loaded Colt.

Now, I understood why. These Navajo children were not *Indian*, at least not in their way of thinking. They were Diné, or, in English, Navajo. *Indians* shot arrows with bows, and wore buckskin and feathers, and hunted buffalo, and killed innocent white women and children. *Indians* bore no resemblance at all to Diné, who herded sheep, wove rugs, attended squaw dances, and were taught to live in *beauty*—that is, in harmony with the universe.

Chinle student Geraldson Begay had been, in a sense, quite

accurate in believing that by turning into an "Indian," he would be going through a metamorphosis. What he had imagined as "Indian," communicated to him through Hollywood, was a pure, negative stereotype.

The entertainment industry has, of course, changed since the days of the portrayal of the *wild*, ruthless Indian. Indians nowadays receive more agreeable coverage in film and on television, albeit scant. And such actors as Will Sampson, Chief Dan George, Iron Eyes Cody, and Graham Green have recently provided Indian children with fine role models.

Unhappily, though, the old movies keep showing up on the tube, and real Indian kids—who, like most kids, tend to believe what they see—still watch them.

27
Many Mothers

"I'M LUCKY BECAUSE I have a lot of mothers," said ten-year-old Landon Manygoats as we walked through the glass corridor that bridged the classroom wings of CBS to the administrative offices. Snow ticked against the windowpanes and swirled through a set of double glass doors inattentively left open a crack. The linoleum floor was slippery with snowmelt from the boots and sneakers of dozens of children.

I yanked the doors shut, contemplating what Landon had just said. We had been talking about our families. He had asked me how many brothers and sisters I had, and I had asked him if he came from a large family. I didn't know it at the time, but talking about family is the first and most natural topic for Navajos to discuss with anyone. I wondered what it meant for a Navajo to have a lot of mothers.

I considered asking outright. But Landon had spoken so offhandedly, so unaffectedly, that I feared I might look foolish. With typical non-Indian equivocation, I said, "A lot of mothers? That's nice," hoping he might elaborate.

Landon looked up at me and asked, innocently, "How many mothers do you have?"

I was caught again in my own trap. How many mothers *could* I have, Navajo style? How many did I actually have? What definition other than a woman who gives birth to a child should I consider in making my own list of mothers? It was obvious that having more than one was part of the normal fabric of Navajo life.

"Uh . . . one," I said.

"Too bad," the youngster offered sympathetically.

Landon Manygoats was a bright boy—beyond ordinary intelligence. He had just skipped a year at school and was now achieving top marks in the sixth grade. I wondered if he perceived my confusion.

Then he said, proudly, "And I don't even know how many brothers and sisters I have. I never counted them."

I wondered if he also had a flock of grandparents.

"Well, look at that," I said. "Sure is snowing hard. Does it snow a lot around here?" I hoped he hadn't seen through this deliberate evasiveness, but I suspected he had.

In the office, Landon took care of his business with the secretary and left. I sat down at the long table across from assistant principal Art Hobson. I rubbed my hand over the table's surface and looked at it; a thin red line of powdery dust extended from the tip of my index finger down to the webbing between finger and thumb.

I had learned this about Navajoland: There was no escaping the red dust. It was everywhere. Even if you didn't see it, it was there. It crept through the minutest cracks between window frame and sill, and under every closed door. An Anglo friend of mine in Red Mesa had tried to bar the dust one winter by sealing her windows with clay and stuffing moistened rags along the base of her front and back doors. The dust would not be deterred. It somehow routed itself around her defenses and left its usual coating on everything in her home.

Another white friend, a teacher at CBS, had told me, "You get used to it. You've got no choice because it gets into every last thing you own. Stick around, you'll be wearing rust-colored underwear before long."

The red dust is very much like the Navajo culture itself. When you are in Navajoland, there's no escaping it. It's all around you and ever-present, be it conspicuously or invisibly.

The red dust is Navajo flesh and blood; it's Navajo thought and vision; it's Navajo *beauty* and medicine; it's Navajo breath. You make note of it. Sometimes you examine it. Sometimes you learn from it. Sometimes you're not paying attention—that's when you run your hand across a tabletop, and there it is, plain as can be.

When Landon Manygoats told me about his many mothers, his words formed another puff of red dust. As I sat in the office, I decided I would ask Art Hobson about Navajo mothers.

"Art, Landon Manygoats just told me that he had a lot of mothers."

Hobson shrugged. "Yeah?"

"I don't really know what he meant by that. How does one wind up with more than one mother?"

"Oh," he said, realizing my dilemma. "Well, you've heard of the Navajo clan system?"

"I've heard of the clans, but I don't know anything about them or how they work." Somehow I had the impression that this situation would be similar to the one in which I attempted to explain to little Geraldson Begay what an Indian was. Only now, I was at the learning end. I listened hard.

"The Navajos follow a very definite clan system. To violate the system in any way is to commit a grave wrong. It's how they avoid intimate relationships with cousins and such. It's also how they break down the responsibilities of individuals to their relatives, as well as how they classify relatives.

"You see, you are born *into* your birth mother's clan, and *for* your father's clan. There are about seventy clans in all. All of your mother's sisters are regarded as your other mothers. That's what Landon was talking about. His mother has a lot of sisters. You'd call them maternal aunts, but in the Navajo Way they are your mothers. You're expected to relate to them just as you do to your birth mother, and they treat you exactly the way they treat any child born to them. If anything happened to your mother and she was no longer there for you, one of your other mothers would take you in without hesitation. Navajo families are extremely close, and Landon feels a mother's love multiplied by the number of sisters his mother has."

"All right so far," I interrupted, "I can follow that."

Hobson laughed. "Hold on to your hat," he said as he continued. "All the children of your mother's sisters, those you would consider maternal cousins, are your brothers and sisters. Your maternal cousins who are the offspring of your mother's brothers are of their mothers' clan, and thus your cousins. Your paternal cousins by your father's sisters are cousins and belong to his clan, while the children of your father's brothers belong to their birth mother's clan."

I sighed. "It'll take a little time, but I'll catch on."

"The clan system also helps control crime," Hobson said. "You see, when anyone commits a crime, everyone in his clan is considered responsible. There's a lot of peer pressure to be good."

I thanked Art for the information and left for my next class. Walking back through the glass corridor, I stopped once again to pull the double doors shut. It was snowing harder. I mulled over what Hobson had told me and knew I would not let it go until I could differentiate the clan lines of Navajo kinship. Maybe I had just shut out the snow, but never the red dust. At least now I clearly understood where mothers came from.

What stuck in my mind was what Hobson had said about Landon Manygoats and his mothers—"Landon feels a mother's love multiplied by the number of sisters his mother has." Landon had a lot of mothers. Landon seemed very happy about that. And, yes, Landon was very lucky.

28
Indian Givers

HANDWOVEN RUGS, TURQUOISE jewelry, hogans, and herds of sheep are all symbols of the Navajo tribe. Less known, but so common among the Navajo that it, too, could be a symbol of the tribe, is the piñon nut. Every autumn thousands of Navajo families climb aboard their pickups and head for the areas of the reservation where the piñon pine trees grow. There, they festively collect thousands of the delicately sweet nuts. For me, the piñon came to represent something special; whenever I worked in the Navajo Nation, I came to see the piñon as a symbol of the giving spirit of the Indian.

This spirit of generosity was nothing new to me when I encountered it among the Navajo. From Indian friends, I had received baskets, beadwork, even a hand-painted sofa pillow. One young Pima-Sioux had given me that most cherished of possessions—a feather from his powwow outfit. It was one of the first gifts I had ever been given by an Indian friend, and remains today one of my most treasured. This book is dedicated to him and to that spirit.

The fact is, Indians honestly *enjoy* giving. It is truly ironic that among the poorest people in the United States there is more giving of whatever material wealth they have than among any other ethnic group I have ever known. But this naturally reflects that part of the Indian worldview that regards material things as nice but ephemeral, and not to be coveted so much as shared. This wonderful trait is so elemental to the Indian that Indian children understand it, at least emotionally, from the moment they recognize they have emotions. And they live their lives by it.

Whenever I return to work with Navajo kids, I am reminded of the Indian spirit of giving. The children, stuck in boarding schools, don't have much to give, but the supply of piñons seems always plentiful. I can't count the number of times I have been stopped in hallways, or cafeterias, or playgrounds, and been handed a dozen or more piñons by young Navajos who, more often than not, simply smile and say, "Here."

If these kids happen not to have any piñons on them, anything will do. In the dorm at Chinle one night, a student bought an ice-cream sandwich, broke it in two, and handed half to me. At Wingate, a student walked into the lounge area and sat next to me on a couch, offering me one of the two cookies he had in his hand. On numerous occasions, kids have showed me pencil or ink drawings they had done in their free time, then said, "You can have it." Beaded and leather key chains, yarn bracelets, and small cardboard and cowhide drums have come my way via the affection of many young Indians.

At first I was reluctant to accept the gifts—the candy bar I took meant one less for the kid giving it. The child who spent his only two quarters on two cookies and then gave me one had given up exactly half of his current net worth. But I realized that to turn down a gift from an Indian was to offer an insult. The spirit of sharing is the important thing, and should not be denied those who would enjoy it. When a kid really likes you and wants to do something nice for you, you don't have the right to decline what's extended in friendship, for the sharing itself represents a seal of that friendship—and that's the way a Navajo sees it, no matter his age. Turn down a gift and you've rejected the bond of friendship. Nowadays, whatever the gift, I always accept it enthusiastically.

One day at CBS a fourth-grader named Kermit Yazzie offered me a plastic bag full of piñons just before class was to begin. I told him I didn't have anywhere to put them, and asked him to hold on to the nuts and give them to me after class. I started the hour by telling the students a legend from the Blackfeet tribe of Montana about a family that ventured to the far north of Canada in search of a white buffalo; they become trapped by the severe winter, and most of them perish in their struggle to return home. It's a story packed with adventure.

While I was telling the story, I noticed that Kermit had opened the plastic bag of piñons and had begun munching on them. I smiled to myself, knowing that Kermit was so wrapped up in the story, he didn't realize what he was doing. Sitting there with eyes as big as silver dollars, he plunked one nut after another into his mouth—he reminded me of a kid at a movie eating popcorn with unconscious, rapidfire compulsion. Midway through the story, Kermit began gagging. He covered his mouth with his hands, but the rasping screeches of his constricting throat couldn't be muffled. The other students looked at him and began to giggle. I figured he had choked on a partially chewed piñon. Trying to cut short the interruption as quickly and smoothly as possible, I said, "Go get a drink of water if you want, Kermit." He did. By the time he returned, the class had settled and I was back into the story. When I finished, I gave the students a five-minute break before giving them the writing assignment. I walked over to Kermit and asked, "What was happening when you were making those terrible noises?"

"These," he said, holding up the bag of piñons.

"Oh, you choked on one?"

"No. I got one of those things."

I didn't know what he meant. "What things?"

"One of those sheep things," he said.

Kermit had gathered those piñon nuts himself, on a harvesting outing with his family just a week before. Inadvertently, he had thrown into this bag a sheep pellet—small, brown, oval, just like a piñon nut. While he was listening to my story, he just kept grabbing at the nuts and throwing them into his mouth. He got hold of the "sheep thing" and, not noticing it to be different from the other nuts, threw it into his mouth and bit down. After hearing this, I immediately offered Kermit the rest of a pack of Certs I had in my pocket. . . . And I had never in my life been so thankful to have delayed the acceptance of a gift.

A couple of weeks later, after another class, sixth-grader Garrett Tso approached me in the hall and held out another plastic bag. "Here," he said. "My mother sent this for you, so you can try it." I took the bag and examined the contents. A bunch of thin, greenish sticks had been neatly broken into even lengths and tied with string into half a dozen little bundles. I momentarily flushed, thinking the boy had given me a bag full of marijuana stems. But that was altogether outrageous, I knew.

"What is this?"

"Navajo tea. Did you ever have it?"

"No. But, thanks to you, I will."

"It's real good. And it's good if you feel sick; it's medicine. But you can use it just as a hot drink, too."

"Thank you so much, Garrett. It's a wonderful gift. I'll try it tonight."

Brewed, the Navajo tea bore a golden-yellow color and tasted delicious, a little like some herbal teas I've had. Later, I found that Navajo tea was a species of what is known as "Mormon tea." "Navajo tea" made a better name, however, since the native people had used these teas for generations before Joseph Smith walked the earth. I also discovered that Navajo tea did, in fact, possess medicinal qualities. To this day, I always keep it around and use it against minor illnesses, especially colds and flu and upset stomachs. It works. Garrett Tso had given me a very special gift.

Because most of the Navajo children's families lived in scattered family camps often miles from the schools, it was nearly impossible to get to know many of them personally. They would come to know of me through their kids, as Garrett's mother had—her sending me the Navajo tea was a recognition of my work that left me feeling honored. I did, however, get to know Navajo adults who worked at the schools and who lived in the government compounds or nearby. They, too, offered gifts, particularly at the end of my stays.

One late spring afternoon, during a final week at CBS, I visited Eric Zah's home in Many Farms. The sixth-grader's mother and father had invited me for a typical Navajo dinner: mutton stew and fry bread. After the wonderful meal—I really do love mutton—we sat in the living room and talked. Then Eric's mother excused herself, and Eric followed her. "Do you smoke?" the boy yelled to me. I yelled back that I did. A few minutes later, the two returned, and Eric handed me a shoe box: "This is for you."

I thanked the family and opened the lid. Inside was a plastic donkey about eight inches from snout to tail—the kind you might find in a souvenir shop south of the border. Eric asked me for a handful of cigarettes as he took the donkey from my hands and lifted the lid off the basket on its back. I gave him four or five, and he dropped them into the basket, saying, "See, it's a cigarette holder." He handed the donkey back.

"Thanks," I said. "I've never seen anything like it."

"But it's a special cigarette holder," Eric said. He now wore a mischievous grin.

"Special, how?"

"Pull down on his ears." Eric giggled. I pulled the donkey's ears forward and down; instantly its tail flipped up in the air and a cigarette shot out of its ass. We all roared. Yes, Navajos love to give gifts; they also love a good laugh. I still have my donkey, and every time I look at it, I think of the Zahs and smile.

Like most people, I, too, had always enjoyed giving gifts. But in my culture, gift-giving is usually restricted to special occasions: birthdays, anniversaries, Christmas, and such. What I learned from Indians is that the pleasure of giving should be experienced any time one is so moved. What better way to seal friendships? What better way to signal the bond of affection? And the element of surprise in giving someone a gift when he or she doesn't expect one only adds to the pleasure.

Often, now, I give things to both older friends and Indian kids on the spur of the moment, for the sheer pleasure of it. Every spring I surprise my best student of the year with a new typewriter. But the other gifts I give are small: chips and soda pop in a dormitory; card or board games; a pair of gloves for a pair of cold hands; a fast-food meal and a movie for three or four kids at a time.

But when is a gift so small or inexpensive as to no longer be considered a gift? Never. The Navajo kids know this. Among the best gifts I receive from them, over and over, are handfuls of piñon nuts. The children hold out their closed fists and say, "Here." Of course, I admit, I now double-check all of the nuts before I eat them, but every time I receive a gift from an Indian child, I get a real charge out of the mutual love that makes these children want to share whatever they have with me.

29
Teachers

WHEN IT COMES to teaching Navajo children, Navajo teachers have a clear edge over outsiders. They know the kids' cultural background inside out—language, clan system, traditional ceremonies. They know the categories of appropriate behaviors in the relationships between adults of one clan and the youngsters of the same or other clans. They know how Navajo sisters relate to each other, how they relate to their brothers, how they relate to girls and boys of other clans, and how boys relate to brothers and sisters and other nonfamily boys and girls. Navajo teachers can quickly spot behavior changes in Navajo kids and pretty well finger the causes and know how to deal with them in the same time it takes a lot of outside teachers to catch on that anything has changed at all.

This is true not just of Navajos, but of Indians of any tribe. The move toward self-determination, self-rule, and self-sufficiency must include the gradual replacement of non-Indian teachers with teachers of the students' own tribes. Within a smaller, less traditional tribe, such as the Pimas, the few Pimas who become teachers often move off the reservation and take jobs in larger, non-Indian communities where the pay may be better, and they see themselves as having risen "above" the conditions of the reservation. Progress seems generally to come faster within tribes that retain much of their cultural heritage. The Navajo, the largest tribe and among the most traditional, turn out new teachers every year who believe it vitally important to return to the Navajo Nation and teach Navajo children. The Navajo are closer than many to a time when very few, if any, non-Navajo teachers will be needed to guide their children toward education's ultimate goal—that is, providing avenues of development that can lead to a happy, successful life. Another advantage for Indian teachers is that they know more about how their own tribes *define* happiness and success, which may not always be exactly the way non-Indians define such things.

But at present there is still an obvious need for non-Indian teachers on reservations. In some schools, like CBS or Wingate, the white teachers represent the minority; in other Indian schools, they make up the entire staff. The best of these educators demonstrate their belief in the move toward Indian self-determination, while the worst are full of the passionate intensity of the old assimilationists. The best go about learning as much as they can about the tribe they work for and attempt to become culturally sensitive, respecting tribal customs and beliefs. The worst fiercely adhere to the paternal idea that Indians must be "civilized." They approach education as though it embodied their own personal mission to convert Indians to thinking that the only way to happiness is the "White Way." The worst of the worst not only believe this—and have failed at it over and over for years—but they remain in Indian classrooms, where the damage they do to native children continues with every day they spend on a reservation. In the Navajo Nation, I met non-Indian teachers of both extremes.

BARNEY

Red Mesa won't be found on most maps. Like many Navajo towns, it's not really a town. More correctly, it's a chapter—the Navajo Nation is politically divided into dozens of these chapters, from which representatives are elected to serve on the tribal council. The residents of each chapter are generally scattered all around the high desert in their family camps, while the center of local political activity in any given chapter is the chapter house, usually like a small community hall. Red Mesa, so named for the immense red mesa that marks its northern border, is in northeastern Arizona between two other "towns," Teec Nos Pos and Mexican Water. It has a trading post–filling station, a tiny community of tract homes, and a public school that serves an area stretching in any direction as far away as fifty road miles.

Visible from various points in Red Mesa are the pine-studded Carrizo Mountains to the southeast, the far-off, usually snowcapped peaks of Utah's Abajo Mountains, the Sleeping Ute Mountain in Colorado, and, to the northeast in Colorado, the majestic La Plata Range—the tallest peak of these mountains, Hesperus, is one of the four sacred peaks of the Navajo.

The public school's grounds contain a housing compound in which many of the staff members live in trailers or apartment units. From this compound, looking west, one catches sight of the monoliths of Monument Valley, thirty-eight miles away. Because of Red Mesa's isolation, a good number of its teachers commute from their homes in the nearest town of any size, Cortez, Colorado, some sixty-five miles off and away from the Red Mesa Navajos. Long drives. Big car pools.

One cold, dry, dusty afternoon, during the first week of a six-week stay, I took my lunch break in the teachers' lounge, resting on a big, cloud-cozy sofa. A high school teacher in his fifties, slim, dirty-haired, and unkempt, sat at a table eating a sandwich that smelled of old potted meat. We didn't exchange words. There are some people with whom you share a mutual instinct of incompatibility. For me, he was one.

The door opened, and in came another one—the junior high school history teacher. This guy wore baggy wrinkled slacks and a plaid wool shirt. Also obviously past his midcentury mark, he proved as coarse in manner as his unruly gray hair. He let out a thunderous belch, sighed "Oh, Christ," unfurled a brown paper lunch bag, and sat down opposite the other man. I hoped it was not more potted meat; the air was thick enough. Both men were white and commuted from Cortez.

"What's a 'matter, Barney," the first man said, "these little fuckers gettin' to ya again?"

"Christ a 'mighty, these fuckin' Navajos," Barney mumbled into his lunch bag. The air was getting thicker with an odor worse than potted meat. I lay on my back, motionless, staring at the ceiling.

"I'll tell ya, Ralph, I'm ready to walk out those doors and never come back."

"Why don't ya?" his buddy chided. "Ya already got your BIA retirement. You could be—"

Barney cut in, "An' if I stick it out long enough, I'll get another pension from this damn place."

"Then just don't let the fuckers get to ya. Just smile an' walk away. That's what I do."

"The thing that gets me most is they got no respect for anything. They don't want to listen to you. They don't want to do their work. They don't want to settle down an' be polite. Even if they're not gonna listen, they could at least be polite. They just don't want to learn, period. How can I teach them anything if they don't want to learn?"

"Just smile an' walk away," Ralph repeated. Sage advice from one bigot to another, I thought. I was finding the sofa less comfortable.

Barney went on, "One asshole—I asked him if he did his homework, and he started talkin' in Navajo again. I know that word for shit, *chin*—he's callin' me shit right in class. . . . I'll tell ya, they're all trash, Navajo trash."

That was it. I was already flashing back to the teachers in the lounge at Sacaton Middle School, the three who had told me I would never get Pima kids to read their poems out loud in front of an audience. This was the same prejudice, only more crudely put in its comfortable isolation (I was clearly not regarded as a presence). I got up and brusquely exited. Before the door came closed behind me, I heard Ralph's complacent, metallic voice sneer again, "Just smile an' walk away. That's what I do."

Johnny Begay, an eighth-grader, was leader of a group of boys numbering six or seven who were not only the physically biggest students on campus, but also the most visibly and vociferously rebellious. They violated school rules and got away with it most of the time. These young men seemed always poised and ready to butt heads with any white person of "authority" willing to challenge them. They rode the buses to school every day, rarely absent, as though they relished confrontations with "authority." They sat at their desks and challenged "authority." It was painfully evident that they were not being provided avenues of development that would lead them to happy, successful lives.

I didn't mind working with students like this. In my own school days, I had been a rebel, and I saw a lot of my younger self in boys like Johnny Begay. I knew that the only way to get through to those kids, and actually teach them something, was to extend courtesy and friendliness, and not to present myself as another outside "authority figure." I made a point of regularly stopping in the halls to talk with Johnny and his group. In the classroom, before the bell would ring, I would join them where they sat in a corner and chat with them. At first, they seemed reluctant to accept this intrusion into what they surely perceived as their own guarded space. But within a couple of days they were beginning to accept my presence. And then, during the classes, they began to go to work and write poems along with everyone else in the class. For one of the initial lessons, I had asked the students to select an emotion and metaphorize it by matching it to a concrete image. One of the boys wrote a short piece in which he compared anger to a bomb going off under a teacher's chair. When I read this poem aloud, the boy eyed me suspiciously, tensely, waiting to see if I might pass judgment and declare the poem's subject and theme inappropriate. Instead, I pointed out that emotions rise up from all kinds of situations, and that this student's portrayal of anger was effective because it was both personal *and* well composed. It was a good poem.

This took the boy and his friends by surprise. In his poem, he had expressed hostility toward at least some teachers, and I had said that such expressions were valid. This sent a message to the whole class, as well as to the rebellious boys: Write what you really feel, what you really think, but try to do so *clearly* and *creatively*.

Needless to say, I never had a problem with Barney's "trash." Johnny Begay himself wound up writing a poem about winter of such imagistic merit that I immediately selected it for publication in the school calendar we would later be publishing. This gave me the added satisfaction of knowing that Barney would see Johnny Begay's writing featured in a school publication. So these kids don't want to listen? They don't want to do their work? They don't want to learn? If I thought it would have done any good, I would have asked old Barney, "Hey, where'd that poem come from? What part of Johnny Begay's spirit and imagination was tapped for him to express himself so elegantly?" I have my doubts, however, that

Barney even bothered to read the literary calendar when it came out.

One Thursday, Johnny Begay didn't show up for class. I knew he was at school; I had spoken to him earlier. His absence puzzled me, since he had come to enjoy our sessions. After the class, I followed his friends out the door and stopped them in the hallway and asked if they knew where he was. One of the boys said, "He's in the principal's office. He's getting suspended."

"What happened?" I asked.

"He had a fight with the history teacher."

Of course—Barney. I asked if it had been an actual fistfight.

"No. They were arguing. Then Johnny just got real mad and called him a damn white devil. Mr. Smith's face turned to red and looked like it was going to explode. Then Johnny said to him, 'Good-bye, motherfucker,' and he climbed out the window."

"What were they arguing about?"

"Mr. Smith said that someone stole his keys. He was accusing Johnny. But Johnny said he never touched them."

I knew I had to be careful of what I said and how I said it. I resisted an intense impulse to side with the boys, but they knew I was sympathetic. For me to have openly bad-mouthed Barney would have been altogether unprofessional, but it was difficult to bite my tongue after what I had heard in the teachers' lounge. I took a different tack. "What's going on in that class, anyway?"

With no hesitation and absolute candor, one boy said, "Mr. Smith hates Diné."

"How do you know that?" I was sure Barney had never said as much to them outright, but I wondered what it was about his classroom behavior that gave the fact away.

The same boy answered, "When he teaches us, he just stands there and talks, like he's talking to someone who's not in the room. He just says these things about history real fast, and we sit there wondering what he's talking about. If anyone asks him about something, he gets mad and yells, 'You're not listening!' But we *were* listening. Maybe we didn't understand. He won't help us. If you don't get what he says right away, then he says you're lazy and that you don't care about anything. He's a stupid white man." When the boy finished this last sentence, the others stirred uneasily in their awareness of *my* color.

"No problem," I said.

Another boy then added, "He never talks to us. I mean, like a real human. It's always 'Sit down, shut up, listen to me.' And then he starts talking about these things that confuse us. I bet he'd be confused at a Yei-be-chei, but Navajos wouldn't treat him like he treats us."

"If that's really true," I said, "what do you guys think is going to happen in that class? You've got to go there every day for the rest of the year."

"We got no choice; we're gonna try to force him out of here—try to get him out of Red Mesa."

"How can you do that?"

"By doing everything we can to make him crazy. If we gotta steal his keys and cuss at him, we will. He hates Diné. He shouldn't be with us. He should stay in Cortez with his own kind." Then the young man added, "Maybe someone should put some bad medicine on him. But none of us is like that. We're not witches." The other boys became noticeably edgy at the mention of witches. "I don't mean. . . . Never mind."

This group of "bad" boys was already late, so I walked them to their next classes, explaining to their regular teachers that I had delayed them. I returned through the corridor, bypassed the teachers' lounge, walked through the office area, and headed straight out the front doors, retreating to the compound, to the apartment I was staying in. There I sat for nearly an hour. I was furious, and I had no one to talk to. Yes, I was on those boys' side. All I could think of was them and Barney, and when I thought of him, all I could smell was potted meat and worse. I wondered how such a man could, under any circumstances, be allowed to remain at that school. He hated it there. The Navajo students hated him—and not just the boys who openly expressed their feelings about him. He wasn't teaching, and the students in his class weren't learning. He couldn't care less about young Navajos as human beings, and they saw him as an incarnation of white evil. And, worst of all, the school's administration would not, indeed perhaps could not, because of teacher-tenure laws, do anything about the situation. The students felt forced to take matters into their own hands. If no administrative "authority" would assume responsibility and remove Barney from the classroom, the kids, then, would make an effort to drive him out. What a pitiful waste of their energy. Of their intelligence and talent. Of their education.

I never talked directly to Barney or to a handful of teachers like him. I avoided them. They all hung out together in the lounge. Presumably, they were at Red Mesa to teach Navajo students, but they taught them nothing but hatred and fulfilled none of the responsibilities associated with the true goals of education. They showed up in their classes and, frustrated, retreated into their lounge for mutually satisfying discussions of Navajo "trash."

I have never been able to shake Barney off. The memory claws. I hope the students drove him out, but I doubt it. And I'm plagued with another question: at what cost one man's second pension?

SUE

Something in her voice, the way she formed her vowels, scratched something in my memory. What, I didn't know, and I had no time to think about it. She had just introduced me to her twenty-four fifth-grade students at Chinle Boarding School, and the kids became my immediate priority. I launched into my introductory stories.

Sue sat down near the back of the room, among her students—indeed, she became *like* one of her students. Her facial expressions during my stories gave away the fact that she was deliberately attempting to experience my presence in the classroom from a Navajo student's point of view. I liked this. Any teacher of reasonable intelligence could easily determine my classroom goals and objectives, but Sue desired a further perspective; she wanted also to observe me as youngsters did, from a student desk and surrounded by classmates.

I guessed Sue to be in her early-to-mid-twenties. Her straight light brown hair hung just below her shoulder line, and her delicately pale face carried a spattering of freckles. Instead of makeup, she preferred to wear an almost constant smile.

When I finished the session with her students, I approached her and asked where she was from. To my astonishment, she had grown up within two or three miles of where I had spent my first nine years, in the suburbs of Philadelphia.

She still retained a bit of the old Philly accent, and that's what I had heard in her voice. I don't know if I ever would have figured it out on my own; the last place in the world I'd have expected to come across an eastern "neighbor" was in the middle of the Navajo Nation.

Sue's students were genuinely fond of her, and she obviously loved them. There existed such good feeling in her classroom that, on many days during the following weeks, I enjoyed popping in ten to fifteen minutes before I was due, just to sit and watch her and the children interact. Sometimes she'd be reading a story as the kids huddled on the floor in a circle around her. Sometimes she'd be darting from desk to desk, individually helping students with their math or science problems. Whatever the activity, Sue was not just involved with her students, she was truly immersed in all of the dimensions of their potential for learning. And this was clear: She made learning fun. The kids in her class never said, "I can't do this"— instead, they asked, "Can you help me?," and she always did. They never said, "This is boring" about *anything*. Sue's enthusiasm was definitely contagious.

As we sat in her empty classroom after school one day, I asked her why she had come to the Navajo reservation to teach and what kept her there. "Well, when I finished college," she said, "I was prepared to be a teacher, but I wasn't prepared to be your normal, everyday teacher in the suburbs. I wanted two things more than anything: to teach somewhere where I could make a difference, and to take on new challenges. I really believe that my work here is more important than it would have been had I stayed back home. Education's vital for everyone, but for Indians it's a matter of survival.

"I feel I'm growing into this place more and more every day. There's something about it. The way the land looks. And the children—I really love them. My friends back East ask how I can take being away from civilization. I tell them that I'm not away from civilization, that there's just a different culture here, one with fewer distractions. In some ways, I feel like a student all over again, learning about the Navajo culture—I'm even learning the language. I love it here, what can I say?"

Barney, the history teacher at Red Mesa School, had been a career BIA teacher, an assimilationist who had by now given up and cared about nothing more than getting his second retirement. I've seen many like him at Indian schools all over. Not all of them are just sticking it out for a pension. Some, in fact, still hammer away at their young Indian charges with the idea that "white equals right." The one thing that teachers of this kind hold in common is a belief, either conscious or beneath their own awareness of it, that Indians are somehow inferior to white people. They retain the old paternalistic notion that the "savage" can be enlightened by the same grace of intelligence that they believe they themselves possess. They want to transform the natives into an image of themselves.

One such teacher, from Round Rock School, called me after an anthology of poetry by the school's students was printed and distributed. She scolded me severely, telling me that I had no business including in the book poems that bore Navajo themes. She said, "Don't you have any sense of the fact that we, as educators, have a responsibility to steer these children away from those old practices and beliefs? Navajos are going nowhere in this world until they give up all this tribal crap."

I replied, "I don't see it that way. In fact, I think the squaw dances and the Yei-be-chei dances and the 'sings' and even the traditional Navajo medicine are not only beautiful but vital, and I hope this tribe never loses them."

In so many words, she informed me that with such ideas I had no business being on a reservation, that if it were up to people like me, the Indians would never be saved. I said, "Well, if *you* had edited the book, it would have been different. But *I* was the editor, *I* made the selections, and *I* stand by my selections. Thank you for your call." Click.

At the other extreme, there are teachers like Sue. I've run across a lot of them in the last few years. They tend to be young, many just out of college. They dedicate themselves to teaching the Indian child useful skills while not making negative judgments on the child's culture. They respect the fact that Indian customs, beliefs, and ideas may be different from, though not inferior to, their own. They attend squaw dances. They learn the native tongue. And, more than anything, they share a love for the children they teach and understand the personal importance of the students' tribal heritage.

To be fair to Red Mesa, I must mention two high school teachers there whom I did get to know and like. The English-drama and the art-photography teachers, Dan and Karen, were both excellent. And they, not surprisingly, had no trouble with Johnny Begay or any other student. The majority of the rest of the teachers at Red Mesa fell somewhere between the two extremes I've described.

Someday, I hope, the Barneys will be gone—retired, or driven away by the Indians, or, better yet, altogether extinct. In the meantime, let's make more room for the Sues, Dans, and Karens, and, most important, for more Indian teachers.

30

Pryor and the Mountain Crow

THE VILLAGE OF Pryor, on the west side of the Crow reservation, maintained a magnetic pull on me that grew stronger over the next few years. The warmth of the Mountain Crow who live there, as well as the beauty of their land, is gentle and hospitable. And the place is steeped in history. The great chief Two Leggins fasted in the forest-shrouded mountains above Pryor Valley; the Crows, here, defeated the Sioux in a major battle of survival; and the last of the Crow chiefs, Plenty Coups, made his home in Pryor, willed his house and land to be maintained as a state park, and is perhaps most famous for his warning to Indian people: "With education, you are the white man's equal. Without it, you are his victim." Plenty Coups is buried alongside two of his wives in the park where his great-great-grandchildren now play under the cottonwoods, ride their horses, and swim in the lazily meandering creek.

The few hundred Crows of Pryor live either in a housing project near the trading post or in homes scattered over the elevated valley. Several miles from the village, by dirt road, one enters the mountains through Pryor Gap. Etched here is the keen division between forest and grassland, mountains and high plains. Pastoral in appearance, the mountains continue to provide the Crow people with an abundance of game, a cool retreat during summer months, and sanctuary for those going on traditional, cleansing fasts. The many square miles of lodgepole pine forest also continue to keep the Crows in ample supply of tepee poles. Tepees are still used at powwows and ceremonies by all Plains Indians, and the eighteen or so poles used for one tepee need to be replaced every three or four years.

Less than a mile after one passes the sacred Castle Rocks and drops into the gap between East and West Pryor Mountains, a pile of rocks on the right side of the road marks the first place a person is traditionally supposed to stop in the mountains. One customarily asks, in prayer, for safe passage, tosses a rock onto the pile, then leaves behind, on the topmost rock, a material offering such as a few coins, a personal article, or, most desirably, some tobacco, which is still considered sacred among the Crow. Such an offering, it is said, is left for the Little People, who still inhabit the Pryor Mountains. A belief in Little People is widespread throughout the world, and no less so among many Indian tribes. The Pryor Little People are reputed to have long ago kidnapped several children at the site of the rock pile, and now, when an outsider places an offering at the spot, any offense the Little People might take at the trespassing is said to be appeased.

From my first visit to Pryor, I knew there existed a difference between the reservation's east-side River Crows and the Pryor Mountain Crows. Most of the Pryor children, when conversing among themselves, spoke the Crow language; the traditional Indian sweat lodges seemed to be everywhere; and Pryor students' classroom behaviors were similar to Navajo and other traditional Indian children. The Crow culture was, no doubt, strong among *all* Crows, but it seemed more so among the Mountain Crows of Pryor. Before the 1970s, they were labeled as "backward." Today, they are more commonly referred to as "traditional."

Their kindliness and friendly spirit became known to me little by little. One June I came to Billings to present a workshop at the Montana Association for Bilingual Education Conference. After my presentation, an Indian couple approached me in the hallway. The man, although big and powerfully built, had a quiet, gentle voice. His wife possessed a charming smile she could barely suppress if she wanted to. Said the man, "I'm

Chris Comes Up, and this is my wife, Barbara. Conrad's in school and couldn't come with us, but he wanted us to come here and give you this letter."

I took the letter and opened it, wondering who on earth Conrad was. Obviously, I had encountered him at a reservation school somewhere in Montana, but I was now visiting several thousand Indian students each year and couldn't possibly remember every one of their names. I unfolded the lined paper; the words, in pencil, were scrawled in the handwriting of a fourth-or fifth-grader:

Dear Mr. Mick,
How are you I am fine. I miss you and your stories. You are a funny man. And I hope I see you pretty soon. In science I am learning new things did you know that the earth goes around the sun and the moon goes around the earth?
Love, Conrad

Under his name, Conrad had written: *Pryor Elementary, Montana*. He was a Crow who lived thirty miles from Billings, and now it clicked—his parents had driven into the city just to deliver the boy's letter. "You tell Conrad," I said, "that I miss him, too. Tell him I'll be back next school year, and that I can't wait to see him again."

Then Chris Comes Up said in his low, soft voice, "When you come back to Pryor, we'd like to have you come over to our house for dinner."

"I would be honored," I answered. The warm friendliness of the Pryor Crows had extended itself unexpectedly, and I felt deeply moved as I shook the hands of Chris and Barbara Comes Up and said good-bye.

The following April, Pryor tugged at me again. I had been working on a creative-writing curriculum guide for teachers of Indian children and planned on spending the following summer in Tucson to complete the text of the first volume. I mentioned this to Saint Charles School's superintendent, Larry Cunningham. (Pryor has both a public and a Catholic school, and I was working a week at each.) A couple of days later, Cunningham asked me into his office and told me that he had spoken to Father Randolph and Sister Mary Paul, and that they had all agreed to offer me the use of a house at the mission as a writing retreat for the summer: "It's a lot cooler here than Tucson. You'll have all the peace and quiet you need. And the mountains around here are perfect for hiking and exploring." I didn't hesitate. Although time did not permit my sharing a meal with the Comes Ups that March, I would later get to know the family quite well.

That summer I settled into one of the mission's houses and was quickly taken by the charm of this small Indian community. By now, of course, television had arrived—three stations from Billings could be received—but, as is true of so many out-of-the-way villages, the "evening visit" remained one of the mainstays of community life. As more Pryor Crows learned of the presence of this "white guy from Arizona," the visits increased. Mainly children at first, then some of the adults. Sometimes we'd play board or dice games, sometimes just chat for an hour or two. Pleasant evenings they were, with the northern twilights lingering well past 11:00 P.M.

One day an older white couple knocked on the door of my summer home and asked directions to the town of Red Lodge. Tourists from the heartland they were, an Instamatic dangling from the neck of the neatly dressed man. Their Kansas license plates stuck out, even from where I stood in the doorway. In Billings, they somehow had gotten on the road to Pryor, where all pavement ends. I mapped for them the quickest route, which included seventeen miles of dirt road before their ride would smooth out again. As they left, the lady said, "Thank you, Father," confusing me with the parish priest. From then on, the name stuck—many of my new Crow friends jestingly called me "Father Mick."

September came too soon. I had already come to feel as though I were part of this tiny community, and now it was time to say good-bye. As one who travels a great deal—used to saying good-bye—I made a relatively quick departure, a little sadder than usual.

By the time I returned the following March, 1988, I was considering moving to Billings. After all, I was, at this time, spending all of the spring in Montana. It didn't make sense to continue returning to Arizona in June, for a three-month bout with temperatures that allowed one to fry an egg on the ground. One afternoon I sat talking to Rose Chesarek, a Crow bilin-

gual teacher at the public school. I said, "You know, I'm thinking about making my home base in Billings. It would be nice to
stay up here through the summers."

Rose said, "I think it's a good idea. But why don't you live
out here in Pryor with us Crows, instead of in Billings?"

I looked out the window at the rolling mountains. "I'd love
to," I sighed, "but first of all I'm a white guy, and second of all
I don't officially work for the schools here [my work at Crow
was contracted through the state Office of Public Instruction],
so I'd never qualify for tribal housing."

"Well," Rose went on, "there's a vacant apartment across
from the high school. It's owned by the school district. You
might be able to rent it."

"How?" I asked.

"There's a lot of people out here who like you and would
like to have you live here. A few of us could go to the superintendent and ask him to ask the school board if you could have the
place. That is, if you want to live in Pryor."

"I'd love to," I said.

Four days later, Rose approached me in the hallway of the
elementary school and said, "If you still want to live out here,
go see the superintendent this afternoon. Permission's been
granted."

That day, in the school district office, I wrote a check for
the first month's rent and deposit. As swiftly and unexpectedly
as the Montana weather changes, I suddenly had a home in
Pryor. This little village's magnetic pull on me was now complete.

In Pryor I found a Northern equivalent to the natural
beauty, the friendly Indian spirit, and the professional support
I had enjoyed in the Southwest. Living on the Crow Reservation
was ideal for my ongoing work in developing "Indian relevant"
materials for Indian students. Sharon Peregoy, whose efforts
first brought me into Montana Indian classrooms, was now a
friend on whom I could rely for advice. Marlene Walking Bear,
another friend and a traditional Crow woman of enormous
talent and goodwill, had become the programs director of Hardin School District, and she, too, provided continual assistance
and encouragement. The staff of the Bilingual Materials Development Center at Crow Agency; Art Pitts, principal of Pretty

Eagle School in Saint Xavier, and his staff; the public school and Saint Charles School in Pryor, all gave me access to abundant materials as well as unwavering good counsel. At the state level, Angela Branz-Spall, now director of bilingual education for the Office of Public Instruction, had become perhaps the single most significant supporter of my work. Each year, she coordinated my schedule on the Montana reservations and provided much of the funding. Professionally, Montana was my Promised Land.

Constant field-testing with Indian children was the basis of every lesson I prepared for the writing curriculum and for a new textbook I had started designed to teach Indian children American-English idioms. In these efforts, Pryor, again, proved an ideal location. Crow kids came by my apartment all the time, and often I'd have them read the latest chapter or lesson on which I was working. They gave clear, concise, and honest criticism, and a youthful Indian perspective that proved, as it had in Sacaton, invaluable. One sixth-grade boy, Darrel Frost, chastised me for using the singular "a woods." I explained it was grammatically correct. Responded Darrel, "Even so, a lot of us Indian kids have trouble with those plurals, and your book is about idioms, not about when and where we should put *s*'s. It'll confuse a lot of kids like *me*. You should just say, 'a forest.'" Darrel's brother, Jeff, often stopped by with idiomatic expressions he had just heard, to see if I had already included them in the book. Typically, he'd knock on my door, and as soon as I opened it he'd say, "*Hold the fort!* Do you have that one yet?" The Frost brothers and other Crow kids became the initial editors of the texts I wrote for them. And to make matters even better, I enjoyed unlimited access to all of Pryor's children in their classrooms. The teachers at both the Catholic and the public schools opened their classrooms to me any time I wanted to test new lessons or ideas.

Support from the community was also strong. The Mountain Crows of Pryor accepted me as an integral part of the village. Young men began stopping by after a hunt to give me deer meat, usually a hindquarter or two and a tenderloin. I learned that such sharing among friends was customary to the Crow.

In the evenings, my apartment quickly filled with youngsters or adults or both. I attended birthday parties on the muddy banks of the Big Horn River and funeral services in the high school gymnasium. I respectfully watched sun-dance ceremonies and pitched in on community youth activity days. I found, quickly, that Crows addressing each other almost always used the Crow language, yet, though I was often the only non-Crow, I never felt left out or uneasy. Someone invariably translated; and the moment anyone looked at me directly, he or she slipped into English. It is estimated that over 80 percent of all Crow children entering school speak Crow.

The Rock Aboves, the Costas, the Big Days, the Flat Lips, all were families I befriended. Maureen Rock Above, expert bead worker, dropped by regularly to show me her latest masterful necklace or bracelet or tie tack. Sometimes I sat in the living room of Oliver and Belva Costa's home, listening to Oliver's stories about his ancestors. The events in his accounts were all historically documented, but he related them from a Crow perspective, with Crow details, such as the spirit warrior who aided a Crow war party in defeating a band of Sioux near Pryor, a presence usually left out of the history books. Other afternoons I huddled around a kitchen table with Jennifer Flat Lip—a teacher at Saint Charles—and her artist husband, Laurence "Scrap Iron" Flat Lip, discussing education or art. Jennifer was easily one the best teachers I had ever encountered, and I always valued her opinions. And I spent many evenings with Jace and Kathy Big Day, chatting or playing board games. Jace's jocular father, Heywood, was known for being one of the most traditional of Crows, as well as for a speaking part he had in the movie *Little Big Man*, in which, he would say laughing, he almost got to kill Dustin Hoffman.

The Comes Up family and I also became good friends. A not-uncommon evening would have us sitting around eating broiled buffalo while watching VCR movies. They lived in a small house near Saint Charles School, the inside of which, like other Indian homes I'd been in, was richly appointed with snug sofas, family photos, Pendleton blankets, hanging feathers, and other Indian paraphernalia. The odor of freshly brewed coffee always lingered in rooms lit by soft table lamps and a bare ceiling bulb.

Chris Comes Up was the first to invite me along for a weekend camping trip high and far back in the Pryor Mountains, to places where few white men had set foot.

Chris, Barbara, Conrad, as well as several other family

members, and I left on a Friday night around 9:00 P.M. Chris's four-by-four pickup climbed a rutted road bent on destroying any lesser vehicle. Under alternating starry skies and sudden downpours, several of us huddled beneath canvas tarpaulins in the back of the truck until we reached an alpine meadow, where we quickly pitched our tents next to a hundred-year-old miner's cabin. Once the skies cleared, we polished off a late dinner, then sat around an ancient oak table in the cabin and talked and laughed till nearly sunrise.

The next morning I crawled from my tent, tracking down the aroma of sizzling bacon. Now, I saw the mountain setting in full sunlight. Twenty yards from our campsite, a spring trickled out from a sloped carpet of emerald grass. The surrounding lush forest of pine and spruce left me dumbstruck. Wildflowers grew everywhere, like points of yellow and crimson light burning out of the earth. This was the remote, sacred land where many Crows, as they had for centuries, retreated for long fasts of purification and spiritual revelation. This was the forest where they labored to cut, strip, and trim their tepee poles. This was the habitat of the Little People and the abiding spirits. This was a land that made you feel as though you had been thrust up into the sky, where the tips of the swaying conifers scratched the blue by day and touched the stars by night. I breathed deeply and felt renewed. We ate breakfast in a pleasant silence.

Then a muffled *pop* brought us to attention. Chris said, "That's Conrad and Ray Scott. They must 'a come across something." A few minutes later, Conrad and his cousin came running into camp. They told us breathlessly that they'd seen a bear. They'd gotten off one shot with Chris's rifle. The bear looked around at them, then turned away and lumbered off into the forest.

It took an entire day for us to come down from the mountains, so rough was the road and so lengthy our wayside stops. But every curve and crest brought new and breathtaking vistas—vertical thrusts of tree-topped canyon walls, sweeping fans of prairie projecting from the mountains' bottomlands, all magnificent enough to keep one's tongue in place but for an occasional "Oh, my goodness!"

After nightfall, Barbara's oldest son by a previous marriage took the wheel; the rest of us sprawled on our backs in the truckbed. Indians had for thousands of years watched the skies, but tonight's observations included a modern twist. Chris Comes Up taught me to see something I had never noticed—the faint, nearly invisible light of satellites whizzing right past the stars. Leave it to native eyes to show a newcomer the trails his brothers have left.

We had made our own orbit around the Pryor Mountains as finally we pulled into Pryor village from the opposite direction we had taken out. It was nearly midnight. I took a last look at the sky. Then I turned back toward the blackened silhouette of the mountains. In those hills, it now occurred to me, we had left behind a bear that at this moment was wandering over moonlit meadows or through thick pines. And I knew, as well, that I had left a small part of *me* up there, to wander in the heights, while another part had come back knowing my bond with the Crows had grown stronger.

31
In the Beartooth Mountains

MOST PEOPLE WHO visit Crow Country take home snapshots of Custer Battlefield; the lieutenant colonel's final engagement was, after all, the most famous action of the Indian Wars.

Tourists arriving in April are also able to get photographs of the Crow hand games, in which teams of thirty or more, all dressed in colorful costumes, take turns hiding small bones in their hands. A "medicine man" directs the action of his own group of players. In this drum-beating, singing, hide-and-seek game, the score is tallied with sticks, and the first team to win all fourteen sticks is the victor. Besides local Crow teams, Northern Cheyenne and Kiowa teams converge on Crow Agency for the competition, and the betting is fierce. A single game may last over an hour, the victory sticks going back and forth between the two teams. But sometimes the games go quickly; I once witnessed an entire fourteen-stick game completed in just over nineteen minutes—a record, the announcer asserted. The games provide fast, traditional action the tourist is not likely to forget.

The cameras of those who visit during the third week of August are treated to a mighty spectacle—Crow Fair, the so-called "tepee capital of the world." Thousands of Indians from throughout North America gather for parades, an all-Indian rodeo, a huge powwow, and the "49." A "49" refers to a late-night gathering, away from the campgrounds, of social singing and, for some, of beer drinking. I've heard several stories on the origin of the term "49." The most common has it that long ago, nine months after the first such evening of social sharing, forty-nine babies were born. Except for the "49," the Indians welcome non-Indians at all Crow Fair festivities.

The images that most tourists do not record, however, are those of off-the-beaten-track activities and places in Crowland. Very few non-Crows, much less out-of-staters, venture into the Pryor Mountains to pay homage to the sacred Castle Rocks and the Little People; few attend the traditional sun dances held in Lodge Grass or Pryor; when Crow men and boys throw long arrows at distant ground targets, practicing for the arrow games, they do so away from the glare of curious lenses; and how many visitors have seen the unphotographable dark inside a sweat lodge?

Not surprisingly, many things go unobserved by the outsider. What does surprise me is that more tourists do not take the acrophobic road that slashes through the Beartooth Mountains from the town of Red Lodge to Yellowstone Park's northeast entrance. The Beartooth Highway was once referred to by Charles Kuralt, of CBS's *On the Road* fame, as the most beautiful roadway in America. Yet the passage taken to Crow Country by most leads them north through Sheridan, Wyoming, via Interstate 90, and either terminates at Little Bighorn Battlefield or continues along the interstate through Billings and west, bypassing Montana's tallest mountains. And the many people coming to see Yellowstone rarely go out of their way to use the northeast entrance, anxious as they are to behold Old Faithful, Mammoth Hot Springs, and the many geysers and thermal pools regarded by most of the old Indians as manifestations of evil spirits. Yet the sixty-five-mile Beartooth Highway lifts one up and over some of the most spectacular mountain scenery in the world.

These heights are at the core of the old Crow territory and remain sacred to the tribe—a place to collect herbal medicines as well as to garner spiritual medicine. Here I have picked mint tea and kinnikinnick with Indian friends, and regularly bottled spring water with a taste so clear and cold people call it "sweet." And I have, on one occasion, seen a direct reflection of what Indians regard as the spiritual reality of the place.

In June 1989, I was visited in Pryor by Marcia Galli and Jesse Soriano, both education-equity specialists with Mountain West Educational Equity Center of Ogden, Utah. My work in English language development among Indian children had grown in scope and success, and Mountain West had decided to sponsor, in July, a teacher-training institute based on this work. Marcia and Jesse had come to Pryor for a planning meeting that we had determined would end by noon so I could take them on a tour of the Beartooth Mountains. Jesse had brought a camera to capture images of the roof of Montana.

Marcia Galli, a Shoshone Indian originally from the Fort Hall Reservation in Idaho, possessed stunning deep-set black eyes that stabbed you from any distance. She was my main contact and supporter at Mountain West. Jesse Soriano, thickly mustached and quietly amiable, had served, during Reagan's first administration, under Secretary Bell as director of bilingual education for the United States Department of Education. Though both had been to Montana numerous times, neither had been into the Beartooths.

We stopped in Red Lodge for a lunch of burgers and onion rings, then drove on into Rock Creek Canyon. The highway paralleled Rock Creek for ten miles through pines and ever more-towering peaks, and then suddenly began to switchback up to the Beartooth Plateau. "Switchback up," Marcia and Jesse soon learned, was an understatement. In five zigzags, we climbed nearly six thousand feet through an alpine wonderland. Jesse reverently whispered, every few minutes, "My God, this is beautiful," or "I've never seen anything like this." Marcia sighed at the mountain beauty and halfway up said, "I really hope we see a bear."

"You're going to see a lot of fantastic sights," I said to her, "but don't count on seeing a bear. They're out there, but they rarely come out to the road. From what I hear, unless you backpack into the wilds, you really don't stand much of a chance to see one."

"I think maybe we will," Marcia answered. I was taken by her charming naïveté. Like a child, she held on to her dream even in the face of adult logic.

We continued on to the upper, then uppermost, reaches of the Beartooth Plateau, where fifteen-foot snowdrifts still crowded the highway at several curves, wiping out the memory of the green, summertime valley we had just left. I don't know a soul who hasn't said, on first reaching the plateau, what Marcia now said. "My goodness, we're at the top of the world."

We stopped every so often for Jesse to take pictures and for the three of us to feel June snow on our fingertips and sip icy water from gleaming streamlets.

We crossed over Beartooth Pass and began descending into a mountain paradise of twisted, wind-haggard pine and spruce, frigid trout-resistant lakes, lichen-painted piles of enormous boulders, and on toward the one and only commercial enterprise located at the top of the world—a tiny, all-purpose establishment called, appropriately, "Top O' the World."

Marcia said, "Maybe this far up we'll see a bear."

This time I said nothing. I wondered now if Marcia was missing everything else by continually focusing her eyes on the invisible bear she wanted so badly to see. Jesse bought another roll of film—he'd already shot thirty-six frames—and we were soon back on the road.

We stopped for photo opportunities at Beartooth Lake; at a rushing waterfall just beyond; at a breathtaking lookout point above Sun Basin; and at various pullovers offering wide views of Pilot Peak and narrow vistas of stream-parted meadows. All of these sights were more than favorably reviewed by Marcia's sighs and Jesse's oh-my-Gods.

At Cooke City, a cloud-high mountain hamlet that in 1988 almost burned to charcoal during the Great Yellowstone Fires, we paused to stroll the main street, then continued on into Yellowstone. We penetrated the park by no more than ten miles, and saw a herd of mule deer, half a dozen shaggy buffalo, several elk, three muscular moose, and one loping ermine. Not bad and, in Yellowstone, not unusual.

Still, Marcia's bear eluded us. As we left the park, she said, tossing strands of her long black hair over her shoulder, "I think we still might see one." Jesse continued to have me pull the car off the road every few miles so he could take pictures of just about everything.

In June, in the North Country, the sun hangs around late into the night, so Jesse was not displeased when we began descending, sometime after 7:00 P.M., the switchbacks toward Rock Creek. Finally, we reached the bottom of Rock Creek Canyon and headed north toward Red Lodge. Not a single bear had shown itself. Less than six or seven miles from town, Marcia began to say a prayer, Shoshone style, to the spirit of Brother Bear:

"Thank you for giving us this wonderful day. Thank you for showing me beauty like none I've ever seen. Brother Bear, I wanted to see you today, but it wasn't meant to be. That's okay, we had a special time in these mountains. You know I'll be back to this place, and maybe next time you'll show yourself. Thank you, Brother Bear. Thank you, Creator."

When she finished her prayer, Marcia raised her head, then gasped, "Oh, my God!"

Just ahead of us, on the left shoulder of the highway, frolicked a black bear cub. I hit the brakes, drove slowly past, made a U-turn, then pulled up to the cub. We held our breaths and watched as, right outside the car, the young bear nosed around, paying absolutely no attention to us.

The animal was a thing of magical beauty. I could hardly believe its presence; it seemed more an apparition out of Marcia's prayer. The cub, no more than two-and-a-half feet long, ambled about, its black fur as slick and glossy as a small pool of water reflecting a midnight sky. This was a physically real bear. Was it also, I wondered, the spirit of Brother Bear?

The little cub glanced up at us several times before it climbed up and over a low ridge. Then it was gone. What may have been two or three minutes seemed like an hour. Marcia finally broke the silence, whispering, "Thank you, Brother."

Coincidence? The traditional Indian does not believe in that concept, preferring to envision the universe as a harmonious creation of both the physical and the spiritual.

Jesse had been so caught up in the experience that he hadn't thought to take a photograph. "That's all right," he said as we turned around and drove on. "Things like that are better left to memory. No way a snapshot could capture it."

32
Cheyenne
Sweat Bath

As LONG AS anyone can remember, and back through prehistory, hundreds of Indian tribes used the "sweat bath," or simply, the "sweat." Typically, a domed chamber was built over a small circular pit. Some tribes, like the Navajo, constructed the lodge, and still do, out of cottonwood and adobe. The Plains tribes formed the hemispherical dome with thin, pliable willow branches, then covered it with buffalo, deer, or elk hides. In a fire just outside the sweat lodge, large stones were heated until they glowed. Then the people, usually from four to ten, climbed into the sweat, and the stones' keeper shoveled several of the rocks into the pit, whereupon the chamber was sealed and the ritual begun.

Sweating had a clear purpose. It cleansed the body, the mind, the heart, and the spirit. I was once told by a Navajo friend, "The traditional Indian did not, and still does not, make distinctions between physical self, intellectual ability, emotional well-being, and religious faith. These four dimensions of humanity are not like cogwheels joined together, because even that implies a separateness. Rather, they are a single cogwheel that is humanity . . . that is life. What *this* wheel is connected to is nothing more or less than the universe and the Creator."

Many Indians continue the sweat ritual today not because

it is a way to keep the body clean—a shower suffices in that department—but because it remains a way to keep *all* of the self clean. It also represents one of the ways in which Indians have retained their Indianness in the face of having to live biculturally. It represents another of the ancestors' many voices.

In the sweat lodge, one blesses and is blessed; one experiences the power of unity and the sereneness of individuality; one knows the intensity of being human—heart, mind, spirit, and body together. The sweat is a reminder that we must keep whole.

My first opportunity to sweat came in 1987 on the Northern Cheyenne reservation in South-central Montana. Adjoining the Crow reservation to the east, Northern Cheyenne is a land of high-rolling plains and pine-covered hills that rise several hundred feet in variable, moundlike formations. Approaching the higher terrain, one is struck by the bands of red earth bisecting horizontally the more typical off-whites and tans of the hills. Lame Deer, the agency town, is nestled in a valley surrounded by the small mountains. More than a hundred miles from the city of Billings, Lame Deer is the seat of the northern Cheyenne government.

The contemporary Cheyenne, who retain only a tiny portion of their once-vast lands, are a proud people of historic heritage. Their greatest moment in recorded history came in July 1876, to the great surprise of George Armstrong Custer. Little did Yellowhair know on that hot summer day that a century later Indians would be driving pickups past the site of his demise with bumper stickers reading CUSTER WORE ARROW SHIRTS and CUSTER GOT SIOUXED.

The Cheyennes' sense of the importance of their victory over Custer has not diminished with the years. An eighth-grade student at Lame Deer Public School once told me, "My grandma says that Custer wanted to be president, and that if he killed enough Indians, he had a good chance. She says if we didn't beat him at that battle, he probably would have become president, and then things would have been a lot more worse for us Indians."

Custer's death lives on in Lame Deer, very much a part of everyone's life; the man who would be president remains, to Northern Cheyenne Indians, a reminder that long ago Cheyenne warriors proved worthy contestants in a horrible war that they ultimately lost—lost, ironically, for the very same reason

Custer lost, because of an overwhelming imbalance of forces. The Cheyenne perspective of the "Last Stand" is justifiably different from that of many of the thousands of non-Indian tourists who each year traipse among the marble stones marking where nearly 260 U.S. soldiers last saw the light of day above the Little Big Horn River, forty-five miles from Lame Deer. Of this famous victory the Cheyenne are with reason proud.

During one of my visits to Lame Deer, the entire sixth-grade class, twenty-some students, were scheduled to leave the school Friday afternoon for a camping trip to Crazy Head Springs, a lovely mountain setting high up in a densely forested area of the reservation. I was invited to go along and accepted immediately. A tepee was to be set up for some of the children to sleep in. Elders would be on hand to tell old Cheyenne stories. And I was asked to narrate, around the campfire, a story from another tribe. Also, a sweat lodge would be built for both adults and juveniles. The sweats would be conducted by a young Cheyenne man named Vance Littlebird.

The sunny afternoon was relaxed, with cooling breezes gently whizzing through the pine trees. I helped the other adults watch the kids as they swam in a large pond, fished for rainbow trout, and played softball in an open, grassy area yellowed here and there with wildflowers. At one point, I took several students in my pickup to a spring where we filled large plastic containers with fresh mountain water.

Before we delivered our cargo to the camp, we lingered awhile, scooping up handfuls of icy water, not to quench a thirst, but for the sheer pleasure of it. Somehow, sipping this water made me feel as though I were part of the land. I lay down and stretched across the soft grass and enjoyed, as a child does, that most simple and perfect blue we will ever experience—the sky. As I lost myself in a pure, unmetaphorical reverie, it was a child's impatience that brought me back to my responsibility: "Hey," young Marty Woodenlegs called out, "let's get this water back!"

At the camp, as the sun made its slow exit, all the boys and girls and men and women fell silent as a tribal elder offered a Cheyenne prayer in low, halting, confident utterances. I watched the sky as I listened; its magnificent blue was now shaded by the encroaching night. I didn't understand his words, but I felt the prayer. The old man's voice became a part of the scene, a part of the natural world; it could have been Old Man

Coyote mumbling, or the stirring wind, or a stream's song. The old man made his prayer. The sky was our cathedral.

Then we ate. Not exactly traditional Indian food—hamburgers, hot dogs, macaroni salad, and potato chips—but it went down well.

Later in the evening, as we sat around a campfire, I got up to get a cupful of water. A voice out of the dark called to me, "Hey, you wanna come sweat with us?" It was Vance Littlebird. He had prepared the sweat lodge and was about to conduct the usual four rounds of prayer for several of the men.

Another Cheyenne man, who had sweat earlier, loaned me his swimming trunks. The sweat lodge was covered with canvas and quilts, the common materials used by modern Indians. I crawled into the dark chamber, fourth of six men, circled to the left, then sat cross-legged facing the little pit. Littlebird came in last and sat just to the left of the entrance. The stones' keeper handed him a pitcher of water and a Styrofoam cup, shoveled half a dozen glowing rocks into the pit, then pulled down the canvas, sealing us in.

Our group consisted of three non-Indians—two administrators from the school and me—and three young Cheyenne men. It felt good to be in on this ritual gathering—Indians and whites coming together to celebrate and worship in traditional Indian fashion. A century after the Cheyenne and the Sioux faced the white man in the Battle of the Little Bighorn, Indians and whites now faced each other in the darkness of a sweat lodge, in brotherhood.

Littlebird started, in Cheyenne, the round of prayers, sprinkling water and cedar on the hot rocks. The lodge filled with steam. Then each of us took a turn offering thanks and asking for blessings for family and friends, while Littlebird continued sprinkling water on the rocks. The inside of the sweat lodge thickened more and more with steam, but as the round drew to an end, I thought the heat was not unbearable, that it was, in fact, comfortable. Between rounds of a sweat, the participants may leave the lodge to cool off. I decided not to.

Little did I know of the sweat ritual's progression, in which *intensification* of heat is the rule. By the end of the second round, I wondered if I could stand it any hotter and hoped the heat had reached its limit. It hadn't.

Midway through the third round, waves of steam lapped over my flesh with such ferocity I imagined they were flames. I rubbed my arms and chest. I rubbed my face and shoulders. Then I noticed what the other men were doing, and I followed suit, slapping at my burning flesh.

Suddenly, I couldn't breathe. My every attempt to inhale met with scorching steam that seared the linings of my trachea and lungs. In a desperate move for oxygen, I threw my head down to the back of the lodge, lifted the canvas, and stuck my nose and mouth outside. I didn't know it, but such a breach of the lodge's seal disrupts the prayer cycle. When I pulled my face back into the lodge, one of the Indian men, sensitive to the embarrassment I would feel as a newcomer, tried to take the blame. He said, "I'm sorry. *I* broke the prayers. I haven't sweat in a while."

I said, "I'm afraid I'm the one who broke the prayers. I'm sorry. I didn't know."

Littlebird said, "I'm the one who should be sorry. We didn't take time to get you ready. When you feel you can't take it anymore, just cup your hands over your nose and mouth and lean down to the earth to breathe. Mother Earth is always cooler than the sweat. Down there you'll always find fresh air. You don't need to lift the canvas."

"Thank you," I said, grateful for the gentle advice.

Littlebird said, "Do you want to get out and cool off?"

I thought about the fact that five other men were sitting around me, and none of them had reacted as I had. The problem, it seemed, was not with the sweat ritual, but with my not having experienced it before. Just moments ago, when I thought I was dying, I hadn't heard a single one of these men gasp for breath. "If I may," I answered, "I'd like to go on."

"Then we'll go on," Littlebird said.

When we finished the third round and the lodge was opened for fresh air, I, like the other men, stayed in the lodge, absorbing through every pore the cool breezes that wafted in through the opened entrance.

The stones' keeper heaped into the pit another mound of rocks from the fire. They glowed so brightly they looked as though they could produce a sunrise. Then he sealed us in. Littlebird spoke in Cheyenne. More prayers. More water. More cedar. More steam. Much more steam. I slapped my body, held my breath, and cupped my hands over my face, ready to lunge to the ground.

Then something happened I couldn't have expected. I

took, through the cracks between my fingers, a breath of steam so hot that I knew instantly nothing like it had ever passed through me before. Instantly, my fingers relaxed. I took another breath, drawing in a little more than before. My arms and shoulders relaxed. I inhaled again, bringing my hands down to rest on my knees. My whole body relaxed and then began to sway from side to side. I took slow, deep breaths that found their own rhythm. The steam filled me, and I felt as though every cell of my body now breathed on its own. I floated in the infinite dark of the sweat lodge. I had become steam myself. The voices of each man, as well as my own voice, saying prayers, swirled around in the darkness peacefully, with a cadence that seemed to arise out of the very earth. My body kept swaying. I felt I could stay there forever, bathed in a mist of cedar and prayer.

As the fourth and final round drew to an end, the only negative feeling I experienced was disappointment that the sweat couldn't go on. It was now over. "That was a good sweat," Vance Littlebird said. Before he crawled out of the lodge, he asked me what I thought of the ritual.

"Incredible," was all I could say. I climbed out into the chilly air and heard the distant voices of children drifting through the moonless night. I stood up, wet to the bone, and started to walk around the lodge to where I had left my clothes, but I couldn't regain my balance. My feet seemed to hover above the ground. Each step I attempted took me higher into the air. I knelt down, then lay in the pine needles, physically spent and in a state of absolute euphoria. I was the nighttime dew collecting in the forest. I was the mist rising.

Never had I known anything like the sweat, and I will always be grateful to Vance Littlebird for his guidance and patience. The sweat ritual remains a voice out of the Indian past too powerful and meaningful to be silenced. That night I slept deeper than I had ever thought possible, with a clean body, mind, heart, and spirit.

33
Andy Small's Death and Memorial

A WEEK BEFORE my second trip to Rocky Boy, when Louise Stump had told me on the phone that I'd be staying at Dorothy's again, I was pleased. Then she gave me the news that Andy had passed away exactly one year ago. My stomach turned over, and I felt a terrible sadness. I had only spent three days in the man's company, but I remembered his handsomely lean face, his determined eyes, and his easy smile. I was truly looking forward to spending time with him again, and now he would not be there. And I wondered how life had been for Dorothy since her husband died.

The house looked no different as I pulled up the narrow driveway. A large grove of aspens that backed the home bore the last flutterings of their October yellow. I looked at the spot in the yard where I had last seen Andy and felt hollow. Before I turned the motor off, Junior Small came out and walked up to the truck. I opened the door, and he said, with more words than I'd heard him speak during my entire first visit, "Welcome back. It's good to see you. Let me carry your bags in."

Inside the house, I hugged Dorothy and offered my sympathies. Zellah Nault, Dorothy's sister, now lived in the home; she greeted me with a handshake.

"I'll tell you all about Andy tonight," Dorothy said. "But right now let's sit down and talk about happy things. I'm so glad you came back. I figured you would. When Louise told me you were coming, I said, 'Tell that white man he's going to stay in my house again.' I hope it's all right with you."

"I felt so much at home here before," I told Dorothy, "that I wouldn't want to stay anywhere else."

"Good. You didn't have a choice, anyway. I'm the boss." I felt immediately at ease. This was the Dorothy I remembered—always ready with a joke; she hadn't lost any of her humor since Andy had passed away. "I'm the boss," she repeated; then, in the routine northern Montana reservation way of letting someone know you're teasing, she chuckled and said, "I jokes!"

The late afternoon sunlight reddened the hills of the Bear Paws. I told Dorothy I would like to visit Andy's grave to pay my respects; the cemetery lay at the top of a hill just north of the house, and I could walk there in five minutes. "Wait a moment," she said, then she went to the kitchen.

When she returned, she handed me a Styrofoam cup containing some bull berries, dry meat, and a little fat. I gave her an inquisitive look. "Leave this food for Andy. Set it on his grave. And Andy liked to smoke, so lay a cigarette on his grave and have a smoke with him."

I was surprised by this Cree custom but thought how wonderful that these people offer this kind of attention to their dead. And I was learning that many Plains Indians, no matter how acculturated they may appear in their dealings with non-Indians, remain very traditional. In the face of a hundred years of repression, they simply have learned to conduct their ancient practices out of the glare of those they don't trust. Dorothy was expressing her trust in me by allowing me to participate in this particular graveside custom.

I climbed the hill to the cemetery and found Andy's grave. Over it lay a Pendleton blanket secured by a frame of sunken two-by-fours. The blanket, with its characteristic Indian-based geometric design, had surrendered to a year of Montana weather; its colors had drained into the earth and left behind only muted grays and tans. It had become the color of the land. I placed the food offering just below Andy's headstone, took out a cigarette and laid it next to the cup, then stood up and lit another cigarette. The brisk northern wind not only whipped the smoke away from my face, it also blew into my bones. I gave my shoulders a quick shudder and headed back to the house.

Before going inside, I walked around back, wanting to stroll for a few minutes in the wind-sheltered aspen woods, something I hadn't done on my first visit. As I approached the trees, I looked up and was caught dead in my tracks by a sight so disconcerting and colorful I had to blink my eyes. Wide strips of cotton cloth of many bright colors were wrapped around and tied to dozens of trees about five feet from the ground. I hesitated, wondering if it might be inappropriate for me to trespass into this ribboned forest. But Dorothy had not advised against it, so I advanced slowly, mindful that whatever the ribbons represented must surely demand respect. About twenty yards into the woods, I came upon the willow frame of a long-unused sweat lodge. Several quilts and a canvas tarpaulin lay on the ground, pushed completely flat by last year's snow. Their colors, like those of the Pendleton on Andy's grave, had bled into the earth. I assumed this had been Andy's sweat. And the ribbons were everywhere; some trees bore only one, others eight or nine. They reminded me of the prayer flags hung in the Himalayas by Tibetans. Indeed, during the next year, as I grew closer and closer to Dorothy and her family, I would learn that these ribbons are almost the same thing—prayer ribbons hung for the spirits. Then I noticed, high in a tree behind the lodge frame, a buffalo skull. No question, this was a sacred place. I disturbed nothing.

Late that evening, Dorothy and I sat in the living room. Junior and Zellah had already gone to bed. Dorothy asked, "Will you be able to stay over Saturday?"

"Yes," I answered. "Why?"

"We're having Andy's memorial feast then. It's exactly one year ago this week that he died. You see, Crees always have a big feast on the anniversary of a death. We'd like you to be there."

I said, "Yes, I can stay. I'd be honored. Do you have the feast here at your house?"

"No. This is gonna be a big one. It'll be at the community center. Half the reservation'll be there. Everyone will bring something. There's gonna be so much food you'll get fat on the spot."

Dorothy got up to make some tea. When she returned and sat down, she said, "I'll tell you about Andy's death now." She took a sip from her cup and sighed heavily. "You see, Andy knew he was going to die. His kidneys were giving out, and there was nothing more the doctors at the hospital could do.

He told those doctors he was going home to die. They said he had maybe two weeks to go.

"He came home and told Junior and me that we had to get ready for him to leave us. He was in a lot of pain, but he was peaceful. He knew the things he had to do before he died. He wanted new beaded moccasins and a belt to be buried in, so we arranged it. Then one day he asked to go to the mall in Havre. He picked out his own burial shirt and pants, and when we got home, he put them in a corner and said he would be wearing them soon."

Dorothy sighed again. "I just couldn't really believe it was happening. I kept thinking, Oh, he'll get better. After all, he always got better before. In the evenings, he told different people to come over, like our son Bobby and our daughter, Delphine, and nieces and nephews, and brothers and sisters, and cousins and friends. One by one he would have them go to him where he sat, and talk very quietly to them for a while. You see, he was telling each one about the things, the old Cree ways, that they should never forget. To us Crees, if you lose those ways, you aren't a Cree anymore.

"Then, on a Tuesday, he told me to come with him down to the basement. So we went down and he opened up the deep-freeze. He said, 'You're going to have a feast next Sunday.' Then he picked out some things to thaw. I kind of knew what he was doing, but I didn't want to think about it. When we came back upstairs, he said he would be real hungry tonight and wanted his favorites. Good beef and potatoes. It made me feel better. I thought if he's getting his appetite back, maybe he's starting to get well. We had a grand meal that night, and Andy acted happier than he'd been in a long time.

"About three o'clock the next morning, he woke me up. 'What is it?' I said. I just wanted to sleep; I thought he was doing pretty good. But he told he that he was going to leave with the morning sun. He wanted me to get Junior up to smudge him. I didn't know what to think. I woke Junior up and told him he better smudge his dad."

I interrupted Dorothy. "What do you mean by smudge?"

"We have this sweet grass up here, and we put it into braids," she said. "It's sacred. You light the end of the braid and brush the smoke over yourself, or someone, or in your house or car. That smoke will help you. It's sacred smoke. I'll show you some sweet grass tomorrow."

She put her teacup down and lit a cigarette. Then she continued, "Anyway, Junior smudged Andy, and then Andy told us to go back to sleep. I still didn't realize how serious it all was. I rolled over and joked with Andy. I said, 'Oh, you can't leave with the morning sun because it's going to be cloudy tomorrow.' Andy said in a quiet voice, 'Maybe it'll be cloudy, but the sun will be there all the same, on the other side.'

"So I went back to sleep. I didn't even know it, but Andy got up at about five. He went to the kitchen and put on a pot of coffee. Then he came back to bed and woke me up again. He said that he was leaving soon. He said he put some coffee on for Junior and me. He wanted us to get up and get ready. I was confused, trying not to believe it, but I got Junior up and then I called Bobby and Delphine to come over."

I could see the strain and the deep sadness in Dorothy's eyes as she spoke. She said, "I think it was around seven when Andy stopped breathing. Delphine knew about CPR, so she did that to him. And he started breathing again. All he said was, 'No, Daughter. Don't do this. I have to leave now.' A minute or two later, he wasn't breathing again. Delphine couldn't just stand there; she loved her father so much. She did that CPR again, and Andy came back again. But he just kept saying, 'No, Daughter. I have to leave. I have to leave now.' When the ambulance got here and those guys came rushing in, Andy was gone. Just like he said, he went with the morning sun, on the other side of the clouds."

The living room where we sat was brightly lit, as were all the rooms of the house. The Crees believe in keeping a home lamp-lit around the clock for a while after a death, to keep away ill-intentioned spirits. But, bright as the room was, I somehow remember it as being darkened while Dorothy told me the final story of Andy Small's life. I remember the look in her eyes as she told it. I don't remember anything else that was there in the living room.

Somewhere between 4:00 and 4:30 A.M. on Saturday morning, Dorothy and Zellah and their two other sisters were in the kitchen preparing food. They completed one dish after another, covering each with aluminum foil. Mashed potatoes and other vegetables, pies, Juneberry pudding, pheasant soup, "spook" soup (made with rice and raisins), pemmican, macaroni and potato salads, deviled eggs, bannock bread, ham, and a huge turkey all took their turns reaching perfection. By late morning, Junior and I had begun loading my truck with steaming bowls and platters, pots full of utensils and napkins and paper cups, and clean sheets. After I backed the truck around and began descending the driveway, Junior looked up the hill toward the cemetery and mumbled, "The old man's gonna enjoy this feast."

At the community center, several men helped us unload. Inside, the sheets were spread out on the floor in the middle of the large hall, and the food was placed on the sheets. By noon, dozens of people were arriving, with more sheets and more food, and by 1:00 P.M., the hall was filled. Everyone sat on the floor against the walls, forming an enormous ring of love and respect for Andy Small. Then Art Raining Bird, most respected of the Cree spiritual leaders, sat down inside the circle of people, lit his ceremonial pipe, and began praying in the Cree language. Three other elder men sat with him, ready to offer their own prayers and share the sacred smoke.

When the men had finished praying, one of them took the pipe and walked around the hall, stopping to give each man in attendance a turn to smoke.

I felt a flush of privilege as the old man approached me; it would be my first time smoking a "peace" pipe, which most Indians prefer to call a ceremonial or sacred pipe—it was, after all, also used during times of war. I made a silent prayer for Andy, puffed several times, and handed the pipe back.

When every man had smoked, half a dozen young men served the food, not a morsel of which was consumed—as is customary at a feast—until after the last spoonful was proffered and Art Raining Bird had given permission to eat. So much food had been piled in front of each person that no one could eat more than a fourth of it; what remained would be wrapped up and taken home. As I devoured what I could, I watched the pipe smoke drifting above our heads, luminous in the afternoon sunlight that flooded through the hall's large windows. The smoke carried many prayers, all offered for Andy. It stirred lightly and reverently in the air above those who had prayed. I thought of how Andy had so meticulously prepared for his own death, not in fear but in acceptance of the inevitable forces. And I wondered how a man comes to such grace.

34
Breakfast at Dorothy Small's

DOROTHY HAD NOT exaggerated. I felt I had gained fifteen pounds from all the eating I'd done at Andy's memorial feast— I felt I'd become *fat on the spot*. Sunday morning at the dining table found me taking in very little of the large breakfast Dorothy had prepared.

I had discovered that Dorothy's house, on any morning of the week, was a kind of family hub. Any number of relatives showed up for eggs, bacon, pan-fried deer meat, potatoes, toast and jelly, coffee, and table talk. This morning, Dorothy, her brother Ned, sister Irene, Junior, and I sat around the table while Zellah puttered in the kitchen. Ned, the oldest of the family, had launched into one of the many stories he told that always left everyone laughing.

"I was drivin' back from Havre when the police pulled me over. They thought maybe I was drinkin' in town. But I wasn't. Maybe I had one or two beers. I don't think so. But maybe.

"Those cops told me to get out of the truck. They said they wanted me to walk a straight line. 'Walk a straight line?!' I said. 'I can't do that. I'm just an old Indian, and I'm lame. Look at this.' Then I hobbled around to show them.

"Then they said, 'Well, okay. Let's see you touch your nose with your index fingers.'

" 'Look,' I told those cops, 'I can't touch my nose. I been workin' as a mason all my life, and nowadays I can't bend my old arms all the way.' "

Ned, in his sixties, but with an eternal impish expression, made a failed attempt to touch his nose to demonstrate for us that his elbows had lost their pliability.

He went on, "So then they told me to count backward, starting from one thousand. 'From one thousand?!' I said. 'How come you have to give me a number with all them zeros in it? I never got through fourth grade, and I failed math. I can't do that.' "

Ned smiled. "I guess I had them pretty stumped," he said. "But then they said, 'Okay, if you can't do that, at least recite the alphabet—starting from the *beginning*.'

"I told them, 'Well, I can give you the A, the B, and the C, but past that, I'm lost. It's been over fifty years since I learned that stuff.' That's when they arrested me." He settled back in his chair, took a sip of coffee, and stared off into space. I waited for some kind of ending, and I knew everyone else in the room knew what it was. But they went along with mock curiosity, always delighted by their older brother's stories. Ned was savoring the moment and suspending his finish like a professional comedian. Then he looked up at me and said, "Well, they took me to the station. They said I would have to take a breath test. 'All right,' I said. 'How do I do that?' They took me to some kinda machine and said, 'Here, blow up this balloon.'

"I was gonna tell them that my lungs wasn't strong enough, but I thought I better not get them mad. So, I said, 'Well, I can do that. I remember how to blow up a balloon.' So, I did. And I said, 'Boy, I wish school had been this easy. If they only ever tested my breath, I probably woulda got all the way through high school.' "

I was laughing through tears by now. Ned finished his tale by telling us that his breath test was the first test he had ever passed in his life. The cops, he said, finally let him go.

After breakfast, Junior helped me load my truck. Another of Dorothy's sisters, Helen, had come over, and everyone was sitting in the living room. I said good-bye and was about to leave when Dorothy said, "Wait a minute. You're not getting outta here so easy, even if you are a white man."

I stopped in my tracks and just stared at Dorothy.

"We have a Cree custom," she said. "We always give a gift to our guests before they leave." As Dorothy walked toward the back of the house, I remembered that on my first visit Louise Stump had given me a beaded cigarette lighter and the Smalls had given me a beaded key chain. I hadn't realized, though, that it was a custom.

Dorothy came back to the living room holding two of the most beautiful small pillows I had ever seen. Their covers were satin. Each bore the traditional Indian star pattern, in greens and reds, over a white background. Exquisite. Dorothy said, "My mother made these. We'd like you to have them."

I hugged Dorothy, momentarily speechless, but then said, "I can't thank you enough. They're absolutely beautiful."

As I drove out toward the border town of Box Elder, over rolling grassy hills and past streams defined by margins of red willow, I silently soaked in the wonderful feeling that came with being touched, once again, with the spirit of Indian giving.

Over the next couple of years, I returned to Rocky Boy, to Dorothy Small's house, again, and again, and again. At first, my visits resulted from my work at the schools; then I began to visit just to visit. Sometimes I returned for the Cree sun dance, sometimes for the annual powwow, and eventually I would spend Christmas holidays with the Smalls. And Dorothy, Junior, Ned, Zellah, Irene, Helen, and Dorothy's granddaughter, Cory, would come to visit me at my home in Pryor. One combination or other of them—Dorothy and Junior always—would spend Easter with me on the Crow reservation.

How Indians and a non-Indian befriend each other takes time—quiet, patient, cautious observation. And what creates that threshold over which a non-Indian may step into the heart of an Indian family often takes that much more time. I had no plans to love and feel a part of a Cree family. I'm sure they hadn't planned on me. But we spent time together—lots of it. We grew to know what it meant to share the same space, to discuss and respect the differences between our cultures, to accept our daily, culturally influenced routines, and to have *fun* together, whether at a powwow or at a bowling alley, whether watching a Cree-style hand game or betting on a furious round of Yahtzee, whether laughing over dinner at a restaurant or at a traditional feast. The paradox: To be taken into an Indian family, or, for that matter, any family, is something that requires no effort and every effort at the same time. It's interest in each other. It's confusion. It's agreement. It's compromise. It's talking. It's silent communication. It's shared happiness and shared sadness. No one decides such things; they either happen or they don't—or sometimes when they do, perhaps they were meant to.

35
Rocky Boy Education

THE HISTORY OF education on the Rocky Boy reservation is no less filled with dreadful stories of the treatment of Indian children than the histories of other tribes. In 1889, Thomas J. Morgan, then United States commissioner of Indian affairs, said that Indians "must conform to the white culture or be crushed by it." His objective was to prepare young Indians for the "new order of things forced upon them."

A government school opened at Rocky Boy in 1918, and its one teacher's aim was to suppress all Indian traditions and language while teaching the first-through-sixth-grade students how to behave and then become just like white people. Students caught speaking Cree or Chippewa were given doses of castor oil or had their hands bloodied by repeated swats from heavy wooden rulers.

Three more schools, Haystack, Parker, and Sangrey, were eventually opened on the reservation, but the policies affecting the students remained intact right through the 1950s. Then, in 1960, the schools were consolidated into one facility near Rocky Boy Agency, and their control, as part of the government's policy of termination, was turned over to the Havre school district. High school students were still forced to attend off-reservation public schools or BIA boarding schools.

Unfortunately, the situation for the students didn't change much at the new Havre-run school. Says Bobbie Murie, in a locally produced history of Rocky Boy education, of an experience he had in the sixth grade:

> I'll never forget that man; that teacher I had at the time, because he slapped me a couple times. . . . He saw that some kids were teasing me and I was getting after them. Pretty soon he said, "You like to fight?" I told him no. He said, "Are you getting smart?" I told him no. Then he said, "Come on outside. I want to talk to you." As soon as he closed the door, he turned around and let go of a good one. . . . Two times he slapped me. I wish I had known state law. I could have got that guy canned and then some.

In the same document, another instance of child abuse is recorded concerning Dorothy's son Bobby:

> Dorothy Small had children attending the school at that time and recalled . . . abuse by teachers. . . . After seeing her own son's larynx half-crushed by an angry teacher, Mrs. Small attacked the offending teacher. Soon after, the teacher was dismissed.

This incident occurred in the late 1960s. As Dorothy told me, "That teacher got so mad at Bobby that she grabbed his neck and shook him until he passed out. He had to be rushed to the hospital. I was so mad I went right to the school and beat the hell out of that teacher. That was my revenge—Indian revenge. At the time, I didn't know about the white man's revenge—you know, suing someone in court. I did feel a little better after I got my kind of revenge."

But Dorothy did more than just punch back with her fists. First, she joined the PTA. Then, late in 1968, she was appointed to the newly created Advisory Education Committee, a group of Indian parents that would serve as a liaison between the Indian community and Havre school district. Besides Dorothy, the most active members of the committee included Robert Favel, Albert St. Pierre, Alice Russette, and Duncan Standing Rock. The committee members began with high hopes of better understandings and relations between the Indians and Havre's Board of School Trustees. They soon learned, however, that their concerns were dismissed just as quickly as before the committee had been set up.

Dorothy told me, "It was in March, back in 1969, that Havre fired a group of teachers. Two of the ones they fired we wanted to keep in our school. They were good teachers who really got to know us Rocky Boy people. They came to our homes, and we went to theirs. They learned about our culture and our special ways. Maybe that's what Havre didn't like about them. But we felt those teachers really cared about our Indian children.

"Our committee got a petition going. We got one hundred thirty-four signatures. We also got the tribal council to write a resolution asking Havre not to fire those two teachers.

"Anyway, we took all these papers to a school-board meeting and presented everything to the board and the superintendent. After we finished, that superintendent just looked right at us and said, "This is not the way we do things." Then he ripped up the petition and the resolution and tossed it in a trash can, right in public. That's when we decided we'd had enough. The only solution was to get our own school district and run our own school."

Dorothy told me this story in her home; she also repeated it as a guest speaker at our first annual Expressive Language Institute in Pryor. Typically, she tells it with a generous infusion of her infectious humor. "We ran around like prairie chickens, visiting other schools to see how they operated and to find out what kind of budgets a school needs. We went to our own tribal council for support. They gave us two hundred dollars and told us we were wasting our time. We were ignorant, uneducated Indians, but we were mad Indians. We knew that no matter how stupid we were, we could do a better job than Havre was doing."

I said to Dorothy, "Maybe naive is a better word than 'stupid.' "

She said, "Naive or stupid, we weren't going to take the abuse any longer. In August, I had to talk on the phone with someone from the Robert Kennedy Foundation. Fifteen minutes was all I had, so I had to talk fast—I'm pretty good at that, you know. The man I talked to sounded sincere, but I was worried that they wouldn't do anything for us. I didn't really trust no darn white man back then.

"Then one day this long, tall white man and a woman came

to our house. Andy let them in and invited them for breakfast—
that's the way we Crees are, inviting anyone who happens along
to have a meal with us. We thought they were lost and wanted
to feed them before we directed them to wherever they were
going. After breakfast, we asked them where they were headed.
'Here,' the white man said. I didn't know what he meant. Then
he introduced himself and his wife—said he was David Robinson and his wife's name was Sandy. They had just arrived, he
said, from Washington, from the Kennedy Foundation. Holy
cripes! I thought, they're here to help get us our own school.
And this was less than a week after I talked to that darn white
man on the phone.

"David and Sandy set up a trailer on a plot of ground the
tribe gave them, and moved in and began to work with us on
how we could get our own school set up."

The work Dorothy and the rest of the committee members,
along with David Robinson, had laid out for themselves was
monumental as well as exhausting. They had to study and learn
state law; locate and research every possible funding source;
incorporate and solidify their group; develop arguments for
the creation of a Rocky Boy school district; circulate another
petition; and present themselves at a public hearing before the
Hill County superintendent of education—all in the face of
unfavorable rumblings from the state Office of Public Instruction.

Then, on February 28, 1970, Superintendent Beatrice
Campbell announced her decision approving a separate school
district for Rocky Boy effective the following July 1. It was a
victory as significant as the winning of the reservation itself back
in 1916, and, as the school's written history of itself states, it
"was the only way the assimilation process started in 1880 could
be reversed." Rocky Boy Elementary would be the second school
in the entire nation—the first was Rough Rock School on the
Navajo Reservation—to be totally Indian-controlled.

It wouldn't be long before Rocky Boy also had its own
Indian-run high school. Education became a top priority among
the Chippewa-Crees. By 1989, not only every school-board
member but every school *administrator* in the reservation district
was a local Chippewa-Cree. And add these to the long, proud
list of accomplishments achieved by the Rocky Boy scrappers:
During 1987–89, school superintendent Edward Parisian

served as president of the National Indian Education Association (NIEA); in 1989, program director Robert Swan was elected the new president of NIEA (both he and Parisian were instrumental in establishing an alcohol-free conference); in 1990, Parisian accepted the post of director of education for the Bureau of Indian Affairs, Department of Interior, under President Bush; Dorothy Small, right up through the present, retains her positions as member of the elementary school board and president of the high school board, and has also served for years as a board member of the local Stone Child Community College; and Dorothy's son Bobby, who as a schoolboy was almost strangled to death by a non-Indian teacher—an incident that provoked his mother to raise her fists and more—has been employed, since 1988, as Rocky Boy High School's *principal*, and he's doing fine, thank you.

36
A Cree Christmas Powwow

THE DECEMBER WEATHER had been rough, and the roads of Montana were either snow-packed or ice-covered. Rather than tempt the hazardous highways, I decided to catch a commuter plane in Billings and fly to Havre, where Dorothy, Junior, Delphine, and Cory would pick me up. It was December 23; this would be the first Christmas I'd spend with my Cree "family."

The skies had cleared that morning, and from fifteen thousand feet the rangeland below sparkled with a two-foot cloak of white—a perfect screen onto which I projected thoughts of Dorothy's house filled with people and bright Christmas decorations. And I looked forward, as well, to the Christmas Eve powwow. Granted, a powwow might not be the first thing most non-Indians think of in connection with the holiday season, but what could be more appropriate, since the very essence of a powwow is the celebration of togetherness.

The flight plan took us over the east flank of the Big Snowy Mountains, where an updraft caught hold of the plane and almost heaved us right up into space and then back down to the ground. I was thankful I hadn't eaten breakfast. The crew laughed—Montana pilots are like that, laughing or chuckling or making jokes at every unscheduled twist and turn their tiny planes take. They're either attempting to help the passengers relax, or they're just having fun. I suspect the latter, since I was definitely not relaxed—a ho-ho-ho into the side of a mountain was not my idea of a happy holiday. It was true, though, that these pilots knew their stuff, knew every corner and stairway of air above the sprawling state. The pilot and copilot were still cheerful when they maneuvered the plane down to Havre and onto a runway covered with six inches of snow. "Didn't know you'd be skiing into Havre, did ya?" The pilot laughed.

Inside the terminal, Dorothy and her family greeted me with hugs. "How was the flight?" Dorothy asked.

"Rocky," I answered. "But better than sliding off the Missouri breaks with my truck."

Dorothy's family, like many Crees, like many Indians throughout North America, celebrate Christmas and Easter, even attend church services, but have not necessarily given up their Indian religions for Christianity. Early missionaries had great difficulty understanding how people could accept a Christian faith while still practicing their own religion, but some of the tribes that retained a strong identity with their heritage saw no conflict in tolerating, even accepting, new beliefs while not giving up old ones.

For generations, most missionaries remained intolerant of this seeming contradiction, and Indians had to conduct their Indian rituals away from watchful non-Indian eyes. Christian values, they figured, were fully compatible with their own. After all, love of family and community, respect of elders, sharing of material wealth, a reverence for the earth, a cooperative work force, a social system based on honesty, loyalty, strength of character, and obeisance to the Creator, made up the fabric of Indian life long before the first Europeans set foot on American shores.

Today, the Indian world is religiously divided; thousands of Indians still practice *only* the old religions; thousands are fully converted to Christianity; while for thousands more, where there's a crucifix there's an eagle feather, where there's holy communion there's smudging with sweet grass or cedar, where there's a rosary there's a medicine bundle, where there's a prayer meeting there's a sweat-lodge ceremony, and where there's a church there's a sun dance lodge, kiva, or longhouse.

On the way out to Rocky Boy, Dorothy asked me, with her customary concern, "Did you smudge yourself this morning?"

I told her I had. A year before, she had taught me how to smudge my truck, my home, and, most important, myself. Whether the effect of the sweet grass was generated in my head, heart, body, or from beyond, it was real, and I still smudge regularly. Smudging produces a certain calm, a feeling of being *right* with the world. I have smudged non-Indian friends of mine, and they all agree. Sweet grass has been used by Indians for thousands of years. They say it is sacred, and I don't doubt it for a moment.

As we pulled into Rocky Boy, clouds from the north gathered into a promise of new snow. The forecast coming over the radio called for up to a foot more over the next couple of days. An assured white Christmas, I thought. An assured Indian Christmas, as well.

Later that night, Dorothy, Junior, Zellah, and I sat in the living room and talked. Dorothy said, "On Christmas Day, we'll have our feast at noontime. Then, at three, we'll go to my brother Roddy's to feast again. In the evening, even more people will come by here to eat. Sometime in the afternoon, you and Junior can take some prayer ribbons and hang them out back. And we'll have to take some food up to Andy. He'll never forgive us if we don't."

I watched, as we talked, the enormous, blazing Christmas tree Junior and Zellah had trimmed before my arrival. Then I noticed, behind an end table near the tree, the wooden dirt-filled box in which Dorothy kept her sweet grass. The braid in the box was burned halfway down, and I knew that tomorrow morning even more of the grass would be turned into sacred smoke. Above the wooden box, on the wall, hung a framed picture of an eagle—traditional messenger between this world and the supernatural. The mix of traditional Christmas and traditional Indian practices heightened the excitement of the season. Indeed, over the next few days there would be church services, a powwow, feasts, exchanges of gifts, sweat rituals, a round dance, and kids sledding down the hills of Rocky Boy.

I said to Dorothy, "Boy, you Indians have it lucky."

"What do you mean, you crazy white man?" she said.

"Well, you not only get all your own Indian holidays, but you also get all our white ones."

Dorothy chuckled and said, "Indians like holidays. Doesn't matter whose they are. We'll take 'em anyway."

Zellah added, "Indians love any excuse to get together and celebrate."

After a moment's thought, Dorothy said, "We take all the holidays except one. . . ."

Somehow I knew what was coming.

"We don't celebrate Columbus Day. We don't even recognize it as a holiday." Dorothy chuckled, but I later discovered she meant what she said literally. On the Rocky Boy reservation, Columbus Day is nonexistent. Tribal employees go to work, and students go to school as on any other business weekday.

I remembered the words of a Sioux leader I'd heard at a presentation on the Sisseton-Wahpeton reservation in South Dakota: "A long time ago, somewhere around 1492, this Italian guy got himself real lost. Boy, did he ever get lucky. Us Indians found him, and gave him food and shelter. Turned out, though, the guy wasn't very grateful."

On Christmas Eve, after dinner, Junior and I drove down to the high school for the start of the powwow. The temperature had already plunged to minus two, and a crisp, clicking snow was falling. Inside the gym, we climbed to the top of the bleachers, stripped off our coats and scarves, and nestled down, rubbing the cold from our hands. At about seven-thirty, six men sitting around a large drum began singing and pounding. The dancers, in their spectacular feathered outfits, started making their way into the gym; they danced to the right and then around, forming, as more and more came in, a huge, moving, counterclockwise circle. The "grand entry" was on.

Indian powwows, to the surprise of some, are not religious ceremonies, as are the sweats and sun dances. They are, instead, social celebrations of tribal heritage; they often bring Indians of many tribes together to rejoice in their Indianness; they provide good fun for the observers and tough competition for the dancers; they reinforce the Indians' connections to the earth and the past.

Competitive powwow dances usually continue late into the night, often until the following morning. The dancers' and observers' stamina is said to come from the drum rhythms, which emulate the human heartbeat. Indeed, one sees little or no body movement among the observers; they keep up with the drumming and singing in their hearts, in the blood pulsing through their bodies.

Powwow dancers compete for cash prizes in distinct categories. For the men, there's traditional, fancy, and grass dancing; for women, traditional, fancy, and jingle-dress dancing. The costumes of each are different. Traditional men's outfits are heavily feathered, and the buckskins, bustles, and porcupine-quill head roaches come in subdued earth colors. These dancers imitate various birds and other animals. The men's fancy-dance costumes are elaborate, brightly colored evocations of the Indian spirit of celebration. Grass-dance regalia, also of brilliant hues, is characterized by yarn fringes.

The main feature of a woman's traditional or fancy-dance outfit is the shawl. In traditional dancing, the women move at a slower, stately pace. Fancy dancers, again more brightly colored, twirl and bounce along quickly, employing remarkably intricate dance steps. Jingle-dress dancers wear dresses covered with small tin cones that dangle from fringes and clack together, thus producing the jingle sound.

I was fortunate, several years back, to attend a powwow with Dorothy Small's family at Northern Montana College in Havre. I'd been to a few before, but this was my first opportunity to learn about powwows in greater depth—Dorothy was one of the judges. I sat next to her all evening. She advised me to closely watch the feet of the dancers, to study their hand and arm movements, and to pay attention to how well their body rhythms synchronized with the drumbeat. For a while, at first, I tapped my feet to the drums. But gradually I settled into the heartbeat, feeling it inside, while the drums grew to be an echo of my physical self. I became, like the Indians around me, outwardly still, inwardly in motion. I was learning how to *observe* and, at the same time, how to *feel* a powwow.

Most of the hundreds of powwows held each year in the United States are intertribal. Tonight's Rocky Boy Christmas Eve powwow was mainly Chippewa-Cree. Some Canadian Crees were there, spending the holidays with relatives, and at least one Blackfeet family from Browning was attending.

A small group of junior-high boys climbed the bleachers to say hello and chat for a few minutes. We hadn't seen each other for several months, and they wanted to hear any new jokes I'd picked up since then. And they told me a couple of new ones. Then they were off, not to watch the dancers, but to look for junior-high girls.

Junior and I settled back. The drumbeats filled the gymnasium, then coursed through my arteries in step with my heart. I gazed at all the dancers. During grand entry, all the different kinds of dancers dance together, and the mingling of the costumes in a circular dance is a thrilling sight.

Then I noticed a boy, maybe ten years old, maybe fifteen, dancing amid the others without a costume. He wore blue jeans, a maroon jacket, and a cockeyed baseball cap. His jerky, erratic movements called attention to him. Completely out of step with the drum, he stomped on the floor, twisting his body this way and that, flailing his arms wildly. Curious, I looked harder.

The boy's mongoloid features answered my questions. He seemed oblivious to all but the drumming and singing. While Indian drumming mimics the human heart, Indian singing sounds like incantations of wind. This boy, twirling about in his own physical chaos, appeared caught in a whirlwind. I felt a deep sadness for him, as I suppose most of us are programmed to feel when we observed the mentally retarded. And I was spared, high in the bleachers, the uneasiness we feel when we are expected to interact with them.

But I couldn't keep my eyes off him. In the middle of such color-splashed regalia, he stuck out in his oddity like a fly on a white wall. I watched in sympathy, and in secrecy, to see if his wayward flounderings would steer him into a direct collision with one of the other dancers; to see if he would tire quickly and retreat behind a group of seated family members; to see if he had an inkling, in his obvious joy, of what was going on in this gym and why he was dancing.

The retarded boy danced and danced. Although he zigzagged wildly, he never came into contact with the other dancers; the twirling and jumping seemed to invigorate him; and although he shook his whole body with abrupt twitches, he moved around the gym in perfect time with the revolving circle of Indian celebrants.

Were the other dancers, I wondered, stepping aside for him? It didn't appear so. Those near the boy never misstepped, never broke a dance pattern. So intent were they on their own movements, they seemed not to notice the boy at all.

And then it hit me. The boy was regarded by all the others as just another one of the dancers—that was the magnificent beauty of it. I felt flushed and somewhat ashamed for paying so much attention to him. He was considered by his people as a part of the larger dance of celebration; he was a part of the Chippewa-Cree community; he was not excluded on the basis of his handicap.

I recall one of Garrison Keillor's tales in which he encounters, on a bus, a group of retarded adults, one of whom happened to have been a childhood friend of his. Keillor knew his friend did not recognize him. As he watched the group, he suddenly felt the distinctions between those retarded individuals and himself vanish. He felt joyous. He felt a part of the *whole* community of humankind. He wondered why we make distinctions among ourselves that keep us apart from one another.

That's exactly what the Rocky Boy Chippewa-Cree were doing—they were *not* making distinctions that would separate the retarded boy from the community, from themselves. He was not hidden at home or in an institution. He was not made to sit off in some secluded corner. Rather, he was being himself, having a good time with family and neighbors. He was part of the grand entry.

Late that evening, back at Dorothy's, I mentioned to her what I had earlier observed and felt. She responded, "Oh, that's no big thing to us Indians. We believe that the Creator made each person in a special way. Some special ways make some people a little different. It's not for us to judge our differences. Everyone is the way the Creator intended them to be. We accept what the Creator gives."

In the morning, I would be honored with a marvelous gift from Dorothy: a beautiful, shockingly vibrant star quilt, which today hangs in my living room and fills the place with a reminder of the warm love of my Cree "family." The quilt also reminds me of Christmas, and of a particular boy. That was surely the greatest gift I received.

37
New Mexico Coup

FROM MONTANA TO New Mexico, I drive through only two other states—Wyoming and Colorado. I stop for a couple of days in Taos, after a lovely, rolling ride through the Sangre de Cristo Range. The days are sunny and warm enough to sit outside on the patio of the small espresso café just off the plaza and sip some cappuccino.

Then I head south through Sante Fe and Albuquerque, then west toward Gallup. This is Pueblo country, high, rocky desert of sage and scrub and juniper. I've never worked at a Pueblo school, and I am curious about these peaceable people. Maybe someday. Past Mount Taylor (one of the four sacred mountains of the Navajo) I reach the plateau-mesa landscapes of northwestern New Mexico. Sheer pink cliffs stretch toward the horizon. I've entered Dinetah. Fifteen miles east of Gallup, I take the McGaffey exit. I can see, directly south, about four miles off, the campus of Fort Wingate Elementary Boarding School. Each year I spend four weeks here, so approaching the familiar, I feel at home.

Four Navajo kids help me unload my truck. I am as excited to see them as they are to see me. I've known these eighth-graders since they were in the fourth grade. I run through my head some of the common Navajo words and phrases I know

I'll be hearing, and using, over the next four weeks. *Ya-ta-hay* for "hello, how are you," or "that's good"; *ou* for "yes"; *doo ga* for "no"; *ge'* for "listen to me"; *hago* for "come here"; *naajoshli* for "I trust you," or "I have confidence in you."

At Wingate I stay in a two-bedroom apartment that adjoins the seventh-and eighth-grade boys' dormitory on one side, and on the other looks out to weekend—when all but a few of the students are gone—parades of campus mule deer. The days are routine: I teach four classes a day; compile the kids' poetry for publication in a yearly calendar; hike in the ponderosa pine forests just south of the school; take most of my meals in the cafeteria, where I talk to, and learn from, the students; watch, in the evenings, an hour or so of television in the dorm lounge or, more regularly, play board and card games with different groups of youngsters; and, after the kids go to bed, at nine o'clock, work on my word processor until midnight.

My stays at Wingate offer me four unbroken weeks of isolation from the rest of the world, during which time I learn more and more about the Navajo tribe while getting the chance to write on a nightly basis without interruption. My yearly month at Wingate is a monastic, creative time for me.

In the middle of the last week of this year's visit, I achieve a small triumph, creating something of a minirevolution in the dormitory.

On Wednesday evening, nine seventh-and eighth-grade Navajo kids and I sit around a long, rectangular table in the lounge, just outside the office of the school's dorm director. Four of the students and I are playing five-card-stud poker; the others watch, talking to each other in Navajo and to me in English. Two of the walls of the director's office contain large windows looking out to the lounge on one side, and to the corridor on the other; the curtains are pulled wide open. Through the glass I see Juanita Claw at her desk, peering down through eyeglasses at her paperwork.

Juanita Claw, somewhere in her fifties, is a beautiful woman, and typically Navajo—thin lips, high cheekbones, oval face—except for her wavy, permed hair. She has worked at Wingate for over twenty years—as a teacher, and now as director of all the dormitories. I've known her for five years, and have greatly appreciated a friendship from which I have learned much. Often, before I retire to my apartment to write, I sit in Juanita's office discussing student concerns, Navajo customs, tribal politics. Each year I leave Wingate wishing I had more time to talk with Juanita.

I'm now looking at a straight, and stand to defeat my Navajo card mates, when a ruckus breaks out on the other side of the large lounge, near the office opposite Juanita's, on the boys' side.

Moments later, emerging from a group of scrabbling students, the dorm counselor marches from the pack, clutching a boy's upper arm, practically dragging him across the lounge. As man and boy near Juanita Claw's office, they slow down, straighten their postures, and dignify themselves for Mrs. Claw. They enter the office, and the door slams shut behind them.

The counselor is new this year at Wingate, a recent transplant from New England. I've talked to him several times; he's a pleasant, affable man somewhere in his forties. But I've witnessed several other scenes like this over the last month. He seems unable to connect with some of the kids.

I lay down my straight. One of the boys sitting across from me says, referring to the counselor, "That guy's no good. Now he got Tommy in trouble."

"What did Tommy do?" I ask.

"Nothing," says the boy. "That counselor wanted to talk to him today, but he was hiding. He didn't want to talk to that guy."

Several students recently mentioned to me in private that they didn't like going in to see the counselor. They said he got too personal, talked about things they shouldn't talk to a stranger about. Now, a girl at our table speaks up: "He acts like he should know everything right away. Like we should tell him our secrets. I hate him." Within moments, six or seven of the students start voicing their complaints.

From what the students tell me, I gather that the man is probably a pretty good counselor—for non-Indian kids, that is. It is apparent that he hasn't taken into consideration, in dealing with these Navajo youngsters, the differences in Navajo culture that would naturally require him to take a different approach in working with them. He is using every counseling trick he knows and still not making progress with the students, because the tricks he uses were learned at a university in the East; they are tricks designed to work with non-Indians. It is also apparent that he himself hasn't been counseled on how to counsel Navajos.

Had he taken, or been given, "Navajo 101," the first thing he'd be doing differently is keeping the curtains to his office windows open, as Juanita Claw does with one exception—when a student is visibly upset and, when asked, says he or she wants them shut. Navajo kids do not feel comfortable cloistered in a small room with a probing adult. I wonder if *any* kid does, but Indian children especially will erect a brick wall between themselves and another if they feel closed in with that person. If this new counselor understood this and, instead of dictating the degree of perceived intimacy, allowed each child to participate in making a decision on whether or not the curtains should be open, he would have broken that first barrier and given the child an indication of respect.

Another thing he would have learned is that in Navajo culture it is considered improper to begin any relationship, including a professional counseling relationship, by asking intimate questions. He would have known, first off, that he, too, would be required to share a lot about *his* personal life with each kid he dealt with—child *and* counselor sharing information about family. Positive information. And he would already know something about the clans, the relationships of extended families. He would share with each student where he came from, what he has been doing in his life, how he came to Dinetah, *why* he came to Dinetah, and what, from his life and experience, he can offer. Navajo kids respond to real people, not to "authority figures," and good for them. Had this counselor been Navajo-patient, Navajo-concerned, and Navajo-sensitive, I am sure he would now be singing praises for Navajo kids, rather than fighting them.

The counselor is a good man. The Navajo children are good kids. The point is simple, and it explains one set of cross-cultural misunderstandings that often leave the non-Indian educator of Indian children baffled, frustrated, accusatory, hostile, burned-out, and resigned. It also explains the Indian students' point of view in such cultural grappling: baffled, frustrated, accusatory, hostile, burned-out, and resigned.

I try to explain all of this to the kids around the table. But they don't like the man, so they're not giving me any slack.

Then I ask them, "Do you know what his job is? The most important thing he's supposed to be doing here?"

"What?"

"He's supposed to be helping you. That's why he was hired, to help you. If you have a problem, he's supposed to talk with you in a way that will help solve that problem."

The kids, watching me, wonder where I'm taking this. I say, "*Does* he help you?"

"No," they all chime in at once.

I ask, "Have you told anyone, like Mrs. Claw, that he's not really helping you, but upsetting you?"

"No."

"Maybe if Mrs. Claw, or the principal, knew he wasn't helping, then they could teach him, or get someone to teach him, the best ways he *could* help you. Wouldn't it be better if he knew about Diné, and knew how to talk to you in a good way?"

The students agree.

I understand why they haven't told anyone, why they have preferred to wage their own battles with the counselor rather than come forward and talk to some other adult about it. They are afraid that whoever speaks up will get into deeper trouble. And they wouldn't know how to present the whole thing; how could one of these children be expected to explain the difficult, complex cross-cultural situation that I've just explained to them? Besides, it is not good Navajo manners for a young person to bad-mouth one adult to another.

I say, "I want to suggest something. If you don't want me to do this, tell me, and I won't—I'll keep my big mouth shut. But if it's all right with you, I would like to talk to Mrs. Claw about this myself. I'd like to tell her that he's not helping you, and that maybe something can be done, or someone can teach him how to do his job better. If no one says anything, nothing will change, so I'm willing to be the one to say something. Is that okay? Can I go to Mrs. Claw and tell her that we've been talking about all this?"

These students and I have known each other for a long time; they're not surprised by my advocacy. And they are, every one, eager for me to go to bat for them.

Finally, the counselor and Tommy emerge from Juanita Claw's office. Tommy looks furious. The counselor looks frustrated. Juanita Claw watches them through her eyeglasses. I get up and walk over to the open door.

"Juanita, can I talk to you for a minute?" I ask.

"As long as you're not bringing me more problems!" Juanita jokes.

I sit down, saying seriously, "I'm afraid I am."

It turns out that Juanita is well aware of the problem. "I figured the kids would open up to you," she says. "But they haven't come out and told me. They're scared. And I can't really bring it up myself; it wouldn't be professional, and besides, our head counselor likes the man. He'd probably think I was just undermining him if I spoke up. I don't know what to do. I'm supposed to punish Tommy now, but how can I except to tell him he *must* see the counselor."

"But now that I'm a witness," I say, "now that the students have spoken to me . . . can't you use that? I'm an objective outsider. Couldn't you go to the principal on my word? Better yet, I'll talk to her myself, if you and I can meet with her tomorrow."

"No, Mick, I couldn't. You'll be gone after Friday, so even if you talk to Beverly, the whole thing will fall back on me anyway."

Beverly Crawford, the principal and a Navajo herself, is a fair, kind, loving woman who keeps the interests of her students as her first priority. But it looks as if bureaucratic snags will prevent her from knowing of the situation.

Then Juanita says, "There's only one way for this thing to come out into the open."

My ears perk up. Juanita goes on: "If some of the students would come forward themselves . . . with specifics . . . and be willing to have what they say documented . . . then maybe we could do something about all this."

"But how can we get them—" I stop in midsentence, noticing the look Juanita has leveled on me. Juanita need not use words to tell me what her eyes are telling me. I say, "I'll try."

"Good luck," says Juanita.

I leave her office and go right to the table where five students remain playing cards. "Mrs. Claw thinks we can work all of this out," I say. "But she needs you guys to tell her what you told me."

The five students, all boys, continue their card game, ignoring me. "Look," I say to one boy, "if you tell Mrs. Claw what happened to you, then we can get something going."

The boy throws down two cards, then looks to the boy at his left, as though he's heard nothing.

I say to another boy, "We can *do* something here. Why don't you come with me right now. Tell Mrs. Claw what you told me. I'll be there. I'll be supporting you."

This boy says, casually, "I don't have anything to say." His attention shifts completely away from me as he reaches for a small half-empty bag of potato chips.

"Come on, you guys," I plead. "Mrs. Claw can do something if you talk to her. That's all it will take."

The boys pretend I'm not there, continuing their game.

Obviously, their telling *me* the counseling stories was one thing. My going into battle for them was another. My involving *them* in the battle is yet another. None is willing. I'm at a loss. Obviously, I have, myself, miscalculated the responses of these Navajo youngsters.

I could let it go here, say good night, walk back to my apartment, turn on my word processor, try to forget it, and work on one of the books I'm writing. Mark it up to good intentions thwarted. I tried to help these Navajo kids in their dilemma, but they don't care to have help.

Or do they? I understand their reluctance, and in a group they can support each other's silence. But what if I confront them one-to-one, when ignoring me probably wouldn't work. I wonder where the two girls and the other boy went and get up to look for them.

Then I see them across the lounge sitting on a sofa watching television. I call to Cecelia, asking her to join me for a moment. We sit in a back corner of the lounge, away from the other students. I explain to her the situation, and in a matter of minutes I'm begging her to come forward, to talk to Mrs. Claw. She resists, but must wonder at this white man pleading like a child. I persist, telling her that if she speaks up, other students are sure to follow. She turns her head aside and then mumbles something that might provide the breakthrough I've been look-ing for.

"I'll only talk to Mrs. Claw," she says, "if Alice comes with me."

I call Alice over. It takes another ten minutes of stubborn

beseeching on my part, but Alice finally agrees to come with us
to meet with Mrs. Claw. Thirty seconds later, the three of us
walk into Juanita's office. I close the door. The card-playing
boys are all staring at us through the window. The girls and I
sit down, and I say to Juanita, "Cecelia and Alice have something
they want to talk to you about."

Once the girls start, they find they're not as nervous as they
thought they'd be. They relate several incidents in which the
counselor's techniques have made them feel very uncomfortable. Juanita Claw asks them, "If we write these things down,
will you sign the reports?" The girls say they will.

Before our meeting breaks up, Alice goes out to the dorm
and returns with her boyfriend, Gilbert, who is now willing to
report several incidents that clearly show the counselor is not
aware of how to approach Navajo youngsters.

The next afternoon, Thursday, I stop by Juanita's office.
"I want to tell you," she says, "this morning two boys came
forward. And about an hour ago, another boy came in here.
They're the boys who were playing cards last night. They're
willing to sign their statements. I think before you leave, both
of us should meet with Beverly. We've got what we need."

As I had hoped, the snowball is now rolling.

The following morning, Juanita and I sit down with Beverly
Crawford. Now, the principal will know the situation, and I am
confident she will do something about it.

The next morning I am in my truck, already past Gallup,
crossing the state line into Arizona on my way to Tucson. The
red cliffs are incandescent with morning sunlight, and I am
feeling pretty good about having pulled off the beginnings of
a successful coup.

38

The Close of the School Year

DRIVING INTO BROWNING, Montana, the first thing I notice is that the huge top half of the Warbonnet Lodge sign has toppled over and rests on the ground below the bottom half. The Warbonnet is where I'll stay, but I drive by, intent on another, more immediate destination, where I plan to spend the afternoon. No rush to get a room—I've never seen the place full in the middle of May.

The second inescapable sight is the terrible litter—it looks as if a plane flew over this capital of the Blackfeet Nation and dropped tons of trash—mainly paper.

As in any level prairie town, another blight instantly becomes obvious: telephone poles. They seem to be everywhere, rising above the single-story homes, surrounding a high water tower that's topped with a tank looking remarkably like the Tin Man from *The Wizard of Oz*.

Past the Warbonnet, I drive by Blackfeet Community College, which consists of a few trailers and a windowless cinder-block building. Where the road curves west, going into down town Browning, I pass a tacky two-story cement tepee replete with little frame windows—a monument to Indian kitsch. The main street of Browning is a dusty, littered mess, lined with a few saloons, Indian curio shops, and a small shopping center.

At the west end of town lies the red brick Museum of the Plains Indian. I decide to check out its gift shop later in the week.

Most accounts of Browning that I have read in travel literature pretty much summarize the place the same way: bleak, dirty, poor. Even William Least Heat Moon, in *Blue Highways*, seems to have put Browning behind him faster than any other town he experienced. Browning looks rough, and most people are happy enough just to pass through. But appearances don't always tell the whole story. I have not spent enough time in Browning to do that, but I have come here each spring over the last few years to work with the Blackfeet students for a week—my final school visitation before summer break—and I have, during those visits, learned a few things about Browning you don't learn if you don't stay here for more than a night.

First, the town looks poor because it is—this is an Indian reservation, and I have yet to see any reservation town whose streets were lined with multileveled six-bedroom homes sporting backyard swimming pools and tennis courts—that's what you find in Sedona, Arizona, and other burgs like it. Browning is neither worse nor better off than most reservation towns.

Second, all the litter blistering the landscape has an uncontrollable force behind its persistent existence—a force also responsible for the toppled-over sign at the Warbonnet Lodge. Namely, the wind.

The fierce, unrelenting winds that surge down the east slopes of the Rockies make the gusts of the Windy City, Chicago, seem like zephyrs wafting over a tropical isle. That motel sign was sturdily built and held in place by three large iron poles, yet the wind chewed it up and spit it out with such thoroughness you'd have thought a tornado struck it.

I have never felt wind with such muscle as I have in Browning. One day, on an earlier visit, I experienced the wind in a way that left me stunned. Walking back to the motel from a convenience market, I was almost physically blown onto the road and into the path of an approaching pickup, while the bag I clutched, full of fried chicken, potato salad, and iced tea, was ripped from my hands, torn, shredded, and deposited somewhere nearby—as more litter.

I understood then why many of the homes on the outskirts of town had single, wooden fences built just ten yards from their west sides. And I understood why Browning was littered—not so much with beer cans and wine bottles as with paper.

Just past the Museum of the Plains Indian, I turn left, headed for East Glacier and a ways beyond. I think of the Blackfeet, with whom I will share company for the next week. These are one of the tribes etched in legend—notorious fighters, buffalo hunters supreme, and, for a while, feared by every white man who set foot in their territory.

The Montana Blackfeet, also known as the Southern Piegan, are actually one of three divisions of the larger Blackfoot tribe. The other two, the Blood and the Northern Piegan, make their homes across the border in Canada. Nowadays, the Blackfeet division numbers nearly seven thousand, and its population is growing steadily. Just like the wind, they persist.

The west side of the reservation is bordered by Glacier National Park. At the tiny hamlet of East Glacier, I turn right, drive another four or five miles, then turn left at Lower Two Medicine Lake. The road climbs along the north shore, enters a thick evergreen forest, climbs yet higher, then dips down to Upper Two Medicine. Here is some of the most beautiful mountain scenery I have ever encountered. I park my truck by the lake, below Rising Wolf Mountain. The lake shimmers and sparkles while, across the water, rugged, snow-encrusted peaks rise straight up into the sky. One peak is so perfectly pointed that it is named Tepee Mountain.

The tourist season won't begin until Memorial Day weekend; the sightseeing boats are locked up somewhere out of sight; the visitor center is still staring at a twelve-inch snowdrift; the restaurant–general store remains boarded up; and mine is the only vehicle in the parking lot. I have the whole wonderful place to myself. For nearly two hours, I walk along the lake shore, sit on boulders and tree stumps, and just stare, breathing deeply of the crisp spring alpine air. Minutes ago I was feeling travel-weary; now I am restored.

A high-pressure dome, centered over Idaho, has kept the winds down to mere breezes. I drive back to Browning under an immense, clear sky. In town, hordes of college-aged Blackfeet are now traipsing up and down the streets, clutching plastic bags, gathering the litter. Apparently, the community is taking advantage of the windless weather. By tomorrow, Browning will be spotless, and will remain so until the next blasts come roaring off the eastern slopes of the mountains.

I check in at the Warbonnet and set up my word processor. I plan a quiet evening of writing. Tomorrow, and for the rest of the week, I will be busy working with Blackfeet children. After my classes, I will spend the late afternoons in a prefab office talking to bilingual education director Joyce Goodstriker and Blackfeet language specialist Darrell Kipp. Goodstriker, from Canada, is an outstanding administrator who, at the same time, is hoping to go through initiation into a traditional Blackfeet Society. Kipp, Harvard-educated and qualified to hold down a professorship at any campus in the nation, chose early on to return home to create the Piegan Institute, an organization dedicated to preserving the Blackfeet language. Both Goodstriker and Kipp are further examples of modern Indians who have opted to live a bicultural life. They are perfectly comfortable in the white man's world, they have used their education wisely, and they practice the cultural ways of their ancestors—great role models for the young Indians with whom they interact.

After working at my word processor for an hour or so, I get up to stretch and to gaze out the second-story window for a few minutes. The emerald plains are ablaze with evening light. Below me, in the parking lot, a plump white woman, dressed in pink slacks and a pink blouse, hoists a 35-mm camera up to her face and points it at two Blackfeet boys. The boys are maybe seven and eight years old; they pose like professionals. The Pink Tourist Lady snaps the shutter six or seven times, then the three of them start to walk back to the lobby.

I have for a long time considered such behavior among tourists abhorrent. They seem to regard the Indian as nothing more than a romantic relic of the past. They don't care that the lens through which they get their Indians serves as a barrier to any real communication with them. They are interested in Indian images, not Indian people. An Apache friend of mine once told me, "Those tourists are really a different species. We gave up trying to understand them long ago. But we can spot them from a mile off—they all have three eyes."

The Pink Tourist Lady has a wide grin plastered on her face. She can go home now and show all her friends snapshots of "real Injuns." I feel nothing but contempt for her—that is, until I look at the faces of the two little Blackfeet boys. Most tourists are at least aware that a posing Indian is also an Indian who expects to be paid for the service. The boys, like Pink Tourist Lady, are grinning widely, grinning no doubt because they now have got some pocket money, and perhaps also because at their age they are flattered to have been asked to pose. My contempt for Pink Tourist Lady is mitigated slightly by the boys' smiling faces.

Ten minutes later, I look out the window again. My God! She's back at it. This time, Pink Tourist Lady has her lens pointed at a young man. He's thirtyish, slender, and neatly dressed in jeans and a sky-blue western shirt. He's got two long braids wrapped in cloth and animal fur that hang over the front of his shoulders. He looks off toward the mountains with that unsmiling expression so common to Indian faces in nineteenth-century daguerreotypes—stern, proud, angry, determined. From my vantage point, however, I can't help but notice what looks like a twinkle in his eye. It occurs to me that such a handsome Indian might be earning a handsome living just by hanging out at the Warbonnet Lodge through the summer.

On my next trip to the window (I am a chronic pacer when I write), I immediately look down to see if the parking lot–photo studio is still in use. Nobody. I walk downstairs and out to my truck to get a dictionary I keep in the back. As I close the tailgate, I hear, carried on a breeze, the voice of a kid. It sounds as though the voice is saying, "Hey, there's Mick Fedullo." I am momentarily stunned but convince myself that what I thought I heard must have been a wind-aberration of other words. I turn to go back inside but stop in my tracks when I hear the voice again. "Hey, Mick Fedullo." Suddenly, other voices begin yelling my name. The voices come from the west. I stare across the road, past the Legion Club. Then I see them, standing on a basketball court several hundred yards away; six Blackfeet kids—obviously students whose classes I had been to the previous year. One of them somehow spotted me, and now there they stand, waving their arms and calling my name. I wave my arms wildly.

Such recognition by Indian kids is something I have, over the years, experienced again and again on many reservations. It is not something, though, that I have ever taken for granted. Tomorrow I will be swarmed upon by dozens of Blackfeet kids in the school hallway. Their love is genuine. These are the Indians I wish the Pink Tourist Lady could see—vibrant, laughing, spirited. And I'd like her to see them through her eyes only, sans lens. I'm almost tempted to hunt her down and invite her to join me at the school tomorrow, but I fear the possibility that she might be left with nothing more than memories of little Indian cartoons and not of real children.

My week at Browning goes by too quickly, a good week of storytelling and writing and sharing. On Friday afternoon, I drive to Rocky Boy, 180 miles due east, to spend the weekend with Dorothy Small and her family. By Sunday evening, I am home in Pryor. I flop back on the sofa, exhausted from so much travel.

Finished teaching for the year, I will spend the summer working mostly at home on the textbook I am writing to teach Indian kids English idioms. I'll also spend some time at the state capital, working with a team of eighteen educators on the Montana State Language Arts Model Curriculum. On this team, working side by side with me, will be Barbara Bacon, one of the two Indian teachers responsible for first getting me to work in Montana. And I will spend time, too, fishing, camping, and hiking through the mountains with my Crow friends and neighbors. I do, however, have one last school-related task to perform. On Wednesday I drive the 110 miles from Pryor to Lame Deer, on the Northern Cheyenne reservation. Each school year, I single out my favorite student poem and buy an electronic typewriter for the kid who wrote it. This year, a seventh-grade Cheyenne boy named Fred Bellymule takes the honor.

The school's superintendent, a Cheyenne herself, and the bilingual director, a Crow, are thrilled; they called a three o'clock assembly for the junior high and now telephone Fred Bellymule's parents to invite them to be there. Another staff member decides, on the spot, to have the poem run off on a laser printer, then mounts and frames it.

I spend the day wandering from classroom to classroom, telling kids stories. In each room I enter, I am greeted with the familiar cries: "Mick's here! Mick's here!" Before I go to the gym for the assembly, the bilingual director introduces me to a reporter and a photographer from the national Indian newspaper, the *Lakota Times*. They will do a story with photos. And they will publish Fred Bellymule's winning poem.

The students are already seated on the bleachers when I enter the gym. I spot Fred Bellymule sitting off to the left, about four rows up. He's small for a seventh-grader but already possesses that manly, chiseled handsomeness typical of Plains

Indians. The bilingual director points out Fred's parents. The boy must wonder why on earth they are here.

I explain to the students the purpose of the assembly, and finally announce Fred's name. He comes forward slowly, fighting back his nervousness. Then I read his poem, called "Sacred Love":

> As the Earth revolves, our
> past is gleaming
> with all the knowledge
> and hope our ancestors give.
>
> And as I walk the Great Plains
> that were planted with love,
> I think of the world
> before us and how the
> Indians survived.
>
> As I stand high on
> top of a buffalo jump,
> I wonder if the Great
> Chief's spirit still walks
> high on the clouds.
>
> As I stand alone
> in a once walked on valley
> I pray for wisdom for
> the children who will
> experience the Sacred
> Grounds of this Cheyenne
> Dream Land.

Fred's schoolmates break into applause. His teachers wipe away tears. His parents beam. And I'm sure his ancestors are proud.

As the students file out of the gym, Fred, his parents, and I pose for the *Lakota Times* camera. The picture, which will be published in a couple of weeks, is not a romantic image of the Indian as a relic from the past; rather, it is a documentation of a Cheyenne boy's accomplishment in the present. And I cannot express how honored I feel to be on this side of the lens.

I am carried home from Lame Deer to Pryor on a strong wind. In Indian belief, the wind is a messenger, a carrier of old knowledge, of wisdom, of spirits, of the song that is life. Just as the Indian drum imitates the human heartbeat, Indian singing sounds like the wind. I believe that I learn from the wind—the wind that blows down from Montana mountains, the wind that spreads the red dust through Navajoland, the wind that surges across the southern deserts, the wind that takes me to reservations throughout the country.

Another year of travel is finished. The first thing I do when I get home is smudge my apartment with sweet grass. I smudge my medicine bundles and the feathers given to me by Dorothy Small. I smudge the feather handed to me, so long ago, by a young Indian friend. The feather was from his powwow costume. His name was Victor. I don't know where he is or what he is doing, but I trust the wind to let him know the feather is still safe.

The next morning, after coffee and a couple of hard-boiled eggs, I sit down at my desk. From my briefcase, I pull out one of those blank calendars, then fill in the months and days, starting with September and ending with May. Referring to a list of schools I had scribbled on the back of an envelope, I begin to pencil onto the calendar a schedule for next year.

There's a knock on the front door. It's four Crow kids. They want to come in and visit. I've been away too long, they tell me, and they're glad I'm back home.

The schedule can wait.

Ah-ho.